CHEAP MOTELS
AND A HOT PLATE

CHEAP MOTELS AND A HOT PLATE

An Economist's Travelogue

MICHAEL D. YATES

MONTHLY REVIEW PRESS

New York

Library of Congress Cataloging-in-Publication Data

Yates, Michael, 1946-
   Cheap motels and a hot plate : an economist's travelogue / Michael D. Yates.
   p. cm.
   Includes bibliographical references and index.
   ISBN 1-58367-143-9 (alk. paper) -- ISBN 1-58367-144-7 (alk. paper)
   1. United States--Economic conditions--2001- 2. United States--Social conditions
--1980-3. Equality--United States--History--21st century. 4. United States--
Environmental conditions--History--21st century. 5. United States--Description
and travel--Anecdotes. 6. Economists--Travel--United States--Anecdotes. I. Title.
II. Title: Economist's travelogue.
HC106.83.Y38 2006
330.973--dc22

                          2006034213

MONTHLY REVIEW PRESS
146 West 29th Street – Suite 6W
New York, NY 10001
http://www.monthlyreview.org

Printed in Canada

CONTENTS

DEDICATION

To Karen Korenoski, my constant traveling companion, and to Clark Strausser, who kept us company from a distance.

ACKNOWLEDGMENTS

This is a book based mainly on personal experiences, so there are not a lot of people to acknowledge. I am grateful for the professional competence of the staff at Monthly Review, especially Martin Paddio. Nicholas Mirra did the copyediting and also gave me thoughtful and useful criticism. My good friend and long-time Manhattanite Louis Proyect made helpful comments on the Manhattan chapter. Karen Korenoski traveled every mile with me and also kept an invaluable daily journal. She always gave me good advice and warm encouragement, and rescued more than one chapter that had gone astray. She skillfully critiqued the book paragraph by paragraph. Without her the book would not have been possible. No wonder I love her!

PROLOGUE

ESTES PARK, COLORADO

Population in 2003 5,695
    White 95.1%
    Black 0.3%
    Hispanic (all races) 5.6%

Median household income in 2000 .... $43,262
Median rent in 2000 .... $541
Median mortgage, including associated costs $1,162
People below poverty level of income 4.5%

Elevation .... 7,522 ft.

Visit the Stanley Hotel, built by the inventor of the Stanley Steamer automobile. Stephen King wrote *The Shining* there. Enjoy lounging on the huge front porch. 333 W. Wonder View Ave. (970) 586-3371. 1-(800) 976-1377. After a week of hiking and camping, do your laundry and take a shower at Dad's Laundry, 457 E. Wonder View Ave., Upper Stanley Village, 80517. (970) 586-2025. Mother and daughter, Carolyn and Heidi, are about as nice as people get.

I wrote this book in 2006 while living in a small cottage along the Big Thompson River near Estes Park, Colorado. I couldn't have asked for a more beautiful setting. The river flows out of the Rocky Mountains down a spectacular canyon onto the plains of eastern Colorado and is gorgeous in every season. It is a pleasure just to watch the cutthroat trout jump, the ducks swim, and the beavers work on their dams, surrounded by the canyon's rocks, ponderosa pines, and aspens. Every morning in winter we observed deer in the fields across the highway follow, dog-like, a man setting food out for them. One afternoon, a red fox skipped across the partially frozen river and stood in front of our living room window. While I was away teaching a class in Massachusetts, my wife Karen saw a bobcat moseying along the flagstone path behind our kitchen. She went to the side door to watch, and the bobcat stopped a foot away and stared at her before bounding up the canyon boulders behind the house. There are also mountain lions in the boulders, but thankfully we haven't seen one of these shy but dangerous creatures.

Our cottage in late summer.

Our house was cozy and trim. We rented it furnished from a businessman and fanatic fisherman who lived in Boulder, about thirty-five miles south of Estes Park. We did have to get used to some minor—

at least they came to seem minor—inconveniences. A freestanding propane stove was the main heat source. It kept the living room and the kitchen warm, but the rest of the house was unheated. We had electric space heaters for the other rooms when we used them, but without one of these our bedroom was usually about 45 degrees Fahrenheit on winter mornings. There was no well, so we had to have water trucked in to the 1,000-gallon plastic container that stood in a shed connected to the house. There was also a 1,500-gallon septic tank, enclosed so that waste wouldn't leach into the river. Since we had to pay for the water (seven cents per gallon) and to have the septic tank emptied (ten cents per gallon), we became zealous conservationists. Any liquid put down the drains went into the septic system, so we kept this to a minimum by collecting waste—from showers, cooking, and dishes—and using it to water the grass and trees. For toilet use, we abided by the adage "If it's yellow let it mellow; if it's brown flush it down." During our stay, we used less than 100 gallons of water per week. There was a satellite dish on the roof, but we decided to forgo a television, the first time in our lives we had done so. We were surprised how little we missed it. We substituted radio, CDs, and movies we rented from a mail subscription service and watched on my laptop computer's DVD player.

The town sits in a lovely valley (or "park" as these valleys are called in the Rockies) surrounded by high mountain peaks. Its setting has been called "the Alps of the United States." We never ceased to marvel at the view we saw on every clear day when we drove the two miles into town to buy newspapers and do daily chores. Winter offered the best vistas, snow-covered mountains often shrouded in frozen mists or blowing snow. Sometimes we would look at the highest mountain, Long's Peak—14,255 feet high and first climbed by one-armed Major John Wesley Powell—and imagine being up there in the swirling wind and cold. The town has the distinction of being the gateway to Rocky Mountain National Park. It is more pleasing to the eye than most such places. Perhaps this is because good design judgment was used in rebuilding after a major flood destroyed the town in 1982. In summer, when more than two million visitors come through and the resident population swells from 5,000 to more than 30,000, the sidewalks are planted with bright flowers, and hanging baskets adorn nearly every business doorway. Although motels can be expensive, there are still bargain places to stay, including campgrounds, and there is plenty of relatively cheap entertainment for families. There is a fee to get into the national park, but it is well worth it. There are hundreds of trails, waterfalls, roaring streams, remarkable rock formations, coyotes, elk, bighorn sheep, mountain goats, magpies, ravens, moose, black bears, and mountain lions. For an exciting day trip, guaranteed to give the most jaded traveler a thrill, you can drive up Trail Ridge Road, which, at more than 12,000 feet in elevation, is the highest continuous highway in North America. The road, closed from October until the end of May due to snow and high winds, crosses the Continental Divide, and on the western side you can stop at a trail and hike to the headwaters of the mighty Colorado River.

Hiking to Gem Lake, Estes Park, Colorado.

The locals, many of whom hail from the Midwest, are friendly, exuberantly so, in the way similar to what they call in another state "Minnesota nice." City sophisticates would probably be skeptical of this, as we were, coming from Miami Beach, but it delighted us nonetheless. The clerks at the grocery store and post office, the workers at the gym and coffee shops, the patrons of the Sunday winter concerts at the Stanley

Hotel, auto repair shop owners, secretaries, airport shuttle drivers—nearly everyone was congenial and polite. Our mail carrier delivered a package to our doorstep after his work hours, and the Federal Express driver left us his cell phone number and said he would make a return trip if we called him and he was still in the area. When I went away for two weeks to teach in Amherst, Massachusetts, the woman who runs the laundromat offered to help my wife in any way she could.

We have learned in our extended tour of the nation that when you scratch beneath the surface of a place, you find that appearances are deceiving. Estes Park was no exception. There is a wide social and economic gap between tourists and townspeople. Julie Dunn tells us in a *Denver Post* article (July 9, 2006) that in 2005, 31 percent of overnight visitors reported an annual household income of more than $125,000. At the same time, the locals often struggle to get by. Much of the day-to-day work is done by immigrants: Brazilians, Mexicans, Nepalese, Byelorussians. To afford substandard housing, workers—whether immigrants or not—must have more than one job and cannot always find year-round employment. In summer it is common for workers to labor eighty hours a week, but in winter they might not have work at all. Too many people, even those in their fifties and older, live catch-as-catch-can, cleaning homes and working in small shops, living in houses without indoor toilets. By September you notice the beaten-down look on their faces, exhausted from long days of toil waiting on tourists. You can almost feel the aching limbs of the immigrant women who have just spent sixty to seventy hours a week cleaning motel rooms.

Many of the houses and condominiums in Estes Park are empty a large part of the year; they are the second homes of visitors. In the *Denver Post* article cited above, we learn that "more than 50 percent of transactions are now second-home purchases." Most are very large—several thousand square feet—and priced beyond the means of the locals. "In late June [2006], 25 million-dollar homes were listed in the area, compared with five homes in that price point two years ago . . . ." So, ironically, there are empty houses and a housing shortage at the same time. New expensive developments are always being built or planned, blotting the landscape, although they do provide construction jobs for workers, who need the employment.

The yearly influx of tourists has given the town a hefty budget surplus (over $13 million), and to some extent the money has been used for the benefit of the community—a good library with free high-speed Internet connections, inexpensive or free entertainment for children and adults, well-maintained streets—but more could be done. The town owns its electric utility and electricity is less expensive than anywhere else we've lived. But the surplus could be used to lower the price further. There doesn't appear to have been a need for the rate increase imposed last winter, unless it had to be used for the inordinately high salaries of town officials. The chief of police earns nearly $100,000 per year. More could be done to provide low-cost housing, especially for immigrant workers and senior citizens. Much praise was given the owner of a mobile-home park who donated the used trailers to American Indians in South Dakota. However, it went unmentioned that his property was going to be used for another high-priced development. Low-rent trailers were eliminated in a town where people desperately need housing. And the trailers were given to people of color, when people of color are those who most need housing here.

At first sight, Estes Park seems like a pristine community. It is certainly the cleanest place we have ever lived. By comparison, Manhattan and Miami Beach were overwhelmed with pollution, congestion, noise, and litter. Yet even here there are troubling signs of environmental degradation. The suburban and industrial development east of town, on the plains facing the front range of the mountains, is sending pollution into Rocky Mountain National Park, reducing visibility and damaging plant and animal life. It is not unusual to see a ring of smog surrounding the nearby towns of Loveland, Boulder, and Denver. The U.S. Forest Service is planning significant land sales to private developers, which will reduce the public patrimony and at the same time further divide rich and poor as more expensive homes are built on this land.

There are other things about the area I came to dislike. Although there is a local peace group, strongly opposed to the war in Iraq, the politics of the town are very conservative. There are quite a few retired military here and, as they do everywhere, tend to make a place less democratic and tolerant. And since Colorado is the national center of extreme right-wing Christianity, this only adds to the conservative tendencies of the community. For a predominantly white, small town, we heard many racist remarks. There is also a notable lack of curiosity about what is happening in the rest of the nation and in the world. This made it difficult for us to build friendships; there is only so much you can say about the weather.

But on the whole this has been a good place to live and write my book. It is quiet, and in winter there is not much to do. I have had a lot of time to think and reflect. At night I could see the stars, and the full moons were so bright that I could see my shadow on the snow. There is a timelessness about things: the river, the rocks, the trees, the animals. Yet close by there were people—working, eating, loving. Struggling, I hope, to understand things. Like me. This book speaks to my understanding of the country. It is not an ordinary travel book, though readers may be inspired to visit some of the places described in it. Instead, it is an attempt to combine a travelogue and an economic commentary. To visit a town or an area and not try to learn how people live, what work they do, what they have done to the land, how they are divided by race, gender, and class, seems inadequate. The United States is a beautiful country, but its beauty is best understood in its full economic, political, and environmental contexts. This book tries to provide this understanding in a personal and concrete way. Hopefully, readers will find this approach useful and interesting.

SUGGESTED READINGS

The demographic data for Estes Park and for the towns listed at the top of each remaining chapter are taken from *http://www.epodunk.com*. The racial percentages may add up to less than 100 percent because not all racial classifications are included for a particular town. These percentages may also sometimes add up to more than 100 percent because the racial categories are not always mutually exclusive. For example, a person can be both white (or black) and Hispanic. All of this data is from 2000, unless otherwise noted.

CHAPTER ONE

THE ROAD BECKONS

JOHNSTOWN, PA

Population in 2000 23,906
Population in 1970 42,476
    White 86.3%
    Black 10.7%

Median household income in 2000 .... $20,595
(50% of the national average)
Median rent in 2000 .... $234
Median mortgage, including associated costs $606
People below poverty level of income 24.6%

Steel employment in 1950 .... more than 20,000
Steel employment in the late 1990s .... less than 3,000

"In 2003, U.S. Census data showed that Johnstown was the city in the United States least likely to attract newcomers . . . ."(Wikipedia). Johnstown has the world's steepest vehicular inclined plane. Visit the Johnstown Flood National Monument, 733 Lake Road, South Fork, PA 15956, (814) 495-4643.

PITTSBURGH, PA

Population in 2000 334,563
Population in 1970 529,167
    White 67.7%
    Black 27.1%

Median household income in 2000 .... $28,588
Median rent in 2000 .... $414
Median mortgage, including associated costs $794
People below poverty level of income in 2003 .... 16.1%

Biggest employers .... Healthcare and Education

Pittsburgh is in Allegheny County, which is the bridge capital of the world, with 1,700 bridges, one for every mile of road. Pittsburgh is number one on a list of most frequently misspelled cities. Check out the largest museum devoted to the works of a single artist, native son Andy Warhol: The Andy Warhol Museum, 117 Sandusky St., Pittsburgh, PA 15212, (412) 237-8300.

ROUTE 22

The distance between Pittsburgh and Johnstown, Pennsylvania, is about seventy-five miles. Most of the trip is on Route 22, a dismal and depressing stretch of highway that perfectly mirrors the drab ugliness of much of western Pennsylvania. Gene & Boots Candy Shop, Dick's Diner, Dean's Diner, Zoila's Western Diner, Country Kitchen (with "broasted" chicken), Dairy Queens, Crest Nursing Home, Spahr Nursing Home, 7-11s, car dealerships, a strip mine, the Cheese House, motels, strip malls, two adult video stores (a clerk was murdered in one of them, but the killer was never found), the country's only drive-thru "Gentlemen's Club" (aptly named Climax), the smallest house I have ever seen, feed stores, Long's Taxidermy, Monroeville, Murraysville, New Alexandria, Blairsville, Dilltown, Armagh, Clyde, Seward, Charles, bad curves, black ice, fallen trees, wrecked big rigs, school buses stopping on the highway, kids walking slowly to the trailer parks and country shacks, mobile homes for sale, a power plant belching smoke and steam in the distance—not an eye-pleasing scene until you get to the Conemaugh Gap, where the waters raged in the Great Johnstown Flood of 1889.

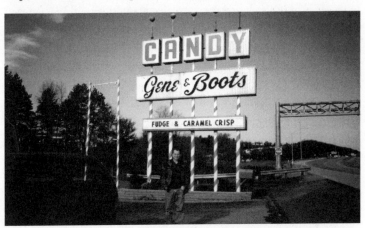

Gene & Boots on Route 22.

When I was young, parts of this highway were three lanes, and you could pass in the middle lane from either direction. If you were traveling east and started to pass a car, you never knew when someone going west might have the same idea. After many accidents, the third lane was converted into a turning lane and a fourth lane added. Progress! Back then, Pittsburgh and Johnstown were steel cities—dirty, yes, but there was work at high wages. And a little pride too. Now both towns are in the rust belt. The famous Homestead Works of U.S. Steel, built by Andrew Carnegie and site of the Homestead strike—where the picketers set the barges filled with Pinkerton strikebreakers on fire with flaming arrows—have been torn down and replaced by an upscale shopping complex. Johnstown's Bethlehem Steel plant, once the center of the industry's technological advances, has been sold piecemeal. Train wheels, steel rods, and wire are still made there, but the size of the workforce is a tiny fraction of what it was when I started work in the "flood city." Hard times have become a way of life. I would wager that there are more drug addicts and alcoholics in Pittsburgh and Johnstown than there are steelworkers. A lot more.

I spent nineteen years in Johnstown, but I never felt that it was my home. I kept moving from one part of town to another, nine moves in all, but a sense of place eluded me. I worried about this until I recognized that I didn't feel at home anywhere. I grew up in a small factory town, and what I am now was shaped by the eighteen years I lived there. Yet I vividly remember coming back after my first two months in college. I was shooting pool in the clubhouse where my friends and I hung out. I looked out the window into the mid-autumn night and realized suddenly that I was just a visitor. Today there is not a single person from my high school years with whom I keep in touch. I enjoyed college, but I have not remained in contact with any of my classmates, nor have I never attended a class reunion. I did return in 2004 to give a public lecture, but I couldn't wait to get out of there. The whole place filled me with dread; it was like being in a graveyard and seeing your own tombstone.

JOHNSTOWN AND PITTSBURGH

I moved to Johnstown in 1969. I had been in graduate school at the University of Pittsburgh studying economics. In 1968, after the government ended graduate student deferments, my local draft board started breathing down my neck. Uncle Sam needed cannon fodder for Vietnam, and I was able-bodied. I was classified I-A (available for military service) in the fall of 1968 and drafted soon after. I spent the next year battling my draft board—appealing my classification, seeing draft counselors, and filing a lawsuit. Fortunately, every time the board ordered me to report for duty I was in the middle of a semester, and the board agreed each time to let me complete it.

In the summer of 1969, during the middle of another term, my academic advisor suggested that, since teachers were still exempt from the draft, I apply for a college teaching job. I told him I didn't even have a Master's degree, so how could I get a job? He said it couldn't hurt to try. So I did, and when a senior classmate turned down a job at the university's campus in Johnstown, I got an interview. I drove along Route 22 for the first time in my life. Johnstown wasn't far away, but it had always seemed like a distant outpost. I remember coming around a bend along

Route 56, the road you had to turn onto from 22 and which overlooked the river valley known as the Conemaugh Gap, and entering the town. I saw a junkyard and then the steel mills smoking in the distance. The first year I worked there, I visited my parents most weekends, and I cried every Sunday evening when I returned to Johnstown and saw the fiery stacks of the Bethlehem Steel plants. I didn't cry that first time. I got lost and barely made it to my interview. I made friendly with the dean and told him I could teach the four wildly different classes (Statistics, Microeconomics, Macroeconomics, and Labor Union Theory) he asked me about. Afterwards, one of his aides took me to a campus eatery called the Tuck Shop and bought me a ten-cent Coke. About a week later I was offered the job, with salary of $7,200 plus room and board for an additional job as Resident Assistant in one of the dormitories. The draft board dutifully reclassified me I-Y (available for military service, but only in the event of a national emergency). If I stayed teaching, I would be safe.

I never planned to remain in Johnstown. I had dreams of fame and fortune and, above all, travel. But our lives are circumscribed by circumstance. The war in Vietnam dragged on until 1975, so I risked being drafted if I quit before the war ended. I had to get a Ph.D. if I hoped to make an academic name for myself. So for five years, I commuted on Route 22 from Johnstown to Pittsburgh for classes. The courses were five dollars a credit. I enjoyed teaching and was good at it. Many of my early students were working-class kids like I was, and I began to feel a sense of duty to educate them. I made friends and some of us began to try to transform the college, mainly by trying to unionize all the workers, first the maintenance and custodial staff and then the teachers. The years began to pass in a not unpleasant succession of writing lectures, playing basketball, agitating for a union, and drinking in local bars.

At the end of my second year, I took a trip cross-country with a friend from high school. We were deep into the dying culture of the Sixties and wanted to pay homage to the Beats and the hippies. We had a great time, sleeping in a church graveyard, in parks, and on the beach in Oregon. We picked up hitchhiking Indians in Montana, who shared with us their tortillas and marijuana, and a longshoreman heading for

San Francisco. We dropped him off and roamed around the city on the bay, making the mandatory trip to Haight-Ashbury. We spent two nights at the home of my friend's aunt and uncle in Stockton. We attended the county fair in 110-degree heat and then went into San Francisco for a baseball game. It was so cold, everyone (but us) wore sweaters and drank hot chocolate. Foolishly we parked our car on the street, and when we returned after the game, we found the trunk lock neatly punched out and our belongings stolen. An anthropologist colleague who had done field work in this part of the city told me that we had probably been the victim of a Samoan gang. We drove east the next day chastened but still thrilled with what we had seen. I promised myself I would do this again soon. As it turned out, soon was quite a while.

College teaching is a comfortable lifestyle. My father used to tell his racetrack cronies that his son worked only twelve hours a week. I would explain that it was more complicated than that. I had to prepare lectures, meet with and advise students, go to meetings, do research, and write articles. However, there was truth in what my father believed about my job. I had control over both my time and the content of my work. I had to teach for ten hours a week and be available to students in my office for six. So except for at most sixteen hours a week, my time was my own. Preparing lectures and writing articles and book reviews were fulfilling uses of my creativity and valuable ingredients for what went on in class. The lectures themselves were a kind of performance art, and when they went well they generated an addictive euphoria. In a small town, a professor is an important person and commands automatic respect. People began to recognize me, and they listened to what I had to say. This was a real ego-booster.

WORK TURNS SOUR

The good parts of the job carried me along for about a dozen years. Then the bad parts began to show themselves. One of my fields of study is work. What is work? Why do we do it the way we do? Can a job make us happy? What I began to learn about work depressed me profoundly, especially when I saw that it applied to teaching too.

I'll put it bluntly: Years of study and observation have taught me that work really does stink. It doesn't have to, but it does in our society. We live in a capitalist system, and what makes it tick is the never-ending drive by businesses to make a profit. To investigate a story, reporters are told to "follow the money." Sound advice. It is hard to find any activity or aspect of life that is not subordinate to the pursuit of the dollar. Work is no exception.

We have been sold a bill of goods about work. Go to school. Get a good job. Work hard. Make money. Buy things. The American Dream. Unfortunately, most of the people in the world never make it over the first hurdle, since they are too poor to afford an education. And those who do find that their jobs do not qualify as good ones. Nearly all jobs necessitate routine tasks requiring us to use a tiny fraction of our ingenuity; nearly all jobs force us to submit to a callous and impersonal hierarchy, and are fraught with insecurity. Mine was no exception. It wasn't horrible, certainly not in the sense that working in a chicken processing plant or a telemarketing cubicle is, but I can say that I found it to be increasingly meaningless. For a few years it was great. The spirit of the Sixties was still alive, and most of my students were working-class teenagers and adults, proud to be the first in their families to go to college. I felt that in teaching them the realities of our economic system, I was preparing most to better navigate the world and a few to change it.

But as the steel mills went belly up in the 1970s and 1980s, Johnstown hit the skids. Those who could left, but many who remained could no longer afford to send their kids (or themselves) to college. We ran out of Vietnam veterans too. So to keep the school going, administrators began to recruit students from the middle-class suburbs near Pittsburgh. These young men and women, better-off and reared in a more conservative time, were not my cup of tea. They tended to feel entitled to a degree without much effort. A college diploma was seen as a commodity, and I was more or less there to see to it that their purchase went smoothly.

Many of these new students exhibited an almost willful stupidity. I used to point out to students in some of my classes the deleterious effects of long hours of labor on a person's intelligence. Karl Marx has a good example in *Capital, Volume I*, where he quotes an English factory inspector whose interrogation of child mill workers indicated that they knew virtually nothing. One child said that a princess was a man, and another did not know that he lived in England. Herbert Gutman, in his book *Work, Culture, and Society*, cites a New Jersey inspector to the same effect: One boy thought Europe was on the moon, while another thought that the word "boy" was a comma. With the new students, I began to wonder what such examples meant to them. I had a student in a seminar on Marx who wrote that the *Communist Manifesto* is a novel. In my introductory class, a student wrote without irony, "The Unighted States." Another said that a good that is not "inferior" (one for which, other things equal, as income rises, purchases fall) is "ferior." Still another asked seriously whether it was "demand and supply" or "supply and demand." In the Marx seminar, after I had explained Marx's concept of the value of labor power (its value equals the value of those consumption goods necessary for the worker to continue working and ensure that the family's children grow up to become workers), I asked the class what Marx says is the minimum value of labor power. A student awoke from a dead sleep (this in a class of ten, sitting around a seminar table) and blurted out "$5.15"!

Although I often took my students' anti-intellectualism personally, I knew that their attitudes had developed in an accommodating milieu. Beginning roughly with the Reagan years, the colleges and universities transformed themselves into businesslike corporations: marketing experts, corporate titles for academic officers, patent shopping, shilling for business paraded as public interest research, distance "learning," grotesquely high salaries for those who bring in the most money, million-dollar coaches, education as product, students as consumers, the defunding of the humanities and social sciences, and the general cheapening of learning. As business values consumed the colleges, class sizes shot up and more part-timers were hired. To compensate for lower pay and harder work, teachers began to cut corners, dumbing down their classes in the process. This meant that less competent teachers could be hired, and this fit in nicely with the work-averse attitudes of so many students. Students flocked to easy teachers and soft majors, like Business and Communications, and the schools got worse and worse.

My students were just products of all these things. But even so, it made me sick. I was almost embarrassed to be a part of it. Some students rebelled against the corporate model, but not many. Most just accepted it, and no wonder, since they grew up in a world where making money and avoiding thought were not just normal but exalted.

Cheese House, Route 22.

THE ROAD BECKONS

I could go on, tell you more about the demise of higher education, and give chapter and verse on my deteriorating mental and physical health, but I am sure you get the picture. In 1988, I moved to Pittsburgh from Johnstown and commuted on Route 22 for the next thirteen years. You probably see what's coming. I got sick of teaching and decided to quit. I turned fifty-five in January of 2001. Our four children were on their own. The stock market had been booming for five years and my pension fund had nearly doubled. At fifty-five, I could withdraw money from it without tax penalty. My wife and I had made two cross-country trips, in 1997 and 1999. We loved driving from place to place, seeing new things. We began to plan for my retirement, and we decided that when that day came we would leave western Pennsylvania for good.

That day did come in April 2001. Our original plan was to move to Manhattan that month. I was supposed to work for *Monthly Review* magazine. But in December 2000, we hit some snags, and it became apparent that we wouldn't be able to do this. At first we were crushed; we had just assumed that this was going to happen. We regrouped quickly. On our two previous trips, we met couples who had worked in national parks and enjoyed it. We liked the idea and applied for jobs at five of them. All offered us employment, and we chose the largest, Yellowstone National Park.

We resolved that we would travel light. We decided to give our possessions—except our clothes, my laptop computer, and an old car—to our children, and what they didn't want we would give to friends or to Goodwill. We made a list of everything and gave a copy to each child. Each chose the things he or she wanted, and then we divided it all as fairly as we could. We filled up several van loads of furniture, beds, book shelves, computers, stereos, radios, filing cabinets, rugs, kitchen equipment, framed prints and paintings, and all the other gadgets and contraptions people collect in a lifetime, and we moved them to our children's apartments. We packed the rest and drove it to friends' houses and to my mother's. We made a dozen trips to Goodwill. I put all my books and journals in boxes I got from a maintenance man at school and had most of them delivered to the college library. The rest I gave to friends and students I liked. My office couch and coffee table I gave to the woman I had commuted to work with for thirteen years. One gloomy day after Christmas, I went to my office and threw away nearly all my lecture notes, files, and personal papers, even thirty-two years worth of grade sheets. I wanted to end the old and begin the new.

My friend, Bruce Williams, with whom I had plotted and schemed and played basketball at school for thirty years, planned my big retirement party for the end of April. On March 27, 2001, he died. His wife and his daughter (my goddaughter) tried to revive him, but he just gurgled and passed away. I lived the next two weeks in a haze. I made small talk for hours at the funeral home. I listened to the orations in the church. I helped carry the heavy casket to the gravesite. Friends insisted on a retirement celebration, and I agreed to have one at the college. The president gave me the traditional silver (plated) bowl, and I was made professor emeritus. Kind words were said about me, and I made some remarks. I cried at the end when I mentioned my friend. The next week, we drove back to the school and took pictures of our favorite places along that Pennsylvania road I had traveled so many times: three nursing homes, Gene & Boots Candy, the Cheese House, Thatchers Motel—where a tractor-trailer truck once hit us—and, of course, Climax Gentlemen's Club.

We packed our Plymouth van, left our apartment in Pittsburgh on April 29, and headed west on the beckoning road. We have been on it ever since.

I arranged this book chronologically, because this helps to give my observations a good flow and offers me a natural way to introduce and discuss the book's main themes. Let me outline our five-year itinerary and present the themes. We worked at Yellowstone through the summer of 2001, me as a hotel desk clerk and my wife as a restaurant host. During our stay there, the New York deal went through, and in November 2002, we moved to Manhattan, delayed two months by the events of September 11. We lasted a year in New York City; then the wanderlust struck again. After a brief stay in Miami Beach, we traveled with our twin sons to Portland, Oregon, where we lived for fourteen months. Before leaving there, we stored our few belongings in a U-Haul storage facility outside the city. We then embarked on a four-month road trip, making a 7,000 mile loop, south to the deserts of California, north and east and finally west, through Arizona, New Mexico, Colorado, Utah, Wyoming, Montana, Idaho, Washington, and back to Oregon.

There, we had a hitch attached to our (new Dodge) van, rented a small U-Haul, emptied our storage space, and drove to my mother's home in western Pennsylvania. We put our possessions, by now down to about twenty boxes, in Mom's basement, and after visits with our children, now living in Pittsburgh and Arlington, Virginia, we drove to Miami Beach, where we lived by the ocean for seven months. On May 1, 2005, we drove north and west through Florida, along the soon-to-be devastated Gulf Coast, across the vast spaces of Texas, and back to our favorite haunts in New Mexico and Colorado. In July, we headed east again to see family and friends. We lasted not quite a month in the hot and polluted regions around Pittsburgh and Washington, D.C., more anxious every day to get back west. After a stop in Joplin, Missouri, to visit Karen's sister, we drove to Flagstaff, Arizona, where we remained for a month. We then drove north to Utah to visit a friend before going to Estes Park, Colorado.

On all of our road trips, we stayed in cheap motels and cooked our meals on a two-burner hot plate—hence the title of this book. We did our own cooking because we are particular about what we eat. We have three sons who work in restaurants, and we know too much about the quality of food served in all but the best of them. Had we not cooked, our health and energy levels would certainly have deteriorated. In addition, it is too expensive to regularly dine out, even at fast food establishments. My pension might have grown during the big bull market of the late nineties, but our income was still modest. Similarly, cheap motels were our only viable housing choice. We learned quickly how to find a decent room at a good price, typically using the motel coupon books found in state visitor centers or by shopping around in whatever town we happened to be.

THEMES OF THE BOOK

Ironically, one of the things we learned in our travels around the United States is that there are people living in cheap motels and cooking on hot plates out of economic necessity. In a run-down motel in Redding, California, we saw Hispanic immigrants hanging their laundry over the second-floor railing. Not long after this, we read an article in the *Washington Post* about computer programmers, downsized out of their jobs, who now roam the country doing contract work and living in cheap motels. And National Public Radio did a segment on the popularity of George Foreman grills for people living without cooking facilities.

People living in motels represent one extreme (along with homelessness) on a housing spectrum marked by grotesque inequality. And housing is just one kind of inequality in a nation where the growing gap between rich and poor is endemic and epidemic. In the aftermath of Hurricane Katrina, our newspapers were filled with stories about the sharp economic divide. If only reporters had taken the time to get to know their own country. Inequality cannot be missed by anyone willing to look and see. You have to be like some of my old students, willfully ignorant, to miss it.

Inequality, then, is one of this book's themes. Another is work. It is hard not to notice—in grocery stores, in Wal-Marts, in drugstores, motels, on road crews, in hospitals, in convenience stores, in restaurants, in retail outlets like Office Depot, Circuit City, Lowe's, Home Depot, Marshalls, and the Gap, in Starbucks, in bookstores, in jewelry stores, in the national parks and monuments, in bakeries, in banks, in laundromats, in post offices, in apartment buildings, in parking garages, at the beaches, in bars, in call centers, in real estate agencies, in visitors' centers, in car dealerships, in insurance agencies, in state and federal government offices, on farms and ranches, on fishing boats, in colleges and universities, in doctor's, dentist's, and optometrist's offices, and on construction sites—that tens of millions of people nationwide perform labor that is neither interesting nor rewarding. Very few of the hundreds of workers we came in contact with during our travels earned high wages, and most of them worked in, at best, tolerable conditions. We saw right away that the more onerous the work, the more likely it was that a person of color did the job. White motel housekeepers were rare, as were white kitchen employees and farm laborers. Just as there is housing apartheid in the United States, so too is there an evident color line in the world of toil.

The destruction of the natural world is the third theme of this book. Two of the most noticeable features of the American landscape are its growing uniformity and our disregard for beauty. With few exceptions, one small or medium-sized town could be substituted for any other: highways leading into and out of town clogged with traffic and crawling with strip malls, the same fast-food restaurants and stores everywhere. The downtown areas, which often show signs of once having been thriving social and commercial centers and possessing an aesthetic sensibility, are now shells of their former selves. Storefronts are boarded up, and only the poor and troubled live there. By early evening the streets are empty. In towns with the good fortune to be located in beautiful settings—such as Flagstaff, Arizona; Santa Fe, New Mexico; and Port Angeles, Washington—you see similar things, although there are variations worth noting. Fine stone houses in central Flagstaff have been subdivided and converted into small businesses or made into apartments, in both cases losing their integrity and charm. Tourists abound, but few live there. In Santa Fe, the downtown is inhabited almost solely by wealthy tourists; you can't buy groceries or sundries anywhere near the famous central plaza. Like the French Quarter in pre-Katrina New Orleans, Santa Fe's central spaces more and more resemble urban theme parks than places where local lives are lived. In both Flagstaff and Santa Fe, the main entry roads are choked with traffic and polluted with automobile emissions. Flagstaff and Port Angeles also suffer foul air from a downtown petroleum plant and lumber mill, respectively.

Throughout the United States, even in places you wouldn't expect— Twentynine Palms, California; Bozeman and Kalispell, Montana; and Newport, Oregon—there is sprawl. Cities expand and give way to suburbs, and what used to be rural areas have become the exurbs *New York Times* columnist David Brooks extols, though not enough to live in one. More people, more roads, more cookie-cutter housing developments, shopping malls, and industrial parks, and on and on, without plan or sense of harmony; the landscape is devoured. Trees are cut down; power lines and power plants are built; dams are constructed; hills are leveled; road repairs and construction go on relentlessly day and night. The constant "development" encroaches on our forests, mountains, deserts, streams, rivers, and oceans. Outside Miami, housing developments have been shrinking the Everglades for decades. The sprawls that are Phoenix, Los Angeles, and Las Vegas have ruined deserts, rivers, mountains, and canyons. Nothing escapes "progress." Even our glorious national parks grow more polluted every year.

Growing inequality, trivial and alienating labor, and environmental despoliation—these are the things we witnessed. We saw many beautiful, exhilarating, and wondrous places, but the excitement we felt was always somehow reduced by our growing understanding that these places cannot be enjoyed by all. And none of them are so safe that future generations can be certain of their continued existence, much less their capacity to give pleasure.

SUGGESTED READINGS

On Johnstown, see: David McCullough, *Johnstown Flood* (New York, NY: Simon & Schuster, 1987); Jack Metzgar, *Striking Steel* (Philadelphia: Temple University Press, 2000). On the steel industry in Pittsburgh and the demise of a steel town, see: William Serrin, *Homestead: The Glory and Tragedy of an American Steel Town* (New York, NY: Vintage, 1993). On higher education, see: Michael D. Yates, "Us Versus Them: Laboring in the Academic Factory," *Monthly Review*, January 2000.

CHAPTER TWO

YELLOWSTONE NATIONAL PARK

JACKSON, WYOMING

Population in 2003 8,825
Population in 2000
    White 89.4%
    Black 0.2%
    Hispanic (all races) 11.8%

Median household income in 2000 .... $47,757
People below poverty level of income 6.8%
Median rent in 2000 .... $642
Median mortgage, including associated costs $1,316

Elevation .... 6,209 ft.

The average price of a newly built house is in excess of one million dollars. They say that in Jackson today the billionaires are chasing out the millionaires. Visit the National Museum of Wildlife Art, 2820 Rungius Road, Jackson, Wyoming 83002, (800) 313-9553. Motels are expensive, but a cozy place to stay, and not budget-breaking, is in a cabin at the charming Kudar Motel, 260 N. Cache Drive, Jackson, Wyoming 83001, (307) 733-2823.

CODY, WYOMING

Population in 2003 8,973
Population in 2000
    White 96.9%
    Black 0.1%
    Hispanic (all races) 2.2%

Median household income in 2000 .... $34,450
People below poverty level of income 13.9%
Median rent in 2000 .... $383
Median mortgage, including associated costs $1,195

Make sure you visit the Buffalo Bill Historical Center, for great Western art. The entrance fee is steep, but good for two days: 720 Sheridan Ave., Cody, Wyoming 82414, (307) 587-4771. Catch a movie at one of the country's few remaining small-town movie theaters, the Cody Theatre, 1171 Sheridan Ave., Cody, WY 82414, (307) 587-2712. On a Saturday night, nearly everyone in town might be there. There were a dozen previews the night I went.

BOZEMAN, MONTANA

Population in 2003 30,753
Population in 2000
    White 94.7%
    Black 0.3%
    American Indian 0.2%
    Hispanic (all races) 1.6%

Median household income in 2000 .... $32,156
People below poverty level of income 20.2%
Median rent in 2000 .... $494
Median mortgage, including associated costs $1,005

A great food store is the Community Food Co-Op, 908 W. Main St., 59715, (406) 587-4039. Montana State University is here and is a pretty place to visit.

Yellowstone National Park is a mysterious and frightening place. It is the nation's first national park and one of its largest. It is not a place to be taken lightly; dangers abound. You might be walking in what seems to be a peaceful and beautiful valley surrounded by mountains, and suddenly your foot breaks through the earth and you tumble into a thermal pool hot enough to scald you to death. You might be driving along the shore of Lake Yellowstone's bone-chilling waters and notice what appears to be smoke rising from the shore. A closer look reveals a small volcano-like opening from which steam is rising. You read on a sign that fishermen used to cook their catches over this hole. Too many people got burned, so the park now prohibits this. You might be taking an idyllic hike in the woods and come face-to-face with a mother grizzly bear and her cubs. Better have your bear spray ready; if the can is capped and hooked onto your belt, you'll be dead if the bear decides to attack. You have three seconds. You might be taking an after-dinner stroll on a dark road and run smack into a sleeping bison. Good luck. If you get back to your hotel room safely, fall to sleep reading the book *Death in Yellowstone*. You'll marvel at the stupidity of the now dead tourists who thought they could make the bears do tricks or who jumped into a thermal pool to retrieve their pet dog.

Karen and I lived and worked in Yellowstone from May to September 2001. I was a front desk clerk at the Lake Hotel, and she was a host in its restaurant.

THE JOURNEY BEGINS

We left Pittsburgh on Sunday, April 29, 2001. I felt like a child before Christmas. Out with the old and in with the new! We were on the road for four days, finding motels in Janesville, Wisconsin (home of a large GM plant, some of whose operations have been moved to Mexico); Chamberlain, South Dakota (overlooking the Missouri River and the stark landscape of South Dakota); Billings, Montana (the rim rock surrounding the town is stunning, especially when hot air balloons are flying above it, and the lightning strikes on a summer night are spectacular); and Gardiner, Montana, the northern gateway to Yellowstone and site of the famous stone entrance archway. It was remarkable how quickly Route 22 began to fade from memory.

We stayed in Gardiner for three days. It is a small town (population in 2001: 851), dependent on tourists but without much in the way of amenities or charm. It reminded us of the town in the television show *Northern Exposure*, except that elk rather than moose roam about. The city life I had known seemed painfully remote when I couldn't link my computer to the Internet through the telephone in our motel room. When I asked the manager about this, she said that the motel had an antiquated phone system. We had to remember, she informed me, that we were in the wilderness. Maybe so, I told her, but she wasn't charging "wilderness" prices for the room. Fortunately there was a pawn shop nearby with an Internet connection.

We were nervous about actually residing and working in the park, and it was sinking in that we had no home and were traveling with nearly all our belongings in our car. So we calmed ourselves with long walks and drives: we drove to a trailhead but were afraid to hike after seeing grizzly bear warnings; we visited an old graveyard on the outskirts of town; and we went to the partially abandoned gold-mining town of Jardine, located at the end of a steep dirt road a few miles from Gardiner. We tried to imagine what life was like in such a lonely and desolate place.

On the fourth day, a Saturday, we drove the few blocks to company headquarters and signed in for work. Like recruits in boot camp, we were lined up and took our turns trying on work uniforms—shirts, pants, ties, jackets—hoping what the clerks threw at us would fit. Karen's long legs made for many trips to the dressing cubicle. After signing contracts and getting our photo IDs, we were instructed to go to Mammoth Hot Springs for lunch and orientation. We drove into Yellowstone National Park for the first time since heading west on this journey. Our excitement rose as we were admitted through the special gate, official employees of the Amfac Corporation.

I don't remember much about the orientation (except a short film warning us of rampaging animals), but at Mammoth Hot Springs I first experienced the strangeness and grandeur of Yellowstone. Thermal eruptions and flowing hot water have created a series of travertine terraces in hues of yellow and brown, remarkable land formations smelling strongly of sulphur. The ground bubbled and belched, and I thought a natural catastrophe might occur at any time.

After orientation, we drove further into the park and headed toward the lake area, to our new home. Yellowstone's main road is built in the shape of a figure eight. The Lake Hotel sits near the midpoint of the eastern side of the bottom loop of the eight, about a ninety-minute drive from Mammoth Hot Springs. South of the hotel, the waters of Yellowstone Lake spread out for more than twenty miles. It is the largest lake in North America above 7,000 feet, and like much of Yellowstone, it was created by an ancient and tremendous volcanic eruption, one which dwarfed the explosion that produced Crater Lake in Oregon.

There is a large complex of buildings at the lake area, including a clinic, a Hamilton Store (gift shop, lunch counter, and grocery store, since sold to another concessionaire), ranger station, Lake Lodge, living quarters for employees, guest cabins, and our workplace, the Lake Hotel—a long and stately wooden edifice built in 1891. We found the Personnel Office and met the director, a young man whom we encountered years later managing a bed-and-breakfast in Key West, Florida. He told us about how some things worked at the Lake, but he and his younger assistant seemed preoccupied and inattentive to our many questions. We were assigned living quarters in a dilapidated shed-like dormitory about a quarter-mile from the hotel. Our human resource specialists told us that this was where married couples typically lived if they didn't own a mobile home.

Since we were among the first arrivals, we hoped to get a clean, quiet room. We didn't. Our room was small and dingy, overlooking the parking lot, next to the dormitory's pay phone, and in direct view of employee RVs. Living in a national park and not a tree in sight! We found a corner room abutting the woods, went back to the personnel office, and insisted on a change. Room 112 in Teal Hall was ours.

The new room was better than the first, but hardly adequate. It was ten-by-ten feet in area plus a tiny shower/toilet. There was a small closet, but half of it was taken up by the water heater, though we never had enough hot water for more than one of us to get a shower. The sink was next to the bed, so close that you could sit in bed and brush your teeth. The space was barely furnished, so we ransacked the unoccupied rooms and took anything we might need to make our new home more comfortable: a compact vinyl-covered easy chair, two dressers, a desk chair, a mirror, and nails. We wiped the floors and walls, unpacked, put together two floor lamps, and hung the photographs and pictures we had brought from home. We prepared an "altar" on one dresser—utensils, sundries, and an expensive Williams-Sonoma coffee maker/bean grinder our kids bought us for Christmas. At least we'd have good

Our room in Teal Hall, 10 feet by 10 feet.

coffee every day. We found one station on the radio, broadcasting from Jackson, Wyoming. We had no television and no place to cook. The room did have a good heating unit that doubled as an air conditioner. All in all, in terms of living quarters we had definitely come down a notch or two—or twenty. We felt pretty low lying in bed that first night. It was so dark, so quiet, and so lonely. Karen started to cry. I tried to comfort her, but I wanted to cry too. What the hell were we doing here, in a room ten feet square? We joked later that if we didn't get a divorce then we never would.

We felt better the next morning. The weather was crisp and clear and the air cleaner than any we had ever breathed, and the food in the Employee Dining Room (EDR for short) was tolerable. Hope springs eternal! We even drove forty minutes north to the lodge at Canyon to buy a Sunday paper and didn't mind the inconvenience.

Over the next few days, we began to meet our co-workers. Most were from the United States, but there were Europeans and Africans as well. There were older couples like us, some living in dorms and others living in large and expensive mobile homes, with expandable sides, full kitchens, and satellite dishes. Most of the RV'ers came every year and had made a little community, meeting at each other's homes for cookouts and looking out for one another's pets. There were also older single people, including my wife's immediate supervisor, a woman in her mid-seventies who had been driving here alone from her home in rural Iowa for many years. There were college students, young people in their late twenties, and a few in their thirties, who were Yellowstone regulars.

TRAINING TO BE A GUEST SERVICE AGENT

While Karen was taking long walks, finding new things for our room, driving three hours to pick up our mail (just temporary until the lake post office opened), getting a tan in the bright warm sun, and waiting for her hostess class to begin the next week, I began training for my job. I was to be a desk clerk at the hotel. I wasn't to be called a clerk, though, but a guest service agent. I was one of a dozen employees assigned to be clerks; more would come on board as the season progressed. I soon found out that the job would be more complicated than I had thought. Two weeks of eight-hour days were being devoted to our training. I had a thick book of instructions, which I had to study at night. Every day, we learned of some new duty we would have. The hardest part was committing to memory all the computer codes and manipulations I would have to use, along with all the room types and activities available. I learned more about hotel rooms than I cared to know.

I noted that the young clerks-to-be were quicker on the computer, but the older hands were more serious about learning the job. I was humbled by the mistakes I made every day, but I was surprised by my desire to master this job. When a corporate bigwig visited our group to give us a pep talk, we were each asked to stand and say why we were here. I astonished myself by almost tearing up and saying that I hoped to prove to myself that I could do something besides what I had done for thirty-two years and was looking forward to working as part of a team. I still can't believe I did that.

I expected that most of my group would be college students, but this wasn't the case. One woman had supervised a bookmaking operation in Las Vegas; another was a retired insurance agent; one man seemed to be a drifter who went from job to job; one odd fellow was a former Census Bureau supervisor and ardent geyser watcher and predictor ("geyser" is the only Icelandic word used in English). Most appeared to be adept hikers. I would come to like my fellow workers. Karen and I have kept in touch with three of them since we left Yellowstone, including the "drifter," who turned out to be an interesting person and is now a good friend. It is curious that I taught at a college for thirty-two years and stay in close contact with just three of my former colleagues, and yet I bonded strongly with a crew of hotel clerks with whom I worked for four months.

Our instructor was a woman in her early thirties who had worked for the company for several years in various locations and in many jobs. When our training was done, she would work as a bus tour guide, driving an original touring vehicle that was as much of an attraction as the tour. She was a person of boundless enthusiasm, full of energy every day. She seemed to believe that nothing was more important than for us to become exceptional guest service agents. She never tired of doing the same exercises on the computer, and telling the same things about the park and its hotels that she must have recounted hundreds of times before. She was recently married, and she and her Dutch husband were also living in a small dorm room. He piloted a tour boat on the lake, wearing a ship captain's uniform. We called him the Admiral. I wondered what kind of a start to a marriage living here would be.

During one of the training sessions, we met our supervisor. He was a young man from Montana, and I don't think he had started to shave yet. Like our instructor, he was enthusiasm personified and friendly to a fault. To show us what the different rooms looked like, he invented a game in which we had to find a particular room from clues he gave us. I found myself participating in this endeavor with enthusiasm, but maybe this was because it was a welcome break from sitting in a classroom, role-playing guest and clerk.

For my work I was paid $6.25 per hour. Part of our room and board was deducted from our pay. There were no benefits, although for another deduction we got some minimal health insurance should we need to use the local clinic. Karen got $6.00 an hour, and I lorded it over her that I made a quarter more than she. I marveled that the company had somehow managed to get reasonably competent people to travel, at their own expense, long distances to work for low wages and feel lucky to be there. No doubt, the setting had something to do with this, as well as the partial room and board. The company tried to convey the idea that we were all in alliance with the National Park Service to preserve the parks, and this helped too, especially among the ecologically minded.

During the second week of training, one of the supervisors announced that two positions were open at the front desk, shift leader and tour clerk. The pay increase was twenty-five cents an hour. The shift leader would start the shift a half hour earlier than the rest of us, do additional paperwork, and deal with guest problems when the supervisors weren't on duty. The tour clerk would handle the many tour buses that arrived every day at the hotel. He or she would have to learn a set of new computer codes and master complicated paperwork. I was surprised when three of the younger people bid for the jobs. They apparently saw these positions as good career moves. This was a large hotel with a complex set of operations, so a job with some authority, no matter how little, would look good on their resumés.

AMFAC'S WORKFORCE

I was curious about Amfac's employment strategy. A fair number of employees were over fifty. The "lead" host in the restaurant was a woman of seventy-eight. Even though she was physically unable to do the work a typical restaurant demands, she was compliant and never questioned the low wages. Here she was useful. What the company lost in productivity, it gained in loyalty and willingness to take and give orders. Some of the older people were retired military, and while they varied in terms of personality (our next-door neighbor was a veteran, but he was also pro-union), they all had a military mind-set, very conducive to the company's typical corporate chain of command. Another vet, of both the Army and the Navy, was a security guard and had all the swagger of a drill instructor and the fake bravado you sometimes find in shopping mall cops. Once, off duty, he officiously told me that I wasn't allowed to have a glass of wine in a public place. (I was talking to someone on the hallway telephone in our dormitory.) Not long after, he threatened to kill someone and was fired.

Many workers were young people doing summer jobs. Only the waiters and bellhops could make good money, since the hotel was almost always full, and the expensive restaurant served over 600 dinners each night. For everyone else, earnings were meager. The company benefited from hiring young people in two ways. First, most were not too concerned with wages and working conditions. Second, a few were serious about careers, and the company could look them over and recruit the best for full-time positions.

There were workers who needed these jobs, and they enjoyed the freedom of moving around from park to park, summer and winter (the company has a contract at several parks and resorts). They also got a place to stay and relatively cheap food. One of these employees, George, was a native of Puerto Rico who grew up in the Bronx. He was a cook in the Employee Dining Room (EDR) and in the restaurant, although he had held a variety of other kitchen jobs. He was divorced and had a fifteen-year-old son who lived with his former wife in Puerto Rico. For George, this was a good job, all things considered, and, while he was not a company man, he would have hated to lose it. George's friend, Jorge, from Guatemala, also worked in the kitchen. In the winter Jorge worked in Key West, while George worked in Death Valley. Both would have been hard-pressed to meet expenses in a city, so this afforded a way for them to live.

The last group of workers was the foreigners. The company actively recruited in Europe and Africa and, from what the workers told us, made promises it seldom kept. Most of the recruiting was done in eastern Europe, in countries like Poland, the Czech Republic, and the Ukraine, and in African countries such as Ghana and Nigeria. Young men and women from these places came to the United States to earn money, learn English, and see the country. They hoped to make enough money at Yellowstone to pay for some travel before returning home. The company representatives promised them full-time work and suggested that there would be overtime too. A wide variety of job types was described, and it was implied that they could qualify for any of them. In all cases, the workers were responsible for their airfare and travel to Yellowstone. Some of them arrived already in debt. None of them had cars, which made it nearly impossible for them to explore the enormous park or get to the nearest towns, all of which were at least two hours away.

Teal Hall, our home at Yellowstone National Park (YNP).

The large number of foreign workers hired served the company's interests in several ways. Even more so than the U.S. workers, these employees would not be disruptive. If they were fired, where would they go and what would they do? They had to save at least enough money to get back home. They could also be assigned to the worst jobs, the ones domestic workers were most likely to quit, like cleaning rooms or working in the hotel's deli. Most of the room cleaners were foreigners (including the Ghanaians, who had been promised national park management training), and I thought that they were assigned to do this work because their English was inadequate for jobs requiring interaction with guests. But this wasn't true. When there was no one to work in the deli, a Polish woman (with little English) was given the job.

I often ate there, and I was horrified to see a long line of tourists trying to order lunch. She was working alone, taking orders and preparing the food. I made the simplest order I could, gave her a large tip, ate, and got out of there. I couldn't stand the tension.

SERVING THE GUESTS

Work began on Friday, May 18. I was up at 5:30 that morning, nervous and excited. I thought that I would be embarrassed to wear a uniform—black pants, black shoes, and green shirt with plastic name tag over the pocket—but I wasn't. Over the summer it was a joy not to have to worry about what to wear, and even better, the low humidity meant that I could forgo changing clothes for several days. I showered, dressed, and hurried to the EDR for breakfast. After eating, I walked slowly across the parking lot, through a side door and into the hotel lobby. I punched in on the time clock, the first time I had done that in thirty-three years. I went behind the check-in counter and into the small room where our "cash bank" was locked up. I got my money, checked it, and went to an open register. I said hello to my fellow clerks, put the fliers I would need in order, placed some pens and a notepad nearby, logged into the computer (I had written my log-in codes on the back of my name tag), mentally went through the codes I might need, tried to remember how to do the most complicated transactions, opened a package of Ricola throat lozenges, and waited for the first customers. My wife stopped by and took my picture. I wished for a second that I was anywhere but here. I wondered what would happen if a guest was someone I knew. I wasn't ashamed to be doing this, but I bet myself that my friends would think I was crazy.

It was busy that first day and every day after, even early in the season when not all of the park was open. I will outline my work duties shortly, but I quickly learned that the key to making the job bearable was to interact with the customers. Yellowstone covers a vast area, and it is impossible for visitors to get more than a glimpse of things in the one or two days most of them spend there. This meant that they came to the hotel tired and frustrated, especially if they had young children along. The hotel was expensive—$169, plus tax, a night for a lakefront room—and had none of the amenities found in a similarly priced hotel. No televisions, no pool, no sports lounge. This added to the guests' frustration. Talking to them helped them forget about how tired they were and how poor the service at the hotel was. Rooms were seldom ready at check-in, and sometimes they weren't cleaned until early evening. Towels and soap were often missing.

I had been to almost every state and I knew something about most countries, so I could gab with the guests and put them at ease and get them smiling. Within a few weeks, I had checked in people from some twenty states, as well as Japan, Germany, Holland, England, Canada, India, and France. I astounded a young Japanese guest studying for an MBA at Yale when I asked him about the former Japanese Finance Minister, Sakakibara, who attended the University of Pittsburgh and knew a good friend of mine. I charmed two Uruguayan guests with my elementary Spanish. They were impressed that I knew the Spanish word for "keys." One guest, a retired ship builder from Newport News, Virginia, was so happy that I remembered his name and occupation that he smiled every time he saw me. Whenever I could I allied myself with guests who had legitimate complaints: incorrect reservations, dirty rooms, small beds, telephones that didn't work, inaccurate room charges, and the like. Some of the worst problems involved the nearby cabins, which we also rented to guests but were not part of the main hotel. These were often musty and in disrepair, and some were rented under false pretenses, especially to foreigners who were bamboozled by their travel agents. The hotel sold cabin rooms to U.S. travel agents, who resold them to their European counterparts. These agents then represented the cabins as rooms in the old hotel. The cabin rate was $87.98 per night, but the guests had paid as much as $300.00, expecting to be in commodious accommodations overlooking the lake. If I could, I got them a hotel room (but they had to pay the difference between the two rates!). I strongly encouraged them to sue their agent and vehemently object to the manager that they had been swindled.

Rapport with the customers was made easier by the requirement that all employees wear name tags giving our first names and the state (or country) we were from. The guests were immediately brought into a sort of personal relationship with us via the tags. What a melting pot this is, they thought, all these people of all ages from all parts of the country and world. It reinforced a national pride for those who were from the United States, and in doing this it served the company rather well. It did not look like just any ordinary business but a very American company, serving the people's needs by helping them to see this American park and hiring an almost all-American workforce. The foreigners hired only emphasized the generous spirit of the company, and America.

But if making conversation with the guests made the job easier, it also tried my patience. I soon realized that clerks did not command the reflexive respect accorded professors. When guests saw a gray-haired man in a uniform wearing a name tag that said "Michael from Pennsylvania," they didn't automatically think that they should defer to him. Rather, they felt a sense of superiority (perhaps tinged with pity); this person was meant to serve them. They found a dozen ways to be rude and condescending. One couple actually accused me of calling them "assholes" when I turned away from them to ask the senior clerk for some help. I did not do this, but they reported me to the supervisor and had a long chat with him. Nothing came of this, but it could have turned out badly for me or for any worker a customer took a dislike to, for whatever reason. When I said to a Frenchman, "Where in France are you from?," he answered, "From Paris, you have heard of it?"

Here is a story to illustrate how some guests viewed us. Karen and I were moving to Manhattan after we left Yellowstone. We had visited the city many times and knew our way around town. Anytime I noticed guests from Manhattan, I asked them if they frequented such and such a place in their neighborhood or asked them a question about where they lived. And I told them our plans for the fall. Invariably a look came over their faces, the kind of look someone might give a child making some outlandish claim. They would say, "Well, it is really expensive to live in Manhattan," as if I didn't have the slightest idea that this was so. After this happened several times, I told the next person who said it, "Well, we have a great deal of money." Without missing a beat, the woman replied, "You'll really enjoy living there."

At least this person spoke to me. So many couldn't bother to treat me like a real, feeling human being. When I taught, I began to see that my students had come to view their teachers as part of something they had purchased, an "education" package, so that they might someday make more money. Similarly, in this job, we were a piece of an "entertainment" package. People often made no eye contact, were inordinately demanding, insulting, downright nasty and mean. It was a rare customer who made a personal remark, much less inquired about our work, where we lived in the park, and so on, or was sympathetic when we were swamped. For the most part, people didn't care about the work of a guest service agent. They had to pay for their vacation; their only obligation was to come up with the money.

An irritating characteristic of the guests was that, though they were in a national park, replete with natural and human-made splendor, they were remarkably unhappy. They came to the check-in counter looking glum, and many of them stayed that way. They couldn't cope with the fact that their cell phones didn't work, or that there was no swimming pool or workout room. One man spent most of his stay asking about his incoming faxes. He had tickets to a Western cookout at a lodge two hours away. He picked up the tickets and rushed out of the hotel when told he had thirty minutes to make a two-hour trip. People hung around the hotel griping that there was nothing to do when outside there were marvels they might never see again. It seemed that many people were here just to take pictures, and never strayed far from their cars.

A NEW RESPECT FOR WORKERS

Analyzing work is one thing; doing it is another. We have all dealt with clerks; there are millions of them in the United States. But many of us don't know much about what it means to be one. Here is what I learned.

The work was demanding. It wasn't factory labor, but it was tiring and stressful. I was on my feet six to eight hours at a stretch, and this took its toll on my legs. The Sunday before Memorial Day, I worked eight hours without a break, neither to rest nor to eat. Guests arrived nonstop, asked a million questions, and had complicated financial arrangements to be solved. Rooms weren't ready even into the evening (there was a shortage of housekeepers); cabin roofs were leaking; people were assigned to rooms without enough beds; and we kept putting guests into already occupied rooms. How this happened I cannot say, but the computer screen would show a room vacant and cleaned, we would assign someone to it, and a while later people would come back to the desk screaming that they had walked in on people in bed. It was a desk clerk's worst nightmare. So I had a steady stream of complaining guests, and these were holding up people still trying to get accommodations, and others wanting to ask questions about tours to take and things to see in the park. And all the while the phone rang, probably five hundred times during my shift alone. The hotel's manager had to deal with so many complaints that he said it was the worst night in his memory. At least he felt so bad for us that he got us some pizza later in the evening to make up for our missed supper. The only good thing about the night was that it was not again equaled. So the worst was over.

This is what I did each day. I checked people in, usually routine but not always. People sometimes wanted to upgrade or split their bills in complex ways or had special requests. I kept track of availability, not just here but in each of the eight hotels in the park. We were expected to make same-day or next-day reservations for any of them. I answered phones, mostly to connect callers to guests (it wasn't possible to dial a room directly from the outside), but often enough to answer some annoying questions—one person from the United States asked if it was safe to drink the water, while working the host position in the restaurant, Karen was asked to give a caller detailed driving directions from Los Angeles. I answered a never-ending barrage of questions: Where is the bathroom? What is the weather report? Can I change rooms? Where is the ice machine? How do I make a dinner reservation? What is there to do? When does Old Faithful erupt? How long does it take to get there? Where is the Elephant Back trail? Where is a good spot to go fishing? How do you get to Grand Teton National Park? What's the best way to get to Cody, Wyoming? Do you have the number of a rental car company in Jackson? Who designed the flower arrangement on our desk? There was nothing we were not expected to know or be able to find out, and after a time I began to take great pride in answering the most arcane or foolish question.

Grand Teton Mountains, Wyoming.

I ticketed and booked activities, of which there were many: bus tours, boat tours, horse rides at several park locations, photo safaris, chuck wagon cookouts, and wildlife excursions. It was tedious and time-consuming to check in a family and then book or ticket their activities, especially if they began to ask questions about them and there was a long line of guests. I kept housekeeping and maintenance aware of any problems in the rooms and other parts of the hotel. I checked people out, which again was usually routine but not always. Most people didn't go over their itemized bills but some did, and if they had questions about particular charges, I had to find out about them, which could involve a laborious search through the dining receipts. Once a waiter, unhappy with the size of a tip, altered a receipt, changing a zero to an eight. It took us a long time to unravel this bill, although it was exciting to catch the crook. I kept careful account of all cash transactions. These had to be posted to the right accounts, or else our book wouldn't balance at the end of the shift. When we were done with our shifts we had to file preliminary reports, see to it that these balanced, and then file a final report, drop our cash into a safe, and put our "bank" away. There were many forms to be aware of and many possibilities for mistakes. One day my cash balance was off by more than $200. Luckily I had written down

all my cash transactions, including the name of the guests giving me
cash. I had forgotten to post a cash payment and so it showed up as a
credit card transaction.

Eventually a job becomes routine, and desk clerking was no
exception. However, a crisis can always undermine routine and then
you learn how little you know. One day in June it began to snow, and by
late the next morning there was a foot on the ground. The entire park
was closed; no one could leave and no one could enter. At the time the
hotel was completely booked, all three hundred or so rooms and cabins.
I began work at 6:30 that morning, and I worked nonstop until about
12:30 that afternoon. The place was bedlam, with guests crowding
around the front desk wanting to know what they should do. Would they
be able to get out? Would they be able to catch planes? Could they stay
another night? Was the snow going to continue and, if so, for how long?
What was the temperature? How much snow had fallen? Were activities
cancelled? And on and on and on. As we tried to deal with all of this, the
power went out every few minutes and the phone rang off the hook. Had
I found someone's cell phone? Why didn't the tub drain? Why hadn't I
made a wake-up call exactly when the guest had requested?

In the midst of the chaos, I took a phone call from a man in
England. Had a fax come through for a guest, the caller's father? We
then proceeded to have a protracted conversation about this fax, which
he said was urgent. It turned out that he had sent it to the wrong fax
number. I gave him the correct number, and he said he would call me
back later to be sure we had received it. I then got back to the nightmare
at the front desk. About thirty minutes later, the phone rang and a
fellow clerk said that there was a long-distance call for me. I thought
immediately that something was wrong with one of our children, and I
picked up the phone fearfully. But it was just Mr. Young asking about the
fax. Yes, I said, the fax had come through and I would notify his father,
who had not yet checked in, that it was here. Well, he said, could I look
at the fax. I got the fax, amidst all of the noise and confusion, went back
to the phone, and spoke with Mr. Young (picture a small space with five
or six clerks rushing around, very loud noise that made it hard to hear,
me with a phone on my right shoulder and a pen in my left hand taking

notes). He insisted I verify that five pages had come and that they were all legible. He asked me to look at a particular paragraph. Did I have a highlighter? Would I highlight the sentence beginning with the word "Hereinafter" and ending with the word "yellow." I did as instructed. He said, "You've been soupah [super], Michael." Later that evening, after the parents of Mr. Young had checked in, my wife received a long-distance call at the restaurant from the son. Were his parents at dinner? How would she know? He had to get in touch with them. Could they be paged? No. Well, he said rudely, she would have to get in touch with them whatever it took. Finally, she said that she would go table to table to find them. She went to each table (remember that this restaurant seated hundreds of people and was as long as a football field) and said, "Are you the Youngs?" Finally, an English couple said that they were. As soon as they learned that their son was calling, they became hysterical. They went to the phone, and, after some business discussion (the fax and the phone calls were about the purchase of a ship), the father told his son not to call him again, because he was on holiday. He ended by saying that he could not take this anymore. Then the mother got on the phone and in a loud and emotional voice told her son to please not call again, because "Daddy is going to have a nervous breakdown." "Please, please, don't call again, Daddy can't take anymore." All the while the many guests at the host stand must have wondered what the hell was going on. And they never offered a word of thanks to anyone for relaying the message to them, nor an apology for such a bizarre conversation.

This story is amusing, and although I was stressed that day, I never lost my composure. The snowstorm was a bonding experience for all the workers, especially the desk clerks who were on the front lines of the bedlam. During all the turmoil, I was thinking about how I would enjoy trading stories with Karen after work. I'd go to the hotel bar and have a few beers while I waited for her shift to end. However, I soon got a better taste of what work stress can do and no doubt does do to tens of millions of poorly paid and disposable workers.

I became ill in late June—cold, fever, chills—and had to miss a day of work. The day before, I had put in a hard shift behind the front desk, coughing, sneezing, and blowing my nose. It was difficult to care about the problems the guests were encountering. At the end of the shift, I printed out my "preliminary" report showing all my cash transactions. It was important that I balance, that is, that the amount I took in matched what I had in my "bank." I also had to be sure that all the activities I sold were posted to the correct revenue center. For example, if I sold a boat or horse activity, this went to the "activity" revenue center; but if I sold a bus ride, this went to the "transportation" revenue center. After some problems with preliminary reports, I had learned to keep scrupulous records of all cash and activity transactions. This particular day, I took in several hundred dollars in cash and sold several activities. When I submitted my report, the printer failed to print it out, which meant that I could not check it and get my final report done and go home. This happened frequently, but this time, no one could fix the printer. As the minutes ticked by and I was feeling sicker and sicker and just wanted to go home and crawl under the covers, I got madder and madder. I started muttering. Eventually, I just left. But I had to return later that evening, feeling worse, to do the reports. This took only five (unpaid) minutes, but I was furious. For the first time in my life, I really felt how working people could get so frustrated with their jobs that they could go into a rage, even at some little thing. Under the right circumstances I might have thrown the printer out the window, or become abusive to a pesky guest, or assaulted the supervisor if he had said anything ridiculous.

The day the printer didn't work was also payday. My friend Bruce Williams used to call our paycheck at the college the "monthly insult." What would he have said here? For two full-time weeks of labor, Karen and I combined cleared less than $600. We had our pension to fall back on, but what if we depended on this job to live? Six hundred would have been more than an insult. And I couldn't have afforded to lose a day's pay. I was lucky, but many aren't.

WORK: ACT ONE, A DEEPER LOOK AT MY LABOR

Clerking reinforced certain notions I had about work. In our economy, skilled jobs are few and far between; there is a natural tendency for employers to eliminate such work whenever possible (by dividing up the labor into routine parts and by using machinery) because it is cheaper. However, management scholars and some progressives have argued that in the contemporary workplace, new skills are needed, so that even if plants no longer have, say, machinists, millwrights, carpenters, and the like, employers must still have people with skills. For example, they say that in the modern workplace, people with good interpersonal abilities are needed as well as people willing to work in teams. Therefore, being able to interact with others and to communicate effectively are the new skills. Or, they tell us, in the computer-driven workplace, people must have computer expertise.

Most of this is pure hokum. In my job as a "guest service agent" I had to get along with people, mainly the guests. I had to know how to keep them from getting angry, and it was useful to know how to make small talk with them. But if this is a skill, it is certainly one that the overwhelming majority of clerks easily could have mastered if they chose to. Since I was older and knew more of the world than most of my co-workers, I may have been better at this, but not much so and the difference did not matter in terms of the work getting done and the company making its profits. I also had to work in a "team," each shift of clerks constituting one. The advantage to the employer was that we were bound to assist each other. If someone got stuck and I could help, it was a natural human tendency to do this, so I did. The work was structured to compel us to cooperate. But this is not a skill; we all do it more or less automatically. I had to know the computer commands necessary to do my job. There were many of these, and it took me a while to learn them. But this was not skill, just memorization and repetition. Some of us were better than others, but again, if there was a problem someone solved it easily.

The way a modern workplace is integrated makes it difficult for workers not to work intensely and give their time to the company. Here, my jobs as teacher and clerk differed greatly. As a teacher, I had considerable control of what I did while working. I could teach when I preferred and prepare and deliver lectures as I saw fit. During a day at school there was more free time than work time. No one ever directly supervised me. At the hotel, my manager set my schedule and carefully monitored me. I had little free time during a shift.

There was the time clock; you had to use it to get paid. It was a shock to me to have to do so, to be compelled to be on the job during certain times and not others. What an ingenious device, just like the factory whistle of old times, but more sophisticated because so precise, and taken for granted by the workers.

Once I punched in it was imperative for the employer to see that I didn't relax, that I worked all day. The employer appeared to have understood the Japanese notion of *kaizen*, or constant speedup. This was achieved by never having enough clerks on duty. We couldn't complete our tasks quickly enough to get some free time. On those rare occasions when customers weren't making demands on us, we were assigned new duties: picking up trash or even making up rooms. So we were continuously "stressed" and thereby forced to work steadily throughout the day. Once, a young woman came to work with a hangover and began complaining immediately that she was tired. She took a break less than an hour after she started, just when most people were checking out. My immediate reaction was to think, what is this?—she is shifting the work onto us. She knew she had to work, so why wasn't she prepared to do so? This is a normal way to think, but it played into the employer's hands. Instead of us thinking about what was wrong with the whole job setup, we immediately thought in terms of personal animosity toward the slacker.

Another aspect of the job was that we worked in the open. There was no place to hide. If we were idle it was immediately apparent. We could steal some time by taking longer-than-normal breaks and meal periods, but then we let down our team members by making them do our work. It was a no-win situation. The only hope would have been a union, but the nature of the workforce at the hotel made that unlikely.

I was always surprised at the ease with which college teachers sided with the administration when there was conflict between it and the faculty. And how quickly a teacher who took an administrative post identified with the employer and forgot what he or she had done not so long ago. The clerks were no different. As explained above, each shift had a "team leader" (called a "senior clerk"), who had extra duties and earned a slightly higher hourly wage. It didn't take long for these "seniors" (aged nineteen, twenty, and twenty-three) to ally themselves with management, to the point of ordering us around and criticizing us in public. They solved problems for us, and, in this sense, they were useful. But it was striking to see how the "seniors" fit themselves into the chain of command without a second thought.

One thing about a routine job is that once you are done, you don't have to prepare for the next day's work. As a teacher, I was preparing all the time; everything I read or talked about might be put to good advantage in a future class, or in something I might write or give a talk about. This kept my mind alert, but sometimes it took its toll. It was hard to relax.

I thought that at the hotel I would have the luxury of not worrying about what I was going to do tomorrow. But while it was true that I didn't have to prepare for the next day's work, it was today's work that took its toll. The job was tiring; I was on my feet all day. At the end of the day I was free, but too exhausted to do anything. I often fell asleep soon after opening a book, as early as seven in the evening. And on some days, especially Sunday, which was the worst day in terms of work intensity and customer complaints, I couldn't sleep at all. The computer keys I had punched all day kept going through my head in an endless loop, and conversations I had with irate guests kept bothering me. Monday morning would arrive and I had to be at work at seven, and I didn't catch up on sleep until about Wednesday evening. Teaching might have generated a lot of anxiety, but this job was both physically and mentally debilitating. Thirty-two years of this would be unimaginable.

We got paid every other Wednesday. People from the payroll department sat behind a table in the EDR (while the rest of us were eating) with piles of money. And just like in a mining company town, workers lined up in front of them to cash their checks. Then they headed for the employee pub and gave the money back to the company. The pub was the most profitable center in the lake complex. Drunken employees carried on late into the night and were broke the next day. There were many heavy drinkers among the workers; one of the few benefits offered by the company was an employee drug and alcohol assistance program.

IN AND AROUND THE PARK

If work offered little compensation, the park and the places around it offered much. The West has its share of what makes the East irritating: too much traffic, too much heavy industry, too many people, too much pollution. But the West also has what the East lacks: a grand landscape and wide open spaces. In Yellowstone, for the first time in our lives, we were in a wild place with time to explore and enjoy it.

Yellowstone was the first of the country's national parks; it was established in 1872. The idea of national parks, however, dates from a few decades earlier. Philip Burnham, in his instructive book, *Indian Country, God's Country: Native Americans and the National Parks*, quotes the artist George Catlin, who had visited and painted in the West, as envisioning "a magnificent park, where the world could see for ages to come, the native Indian in his classic attire, galloping his wild horse, with sinewy bow, and shield and lance, amid the fleeting herds of elks and buffaloes." I will have something to say about American Indians later in this book. They were evicted from Yellowstone, and other national parks as well. But the elk and the bison are still there, along with many other animals, living in nature and not in a zoo. During our first three weeks in the park, we saw six grizzlies (three only twenty feet away), two coyotes, numerous bison, ducks, geese, elk, cutthroat trout, a pelican, a porcupine, an osprey (a large fish-eating raptor), and an eagle in the Grand Canyon of the Yellowstone.

We often drove from the lake north to Roosevelt, through Dunraven Pass. From a lookout along the narrow road, you could see the caldera shaped by the original volcanic action that created much of the park, as well as the great gorge through which flows the Yellowstone River, the longest un-dammed river in the continental United States. In July, when the wild flowers were in full glory, we took the long hike up to the fire tower on Mt. Washburn and were greeted near the top by a group of bighorn sheep. Later we spotted five black bears. One of them climbed part way up a tree and, after climbing down, stood and scratched its back against the bark. It looked for all the world like it was dancing. To top things off, we saw four golden eagles. Two of them flew directly overhead. They looked as if they had been on an Indian totem pole, good evidence that the Indians understood the power and beauty of these great birds. Through our binoculars we could see the underside of the eagles' wings. They were a beautiful yellow color, almost translucent. If you used your imagination, they looked like gigantic butterflies soaring through the sky.

One evening we saw something worthy of a television nature show. A bison had died in the Yellowstone River, and a large male grizzly was feeding on its carcass. The bear was camped out on the shore, wading into the shallow water to eat whenever it was hungry. It was so stuffed with meat that it could barely move. When we saw it, it was sleeping. Out of the woods a gray coyote crept down to the shore to the left of the bear and slowly made its way toward the carcass. The bear roused from its stupor and chased the coyote away. But the coyote was determined and moved back into the woods, only to sneak down around the bear on the right side, about fifty feet downstream. When the bear noticed it this time, it got up again and forced the thief to leave. But in the process the coyote had gotten the bear to move from its initial position close to the dead bison. Then the coyote maneuvered around once again to the left of the bear and this time got to the water, much closer to the meat. Just when it looked like it might get to eat, the bear charged and the coyote ran away for good. The speed of this bear was astounding, dispelling any notion that a human could outrun one in an encounter.

As the summer wore on, we began to trim our work schedules whenever we could. This was easier for Karen; the kitchen and dining room were always overstaffed. I began to give my hours to other clerks whenever they asked. For this I was called on the carpet by a young assistant manager, who said I was setting a bad example by working so little. I kept doing it anyway. We wanted to hike, explore the park, and see the surrounding towns and natural attractions. We soon became addicted to hiking. It is nearly impossible to have even a superficial knowledge of the natural world unless you get out of your car and look around. If you do, you will be rewarded. On our excursions, we saw so many marvelous things. We saw two bald eagles in a nest high atop a lodgepole pine parenting their two eaglets. One adult eagle watched and waited while the mate came back with food. When one landed, the other took off. A magnificent sight. Unfortunately a tourist retrieved a hammer from his car and repeatedly struck the tree trunk. Rangers had to put a barrier around it, so that the eagles wouldn't become upset and abandon their home. We saw a bull moose up close munching on leaves. We also observed many bison with their bright red calves in Hayden Valley, where we often drove. There we witnessed a large herd run to the river, swim across, and march up to and over the road, directly in front of us. Then they started rolling in the dust. You have to be impressed with these animals and the American Indians who hunted them. It must have been a daunting task to kill, and then skin and clean a bison, and to use every part of it for survival. And to think that there were once sixty million of them on the plains.

Though they came out much later than in the East, wild flowers blossomed continuously, numerous in variety and beautiful to see. We went on hikes with our friend, Dwight—who was sixty-seven and in better shape than either of us— and he told us the names of the flowers and plants: paintbrush, wax currant, mountain mahogany, yarrow, thistle, prairie sunflower, goldenrod, tansy, columbine, larkspur, Queen Anne's lace, and bluebells. We could never keep them straight, but we were delighted to see blooms we had only read about. The weather was unpredictable, which made our excursions more exciting. At any time, it might storm, hail, or even snow. Rainstorms came up suddenly and the wind whipped through the trees at night, sounding like a gale at sea. One day, the skies darkened over one half of the great lake while the sun shone over the other half. An enormously wide rainbow formed to the amazement of everyone who saw it. We walked or drove to the shore at night whenever there was a full moon. The light shone so brightly on the water that it might have been possible to read by it as you rowed your boat.

Yellowstone is an isolated place. At Butte Overlook, a few miles east of the hotel, there is a sign that says you are farther away from a regular road—other than a park road—than at any place in the lower forty-eight states. The park is vast, larger than some states, and it is a long distance between attractions. There are towns outside the park, with the nearest one a trying ninety-minute drive away. Sometimes visitors would stop at the front desk late in the evening hoping we had a room available. This even happened on holidays. We almost never had an opening; they were booked solid, sometimes months in advance. When someone made such a request, I checked availability at all the hotels in the park, and every now and then I'd find a room. Most times, however, I would direct people to the outside towns: Gardiner, Montana, Jackson, West Yellowstone, and Cody, Wyoming. To get to any of them required long and dangerous nighttime driving. And if roads were closed, as they often were for repairs, fires, mud slides, and snow, a two-hour drive could turn into a five- or six-hour marathon.

We especially liked Cody. We stayed there for three nights in late May, at a motel that rented its cabins to Yellowstone employees at a discount before the tourist season begins after Memorial Day. Cody is named for Buffalo Bill Cody, the Western "hero" and huckster. The main street of the town is filled with shops selling Western paraphernalia and American Indian "art." The back streets, however, are lined with attractive houses in the arts-and-crafts style and immense cottonwood trees, some over one hundred years old. Cody's legend still permeates the town, and the hotel he built, the Irma (named for his daughter), still stands, site of a nightly "shoot out" among fake cowboys. The cowboys were scruffy characters who sometimes looked the worse for wear from drinking too much. Each summer night at six they put on a show, which always ended in an orgy of gunfire, with people falling down dead, sometimes after dropping from the Irma's balcony.

The best thing in Cody was the Buffalo Bill Historical Center, a vast complex that included the Whitney Museum of Western Art (rich Easterners managed to get their fingers in nearly every pie in the West). In addition to the Whitney, the center contained the Buffalo Bill Museum, the Plains Indian Museum, a large library, and the Cody Firearms Museum. The gun museum contained the largest collection of firearms in the world. The exhibits describing the making of the guns, especially the use of a complicated division of labor to make interchangeable parts—without assembly lines—were fascinating. The guns themselves didn't interest me, although it is obvious that the history of these weapons is intimately connected to the development of our economic system. Ask the Indians.

We loved the many paintings, sculptures, engravings, and illustrations at the Whitney Museum. The great artists of the region—Bierstadt, Catlin, Moran, Russell, N.C. Wyeth, among many others—were well represented. The works of Frederick Remington were also much in evidence, although this artist, whose studio is also exhibited here, never spent much time in the West. Some of the works portrayed the area and the Indians idealistically, and many of the earlier ones showed the Indians as savages impeding "progress." Others presented them with respect, even reverence. But except for the few Native American artists represented, the indigenous peoples were treated as something from the past, part of a regrettably gone and noble culture perhaps, but not as people surviving and living in the present. A similar impression was given by the exhibits in the Plains Indian Museum, although here contemporary voices were heard, sometimes movingly. All in all, though, it is fair to say that the politics of Indian-U.S. relationships was missing in the museum. Fortunately, you could fill some of the gaps by browsing the well-stocked gift shop, which contained many useful books (and a good collection of Western music), and the comprehensive library.

INEQUALITY: ACT ONE: JACKSON, WYOMING

We first visited Jackson, Wyoming, in the late spring of 1997, after a long drive through a snow-filled Yellowstone National Park. Jackson sits just south of the Teton mountains, the most important land formations of Grand Teton National Park. You have to drive through this park as well, since it is nearly contiguous with Yellowstone. The Tetons are classic western mountains, one after another in a chain of sharply etched peaks rising high into the blue sky. Much of Grand Teton National

Park was once the private property of the Rockefeller family. During our sojourn at Yellowstone, we encountered hordes of Secret Service agents in Jackson protecting Vice President Dick Cheney, who was in his homestate to accept a gift of the Rockefellers' Yellowstone River ranch, the last remaining parcel of Rockefeller land, which is now also part of the park.

Thirty years ago, Jackson was a tiny cowboy town, charming in its way, with a beautiful natural setting, surrounded by mountains and close to the picturesque Snake River. Even in 1997 it was possible to get a cheap but decent motel room and a moderately-priced meal, and take a leisurely stroll around the town admiring the park, whose entrances are made of elk antlers, and the stark dry hills overlooking the streets. Rafting, hiking, and skiing were readily available recreations. An excellent art museum, dedicated to nature paintings and sculpture, was just outside town.

Things have changed dramatically, due primarily to the striking growth in economic inequality since the mid-1970s. Both income and wealth have become increasingly lopsided. To put it simply, money has been transferred from the poor to the rich. For example, incomes in the United States grew considerably between 1979 and 2000, as we would expect in the world's richest nation. But who got this growing income? The richest one percent of all households, whose income is mainly from dividends, interest, rent, profits, and capital gains, grabbed an astonishing 38.4 percent of the income growth produced over a thirty-one-year period. The poorest twenty percent of households took home a mere 0.8 percent. Consider that in 2003 there were 111,278,000 households in the United States. One percent of this number is 1,112,780 households. These rich households got a share of the income increase forty-eight times higher (38.4 divided by 0.8) than the 22,255,600 families that comprise the poorest twenty percent of households. The overall distribution of income is more unequal now than it has been at any time since the 1920s.

The distribution of wealth is much more unequal than income. The richest one percent of households own the lion's share of all assets and they keep getting more of them. There has been an incredible growth in the number of millionaires and billionaires in the United States. In 2004, for example, there were roughly 77,500 households with net worth, excluding residences, of at least $30,000,000, a number that has been rising rapidly since the 1990s. There are in the United States literally millions of millionaires, and in 2004 there may have been more than 350 billionaires. Such numbers must be taken with a grain of salt, and I offer them as approximations, but there is no doubt that the number of rich and very rich persons has increased dramatically. What is important here is that these people have more money than they can spend on ordinary consumer goods. So they look for ways to use their money so that it not only grows but offers them pleasure as well. One such venue is real estate, and what we see in every geographically well-situated place that is habitable is an influx of affluent property seekers and visitors. Inevitably this money transforms a town: there is a building boom; more roads are constructed; upscale stores and restaurants replace older, local establishments; housing prices skyrocket; immigrant workers are recruited to serve their betters; and political power changes hands.

In Teton County, where Jackson is located, the median home price has risen threefold in the past five years and is now more than $600,000. The mean cost of a new home exceeds $1.5 million; sales of homes listed at more than $5 million tripled between 2003 and 2005. Vice President Cheney, former World Bank president James Wolfensohn, actor Harrison Ford, and many other members of the rich and famous have homes in Jackson. Most of these people are actually in the town and county for only a few weeks a year; their houses are otherwise closed. Locals have coined a name for this privileged set: "two-two-eighters"—couples who spend two weeks a year in town, living in their 8,000 square feet houses. I suspect that the best job in town is that of realtor. Jackson is home to nearly as many real estate dealers as restaurants. Once home prices start to rocket upward, land and homes are hyped beyond belief. One realtor actually advertised "antique" land for sale; the land was guaranteed to have been hunted by Indians and worked by prospectors and other romantic Old West types.

The Teton Village ski complex lies a few miles north of Jackson. When we visited, it was a typically tacky ski area, with mediocre restaurants, gift shops, ski lifts, and concrete and brick condominiums. However, Teton Village has recently undergone a makeover, so that it could become a fit rendezvous for those with too much discretionary income. Now there is a Four Seasons restaurant with a top chef. At the Jackson Hole Mountain Resort, there are heated pools, an 11,685-square-foot spa with sixteen treatment rooms, and in-room boot fitting for hotel guests. Closer to town there are $700-a-night hotels and fancy dude ranches for the discriminating traveler.

When a town is gentrified, low-wage workers are needed to clean hotel rooms, to attend to rich households, to wait tables and do dishes in restaurants, and to construct new homes and buildings. In much of the West, Hispanics do this work. Ten percent of Jackson's population is Mexican. The foreign workers, and nearly all others, including teachers, nurses, and police officers, cannot afford to buy or rent housing. So they live either in makeshift trailer housing— sometimes on hotel or motel property—or out of town, usually across the dangerous Teton Pass in Idaho. Workers are poor and invisible, and the gap between their economic circumstances and those they serve is enormous and growing. Oftentimes the older, more middle-class residents take out their anger at the changes towns like Jackson are experiencing on the new mainly foreign-born workers. They don't see the economic system that brings forth the changes in the first place.

THE SUMMER ENDS

As the days passed, I began to wear out. Romantic notions about working in a national park were eroding under the monotony and drudgery of the work and living in a 100-square-foot room. The company, like all others, tried always to keep its labor costs down. Within a month of our arrival, the food in the employee cafeteria deteriorated so markedly that I often skipped meals. Even the drinks we got were watered down, as I discovered when Karen brought me some orange juice reserved for the guests when I was sick. The people who prepared our food could only be called cooks by debasing that word. Karen and I revolted against the serving of our food prison-style, slopped onto still-wet plastic trays, without plates. We bought paper plates and insisted that our food be placed on these. Many people commented on this, wondering why we were doing it. I told them that the only people I knew who ate from such trays were in prison. A few said that they admired our nerve. But more than one said that we were being environmentally incorrect. One young man who told me this smoked! And he knew next to nothing about what goes on in the world. So instead of criticizing the corporate polluters—including the company he worked for—he went after us. He reminded me of some of the young people I worked with for the United Farm Workers Union, in Keene, California. They would dress in rags, keep their rooms a mess, and not take care of their health. They thought that this brought them closer to the poor farm workers. Some of our co-workers seemed to think that being in the park, taking hikes, and eating from plastic trays made them environmentalists.

Tray our food was slopped on in the Employee Dining Room.

The inadequacy of our wages and our remote location disturbed us as well. After room and board deductions, we cleared no more than $3 per hour. We could almost have rented a space as large as our room in a city and fed ourselves more cheaply than the room and board deduction here, which amounted to $544 per month. The isolation was sometimes difficult to cope with. We longed to be in a city, to see a variety of people, to eat decent home-cooked food, and to feel more a part of humanity.

So many here took pleasure in being divorced from the world. For me everything a person does ought to be connected to and integrated into a political life. For the things we do to have meaning, we have to try to connect them to the larger society's problems and potentials. A few workers did that and were involved in environmental politics, but most were satisfied to harp about our paper plates. In the meantime, the company paid such paltry wages that no one but the waiters and bellhops saved any money. Almost no one cared to learn anything about the company, its connections to the Park Service, and its sordid history.

A serious illness compounded my growing irritation with work, food, and co-workers. One morning in mid-July, I awoke at 4:30 with sharp pains and cramps in my left side and stomach. These were classic signs of kidney stones, which have afflicted me for twenty years. Karen took me to the emergency room at the lake clinic, where I got a shot of Demerol and some codeine tablets. This facility, a private hospital affiliated with one in Cody, accepted no insurance and had signs throughout reminding patients that while they "don't provide service for money they must have money for service." The doctors were quick to give out pills. A fellow worker told me that some employees faked sickness just to get painkillers. When allergic reactions were epidemic, the doctor prescribed steroids to everyone.

I went to bed and then suffered acute pain even under the Demerol. I thought I had passed the stone. But a few days later, I got sick again. It felt like a urinary tract infection, and I went back to the doctor. My urine was clear, which should have alerted the doctor to the likelihood that I did not have an infection. Unfortunately I told him that I had suffered urinary tract infections before, so he assumed that this was what I had. He prescribed a sulfa-based drug called Bactrim. It seemed slow to work and made me nauseous. This made the food more disgusting, so I ate even less. I also had a low-grade fever and a hacking cough. I wanted to sleep all the time.

The combination of illness and poor nourishment made me sluggish. It was all I could do to drag myself to work. My condition was probably similar to that faced by a majority of the world's people, except that they don't have my money or history of good health. We wonder why the poor cannot pull themselves up by their bootstraps. Maybe if they had clean water to drink and air to breathe, as well as decent and healthy food to eat, they would do exactly that.

Matters got worse, and we made a four-hour drive to Billings, Montana, with the hope that in a city I would get better treatment. An emergency room doctor ordered a CAT scan, and it showed that I hadn't yet passed the kidney stone. This had produced considerable discomfort, since the stone was lodged in a particularly sensitive place. In addition, blood work indicated that I might have suffered liver damage, and the doctor was worried that I might have contracted hepatitis. He ordered me to stop taking the Bactrim and made an appointment for me with a specialist for the following week. By mid-week, my fever broke and the rest of the symptoms began to go away. The examination with the specialist established that, while my liver enzymes were still not normal, they were much better than they had been the week before. This confirmed their suspicion that it had been the drug that had done the damage.

Like so many workers in the United States, those at Yellowstone did not have easy access to good health care, though given the work and living conditions, they were likely to get sick. Many of them had no health insurance. The company provided a discount plan, for a fee, but the discount was not enough to make certain that a sick worker could afford care. Remember, if they went to the clinic, they had to have cash. My bill for two hours in the emergency room was over $800, reduced to $233 by the limited coverage. If not for the insurance from my old employer, which was good through August of that year, I would have had to pay thousands of dollars for my care in Billings. The alcoholic head chef at the hotel had two heart attacks. His skin was the color of alabaster, and he wore a turtleneck and jacket no matter how hot it was. But he didn't have money, so he did not go to a hospital and get treatment. When a friend told a supervisor that he was worried that the chef was going to die, the supervisor said not to worry, the company would take care of things. But the company did nothing. We wonder if he is still alive. Toward the end of summer, a French tourist came frantically to the front desk to tell us that her husband was having a heart attack. A clerk called the clinic and asked for an ambulance. It turned out that the man was just suffering altitude sickness, but he was billed $800 for a two-block ambulance ride—payable immediately in cash.

THE ENVIRONMENT: ACT ONE, THE COMPANY

The name of our employer, Amfac, was short for American Factor. Amfac had its origins in Hawaii. Among the earliest white immigrants to the islands were Germans, including German-American Lutheran missionaries. As the whites began to exploit Hawaii and expropriate the land of the Hawaiians, missionaries traveled there to Christianize the natives and provide an ideological underpinning for Great Power imperialism. By the time the German sea captain Heinrich Hackfeld got to Hawaii, the theft of the islands was well under way. Hackfeld opened a store, Hackfeld Dry Goods, in Honolulu in 1849, and from this base, built a powerful corporation, not just in retail sales but in the sugar industry. Hackfeld became a "factor" or agent for the sugar growers, an entity that connected the growers with the buyers of sugar. The sugar factors parlayed their control of the lucrative sugar market into control over the plantations themselves. This gave them large tracts of land and the power, both economic and political—Hackfeld had close ties to the Hawaiian queen Liliu'okalani; a shipping friend's son was the queen's husband—to gain control of many other businesses. Eventually five conglomerate corporations, named the "Big Five," came to dominate Hawaii's economy and politics, so that the entire nation was, in effect, a company town. The companies ruled through a combination of force and benevolence, the latter reflecting the missionary stock of many of the companies' founders. One of the "Big Five" was H. Hackfeld & Company.

Sugar production was ruinous both to the culture of the Hawaiians—who soon couldn't even get employment in the fields and mills as the corporations began to import Japanese, Chinese, and Filipino labor—and to the land. Sugar eventually destroys the land's health and that of the workers.

The entry of the United States into the First World War spelled disaster for Hackfeld, whose owners were now enemy aliens. The company's property was confiscated by the government and sold to the other four corporations, whose owners reorganized it and patriotically renamed the company American Factor, Amfac for short. The company's retail stores were renamed Liberty House. Amfac prospered after the war but began to decline in the 1970s and 1980s, as Hawaiian sugar lost its government subsidies and could no longer compete in world markets. Amfac sold off its properties and was eventually bought by a Chicago-based realty company, JMB Realty Corporation. JMB removed itself from Hawaii, and Amfac, now a subsidiary of JMB, entered the hospitality industry, concentrating on obtaining the concessions at national parks. In 2002 Amfac changed its name to Xanterra, probably to completely dissociate itself from its former enterprises and to give itself a new focus. The name Xanterra conveys exotic and beautiful places (*Xanadu*) on earth (*terra*).

Today Xanterra owns the concessions at many national and state parks, including Yellowstone, the Grand Canyon, Zion, Bryce, the Everglades, and Crater Lake. The company continues a long history of private enterprise in national parks. First the railroads saw a chance to make money bringing in tourists and building hotels for them; other businesses soon followed. Today, profit-making operations are integral to the parks. This rampant commercialization is depressing. When you can see a spectacular full moon shining luminously over the lake amid a million stars, or see trout swimming upstream to spawn, or a moose eating by a mountain river, why would you be attracted to a corny stagecoach ride?

It is ironic that Xanterra, which in its past identity as H. Hackfeld & Company and Amfac wreaked environmental and social havoc in Hawaii and treated its workers and resources as exploitable commodities, now promotes itself as a steward of the parks and an environmental watchdog. The company pitches itself to its employees and customers as a leader in corporate environmental practices: recycling, composting, green cleaning products in the hotels, pollution controls for the tour buses, cleaner engines for rented snowmobiles, propane boilers, and no overfished seafood and some organic foods on the menus. Environmentalism on the cheap. The company has created a name for its environmental programs—Ecologix. Of course, it is better that the company do these things than not, but it would be better still if the national parks were run as nonprofit public entities; there is no social need for Xanterra.

When people visit the national parks, they miss a lot. They think they are experiencing a primitive nature. As I note in later chapters, this is not the case. When the parks were established, there were often Indians, and sometimes white farmers, living on the land. People, especially Indians, were forced out so that the parks might appear uninhabited. Tourists also seldom realize that the parks are big business, and are, in fact, very large workplaces. They see park rangers and the employees of the concessionaires, but they don't witness workers doing often unpleasant work for low pay under abysmal conditions. They see "Michael from Pennsylvania," not Michael the clerk, on his feet all day, living in sub-marginal housing, being fed slop, and taking abuse from customers.

Toward the end of summer, we had an "employee appreciation" dinner. To appreciate the condescending nature of this event, recall my descriptions of the food we ate. I had developed such a distaste for it I dreaded going into the EDR. On this day, however, the managers, both high and low, were decked out in restaurant costumes. They served us with china plates, kept our glasses filled, and bussed our tables. The meal was several cuts above our usual fare and included sauces, fresh vegetables, and a variety of desserts. A more disgusting spectacle is difficult to imagine. Yet I heard no one say, "Why can't we get food like this most of the time?" or, "Why can't we always eat from real plates?" Instead, everyone said how great the meal was. It was time to move on.

We had agreed to remain at work through the Labor Day weekend. But Karen's boss refused her days off during a visit by our daughter, so we gave our notice and left before the holiday. The personnel director told us that we could leave our uniforms in his office, but when we got there early in the morning, his assistant said we had to turn them into the housekeeping department. We had a bitter argument, but

we lost and had to wait until that department opened. Wage work is
painful no matter what you do or where you are. Leaving it behind is
always sweet.

SUGGESTED READING

Most of the economic data used in this book is from the Bureau of
Labor Statistics website: *www.bls.gov*; the Census Bureau Website:
www.census.gov; and Lawrence Mishel, Jared Bernstein, and Sylvia
Allegretto, *The State of Working America* (Ithaca, NY: Cornell University
Press, 2005). For some useful and interesting materials on the national
parks, see Philip Burnham, *Indian Country, God's Country: Native
Americans and the National Parks* (Washington D.C.: Island Press,
2000) and Robert H. Keller and Michael F. Turek, *American Indians
and National Parks* (Tucson, AZ: University of Arizona Press, 1998). For
how foolish tourists can be, read Lee Whittlesey, *Death in Yellowstone:
Accidents and Foolhardiness in Our First National Park* (Lanham, MD:
Roberts Rinehart Publishers, 1995). One of the best books on bad jobs is
Barbara Ehrenreich, *Nickel and Dimed: On (Not) Getting By in America*
(New York, NY: Henry Holt and Company, 2001). For a good social
history of Hawaii, including a history of the "Big Five" sugar companies,
see Lawrence H. Fuchs, *Hawaii Pono: A Social History* (New York, NY:
Harcourt, 1984).

CHAPTER THREE

MANHATTAN

MANHATTAN

Population in 2000 1,537,195

    White 54.4%

    Black 17.4%

    Asian 9.4%

    Hispanic (all races) 27.2%

Median household income in 2000 .... $47,030

People below poverty level of income 20%

Median rent in 2000 .... $796

Median mortgage, including associated costs $3,615

Our favorite museum is the International Center of Photography Museum, 1133 Sixth Avenue (at 43rd Street), 10036, (212) 857-0000. Our favorite bakery is Sullivan Street Bakery (recently renamed Grandaisy Bakery), 73 Sullivan St. (in Soho), 10012, (212) 334-9435. Try the bianco or funghi pizza, both unlike any pizza you have eaten. Wear comfortable shoes and walk the city's streets. Almost every street has its charms.

9/11

We drove south from the Lake Hotel toward Jackson, Wyoming, stopping at the south entrance to the park to take last photographs. After a day of sightseeing in the town, we drove our daughter to the small airport and watched her plane take off through the mountains. As we left Jackson, we saw an eagle gliding overhead and thought that this was a good omen for our future. We journeyed south and east to Boulder, Colorado, where one of our sons had decided to reside. He had been camping in a tent near the city while looking for a job and an apartment. He found both, and we helped him set up his new home. He would be the first child to live far away from us. We bade him a tearful farewell and drove 1,500 miles to my mother's home north of Pittsburgh, Pennsylvania. Back to the East! As would happen several times during the next four years, our spirits sagged as we neared Chicago. The countryside became increasingly unattractive and more clotted with traffic and suburban housing developments, the latter built on what had recently been farmers' fields. We began to choke on the polluted air, and we bemoaned the disappearance of the open and blue Western firmament. From Chicago to Pittsburgh the sky was usually a leaden gray or washed-out blue. When we were in the West, we would say, "Why didn't we ever look at the sky in Pittsburgh or Johnstown?" The answer is simple: the Eastern sky is seldom worthy of observation.

I had met a guest at the Lake Hotel who lived in New York City and knew of an available apartment. I had taken his name and phone number. I planned to call him from my mother's and then go to Manhattan to see that place and, if necessary, begin the search for our new home. We would stay with a friend who rented in a high-rise building on East 91st Street.

I called the guest, and he gave me the address and the landlord's phone number. Because I lost a dental filling, I had to see a dentist in Pittsburgh on Tuesday, September 11. Karen was driving, and I was looking at a book of block-by-block maps of Manhattan's streets to find the location of the apartment when we heard that the first plane had struck the World Trade Center towers. Like everyone else we were glued to the television for the next few days, watching the horrifying scenes from New York City, Washington, D.C., and Shanksville, Pennsylvania. The plane that crashed in Pennsylvania was not far from where I had taught. As relatives and friends searched for the missing, as fear and anxiety mounted, as the stock market tumbled, and as the government began to implement its draconian plans, seeing the crisis as an opportunity to bring us a few steps closer to a police state, we wondered if moving to Manhattan was such a good idea. We had no backup plan, however, and we couldn't stay at my mother's. So we stuck to our original strategy. And selfishly, we thought, maybe rents would fall.

APARTMENT HUNTING IN THE SHADOW OF DISASTER

Manhattan really knocks you for a loop. No matter how you come into the city, you are thrown into a mass of pulsating humanity. We usually entered the maelstrom through the Lincoln Tunnel, Karen a nervous wreck, worried that we would have to stop somewhere under the Hudson River. We exited the tunnel and went north to our friend's apartment. We had finally reached the owner of the apartment that the hotel guest had told us about and made an appointment to see it. We would scour the newspapers—we had already begun to do this online in Pennsylvania—and begin our search, starting with this one, on fabled Christopher Street in Greenwich Village.

We spent five days in the city, meeting real estate agents and apartment owners; we devoted more than eight hours to this each day. Nothing prepared us for apartment hunting. You can't just drive from place to place; you must take a bus, a subway, a cab, or walk. You are at the mercy of the realtors and building owners; demand almost always outstrips supply. And Manhattan is an intimidating place to a newcomer. Pedestrians walk faster there than anywhere in the world, and night and day on nearly every street, there are thousands of them. Everything is done at warp speed. And everyone seems more sophisticated and in-the-know than you. You feel like a rube no matter where you're from.

The calamity that had just struck the city dampened rental prices but not by much; the agents and owners we met acted as if nothing had happened. Rents were unbelievable, especially considering how little was offered for the money. The place on Christopher Street sounded like a deal. A three-bedroom apartment for $3,000 a month, and the owner made it clear that she was willing to negotiate. We were excited—a place much larger than we could ever have expected and at what was, for Manhattan, a bargain-basement rent. But they say that you don't get anything for nothing. If something seems too good to be true, it inevitably is. This first apartment was a third-floor walk-up, meaning that there was no elevator, not unusual in the city—some tenants have to hike up six floors—but still surprising to us. Inside, we were met with three of the tiniest bedrooms imaginable; two of them could not have held even a double bed, and the master bedroom was smaller than our room in Yellowstone. Considerable repair work had to be done. The owner told us it would be finished by December, which seemed unlikely. She would give us a break on the rent while repairs were in progress. Just what we needed, living for a few months while workers tore up floors, ripped off wallpaper, did kitchen and bathroom work, and dropped paint cloths everywhere. We left disappointed but told her we'd be in touch.

Things went downhill from there. Every time we called to ask about an advertised rental, we met a new agent, and each one had many listings. We were dragged around the Village by a fast-talking agent from Australia, who showed us one unit that had the refrigerator in the living room and another with a floor so uneven that a ball would have rolled from one end of a room to the other. I had foolishly worn dress shoes that day, and my feet were in such pain that I had to buy a pair of sneakers before we could continue our search. We then met a pair of agents in an office in the Empire State Building, one with an open shirt and gold chain, who tried to get us to rent spaces beyond our means and pay them a finder's fee of thousands of dollars for the privilege of using their services. We saw dirty apartments, apartments with kitchens in which only one person could be at a time, and apartments with bedrooms barely fit for the most self-abnegating monk. The stink of freshly applied polyurethane rose from the cheap and worn wooden floors of every site advertised as "newly remodeled." A couple of rentals were in buildings so shabby and surrounded by trash that we didn't bother to ring the bell. In one apartment there was a partition in the living room and two entrances into the kitchen; by such makeshift means are one-bedrooms converted into two, especially useful for unrelated persons who can share the rent. At a swank Madison Avenue address, we walked up a garishly painted hallway, overwhelmed by the smell of nail polish remover from the salon on the ground floor. Another bell we didn't ring. Wherever we went we saw reminders of 9/11. Hundreds of faces stared at us from the "Missing" signs posted by the distraught families and friends of those still not accounted for. People were unusually subdued; the normally frenetic pace of the city was noticeably slowed down.

On the fourth day, we saw an ad for an apartment in the East Village. I called the number from a pay phone and begged the owner to let us see it immediately. After some wrangling, he agreed. We walked a mile or so to East 10th Street, found the number and walked around the neighborhood. It was a tree-lined street, tucked between the hustle and bustle of Second and Third Avenues. The apartment was in a six-story building, which, we learned that day, had once been a single-family house (we also found out that the landlord had evicted Robert Frost's daughter when he bought the building). Next to it was the leafy courtyard of St. Mark's Church, and across the street was the intersection of Stuyvesant and 10th Streets. This was one of the few places in Manhattan where a street was off the rectangular grid that makes the city so easy to navigate. It was also the scene of three a.m. traffic jams and wildly honking taxicabs.

We dialed the landlord's number on the intercom and were met by a portly, balding, and overbearing man. He and his wife owned the building. He took us up three flights of stairs—we noticed that the floor was marked "4," which turned out to be some sort of security measure— and knocked on a door. The occupants answered and ushered us in. A couple and their infant child lived there, amidst remarkable clutter. We were embarrassed by the mess, but no one else was. It didn't take long to look around and get the details of the rental. There was a short, narrow entrance hallway, a good-sized kitchen, a large living room, a tiny bath, and a small bedroom. There was a fireplace, bookshelves, high ceilings, and a large somewhat inaccessible storage area above the built-in bedroom closet. Though less than 500 square feet, it was the nicest apartment for the rent we had seen, and the location was exceptional. We told the landlord we'd talk it over and get back to him. That night we mulled things over as we always did and decided to take it. We walked the four miles from 91st to 10th Street the next day, deposit check and financial data in hand—our income was low relative to the rent, and I had to rush to get our pension information from the offices on Third Avenue—and met the owners. We sat down at their dining room table in the most lavish city apartment we had ever seen: two full floors, fifteen feet ceilings, professionally decorated with antiques, and a garden in the back. We felt that we were in a museum. They meant to impress and intimidate us and they succeeded. They had all sorts of complicated provisions in the lease. We'd have to buy a large rug for the living room and a smaller one for the bedroom, but they would buy them back from us minus 10 percent per year when we left. We couldn't move in for a month. And they would have to do a background and credit check. They asked us, as though we were children, if we were sure we could

Our apartment building on E. 10th St. from St. Mark's courtyard.

pay the rent. Almost like a loan shark might ask if you were certain you'd pay back the loan, the implication being that he didn't want to hurt you, but would. While I had pen in hand, he said that he had changed the terms from a single-year to a two-year lease. We agreed to everything, gave them our Pennsylvania phone number, and left, dazed and feeling vaguely uneasy. Five days and thirty-nine apartments later, we finally had a home.

A DREAM COME TRUE

I brought Karen to Manhattan in 1993. It was her first visit. We were there to celebrate the eightieth birthday of a friend and mentor of mine. The party was at a church in Midtown. We had our teenaged twin sons with us, and during the rather lengthy speeches that preceded the festivities, they started to fidget. So we sent them out to help with the party preparations. "Don't embarrass us," I admonished.

Given the old age of so many of the guests, we were worried that there wouldn't be anything to drink. We needn't have. After the long eulogies to the guest of honor, we went out into the banquet room, where we were greeted by our sons, who proudly showed us the scores of champagne bottles they had set up on the tables. They began to introduce me to people, including the editor of my upcoming book, a woman I had never met. We settled in for an enjoyable evening, and we left with three bottles of champagne that my boys had been given for helping. We headed back to our hotel at Gramercy Park, carrying the bottles in a bag onto a bus. We struck up giddy conversations with some of the other riders, one of whom told us she had worked for years in Pittsburgh, where we were then living, and another who gave us instructions on our stop. Cheered by such friendliness in what was supposed to be a notoriously impersonal city, we wound our way through the streets back to the hotel. I am ashamed to admit that my bladder gave out before we arrived, and I relieved myself through the fences surrounding the city's only private park.

When we returned to Pittsburgh, my wife stated that Manhattan was where she wanted to be. I thought she was joking, but she was serious in the way that only a girl who grew up in a poor mining town surrounded by boney piles of waste coal in what can charitably be called troubling circumstances *could* be. Say what you want about the charms of small towns, we found them boring and stifling places, with too many narrow-minded and bigoted people. I loved my father's factory buddies and I spent many pleasant evenings with them at the racetrack. But living among them was another matter.

So, at last, on November 5, 2001, we were moving to Manhattan. Since we had given our household goods away when we moved from Pittsburgh to Yellowstone, we had to restock. To transport our new things, we rented a U-Haul truck. At three o'clock in the morning, we drove it out of my mother's driveway, heading north through the towns of my childhood: Kittanning, Rural Valley, Dayton, New Bethlehem, Brookville, all good examples of the nondescript villages that dot the western Pennsylvania landscape. Then we headed east across the empty expanse of Route 80 to the Delaware Water Gap and New Jersey. Traffic picks up as you near Interstate 95 and approach the George Washington Bridge. Navigating the truck across the bridge and down the Henry Hudson Parkway, which becomes the West Side Highway, then across town on 14th Street, south on Third Avenue, and finally east on 10th Street, tested our skills. But we figured that cars, even New York's risk-taking cabdrivers, wouldn't want to have an eighteen-foot U-Haul crash into them, so when we couldn't tell if it was safe to change lanes, we just did it anyway.

When I couldn't sleep the night we left, I visualized how we would park on our new street. Finding a space in Manhattan is difficult with a car; how would we find one for a U-Haul? We would probably have to double park and hope that no trucks came down the street. At least 10th Street, like most Manhattan streets, was one-way only, so we wouldn't have to worry about cars coming at us from both directions. A few months later when we brought our car to the city, I learned the town's driving rituals and etiquette. The most important rule is never pass an empty parking space. I once backed the car a half a block against traffic on 10th Street, with vehicles swerving to avoid hitting me, to get a coveted spot. But that night I was afraid. Imagine our joy when we found a double space in front of our building. It was street-cleaning day and not all the moved cars had returned to our side of the street. A hopeful sign. Maybe a miracle. We locked the truck and walked down the stairs to the apartment building.

I pushed the intercom button with great excitement. One of the landlords came to the door and after an awkward attempt at small talk, said things were not ready yet. We walked up the three flights of stairs wondering what we would find. When we looked in, we were astounded to see such disarray—tools, paintbrushes, paint cans, an old table, a fan, a kitchen chair, a filthy kitchen, dust and dirt everywhere, and the wooden floors unvarnished. The landlord apologized, but we weren't in the mood. Our truck had to be returned to a U-Haul dealer that day. We had to move the stuff into the apartment. We cut short his offer to have his Polish workmen help us carry things up the stairs. For three hours we hustled our belongings from the truck, filling to overflow the kitchen and bathroom, the only two places we could stack boxes. We put our framed pictures in the bathtub. Fortunately, we didn't have any furniture.

We were exhausted. The landlord again sheepishly apologized and said he would put us in a hotel for the night. He assured us everything would be ready, gorgeous in fact, the next morning. We doubted this, but we couldn't worry about it; we had to return the truck, get a bus to the hotel, check in, and eat something. We both slept fitfully. The next morning, the apartment was ready. Not gorgeous exactly. I had never seen a worse job done on wooden floors. But we were in New York City!

The next few weeks passed in a haze of my starting a new job and both of us searching stores for a bed, mattress and box springs, a couch, a kitchen table, chairs, the rugs we had agreed to buy, pictures large enough for the high-ceilinged walls, and places to buy food. Here we were, from Wyoming, the country's least populated area, to its most—in a Manhattan reeling from catastrophe and mired in a dangerous economic slump. We moved in while others were leaving. Would they find things so different in their new city? Car alarms shrieking and people shouting at all hours of the night. Streets insanely crowded. It took us weeks to get a phone book, and when we did, it came by FedEx. We moved the larger household items we bought by cab. We'd buy something, and the clerk would hail a taxi. The driver stopped, got out, popped the trunk, and helped us put the new merchandise inside. Amazing! When something we purchased was delivered, the service fee was sometimes larger than the price. We were almost always the only people doing our own laundry; everyone else paid for drop-off service. Our apartment door was so narrow that our couch and chair, ordered in Pittsburgh, wouldn't fit through. We had to send them back. We lived on a futon for five weeks and slept in a bedroom that would make a small child claustrophobic. We were both in shock.

But even amidst the hassle of daily life, there were compensations. I could walk to work, and on the way choose among more than fifty delis selling cheap breakfast sandwiches. I could gaze at the Empire State Building as I munched on my morning repast. We could amble down the street and see where Allen Ginsberg lived and where William S. Burroughs had his famous bunker. Hundreds of stores, museums, theaters, restaurants, libraries, bookstores, and every other kind of shop imaginable were close by. There were at least twenty Japanese restaurants in our neighborhood. On the morning of Karen's birthday, I bought her an orchid, a greeting card, a good loaf of bread, croissants, and a piece of lemon cake during a fifteen-minute walk at eight o'clock in the morning. We could live without a car. The bus drivers and cabbies were friendly. There was a hair salon on every street! There were so many people with unorthodox views on every subject under the sun, expressed in nearly every human language. Where else was there a shop named "Religious Sex"? And a man selling rosaries hung on a long stick he carried on his arm? Yes, it was a wonderful town.

ANOTHER JOB

While we were living in Yellowstone, I was made Associate Editor of *Monthly Review* magazine. This venerable journal of the Left was founded by Paul Sweezy and Leo Huberman. Sweezy was a radical economist at Harvard University, and Huberman was a writer and labor educator. Paul gave up his university position when it became apparent that his politics would prevent him from getting tenure, and after some time off he decided along with Leo to start a magazine. It wasn't an auspicious time to be a left-winger much less to publish a radical journal, but with the help of some friends, including money from the literary critic F. O. Mathiessen, they began the magazine in May of 1949. The first article was written by Albert Einstein and was titled "Why Socialism?" The journal did well and the founders were able to expand into book publishing, first with I. F. Stone's *Hidden History of the Korean War,* and over the years with the publication of hundreds of classics of socialist thought.

I discovered *Monthly Review* in 1969, my first year of teaching. After a particularly awful class, I went to the college library to read sports magazines. By chance, I came across this small "independent socialist" journal. I read every article and then went into the stacks to find more. I began a subscription in 1970. In 1972, I submitted my first article. It was rejected, but Paul Sweezy sent me an encouraging note, which I still have. Anyone who writes knows how unusual it is for an editor to send a personal reply to an unknown scribbler. I eventually got a few book reviews accepted, and I became a supporter of the magazine. I invited Sweezy and Harry Magdoff—who became co-editor after Huberman's death—to speak at a conference at my college. They came, and we met for the first time. It was an exhilarating experience. Both editors were economists, and I had been using their analyses from the magazine in my classes for years.

My commitment to *Monthly Review* deepened, and I contributed more reviews and articles, participated in conferences on panels sponsored by *MR* (as it is known to its friends around the world), co-edited a special summer issue, and visited the office in Manhattan. It was Harry Magdoff's eightieth birthday party that I described earlier in this chapter. I decided to go to New York City and work for *Monthly Review* after I retired. Now, after some initial delays, I was doing just that.

I began work the day after we moved into our apartment. I was traumatized by the move, but I got up early and left the apartment to walk the mile and a half to the office. Karen took my picture, and I nervously walked on 10th Street toward Third Avenue.

I don't remember the route I took that day. I had several. Sometimes I walked to Union Square and then north on Broadway to 27th Street. *Monthly Review*'s office was between Sixth and Seventh

Avenues, not far from the Fashion Institute of Technology, where I once sat through an interminable birthday party for a well-known advocate of union democracy. Sometimes I just walked directly west from our apartment to Sixth Avenue and then north the seventeen blocks to Twenty seventh. Both walks were interesting. Union Square was full of

The Flatiron Building, Manhattan's 1ˢᵗ skyscraper.

people—heading toward the subway station, selling newspapers, setting up for the year-round farmers' market—even early in the morning. On Sixth Avenue there was a steady flow of cars, cabs, and delivery trucks, all dodging the constant construction. Once I watched in amazement a parade of about one hundred tank-like cars celebrating the Lubavitcher

sect of Judaism. Music blared from the trucks' loudspeakers, and the sides
of each vehicle announced the coming of the Messiah. Double-parked
trucks and the busy Asian and Latino garment workers loading and
unloading them made 27th Street roar with noise. Sometimes a homeless
person would push a wheelbarrow loaded high with refundable bottles
down the middle of the street.

My work at *Monthly Review* was as unlike my job at the Lake
Hotel as could be imagined. No managers, no senior clerks, no schedule.
I had no fixed assignments. I became a jack of all trades. I helped prepare
the magazine for publication each month. I read every submission and
participated in the Wednesday planning meetings. We often accepted
articles that needed additional work. I took the worst and turned them
into publishable articles. I did some copy editing. I xeroxed articles,
prepared packets of submissions to mail to the editorial committee
members who lived outside the city, helped plan the annual Christmas
party, and took book orders over the phone. I began to answer the non-
routine correspondence, replying to queries from prospective authors
and readers who had comments or questions about things we had
published. I made a list of possible writers and began to correspond
with some of them. I assisted the director of Monthly Review Press,
taking editorial responsibility for one of the press's forthcoming books.
I helped write copy for books and fundraising letters. I brainstormed
book titles with my office mates. Whatever I was asked to do, I did. I also
contributed to the magazine, so I usually had a writing project going.
Shortly after my arrival, I was asked to write another book for the press.
I had previously written two and co-edited a third. My books had done
well and made the press some money, so everyone was happy when I
developed a proposal for another.

Editing and writing are demanding jobs. A submission might
arrive from a writer whose first language was not English. If we accepted
it, it would have to be "Anglicized," a tedious task. Since *Monthly Review*
is known for its economic analyses, we frequently received articles from
economists, typically academics. Academic writing is usually clumsy,
and the compositions of economists are almost always good examples
of scholarly obfuscation. They often assume they are writing for readers

who know the special language of this dismal science. Few readers do, and I think that unclear language is a sign that writers themselves are unsure of what they mean. In any case, the economic prose usually required major editing or surgery.

My days at work quickly fell into a routine. I arrived early, by 7:30, but the office manager was always there ahead of me. I had a complicated set of keys—two for the outside doors, one for the elevator, one for the office—so I was glad I seldom had to use them. I'd spend a few minutes chatting with him and then settle in at my desk. The building was an old one, and it was hot in winter, with creaking pipes and odd noises. I could hear sounds from the street but, except for sirens, they were muted. The space was large, taking up half of a floor, but cozy at the same time, with books and magazines everywhere. There were easy chairs, a couch, and a large meeting table, arranged somewhat haphazardly around the central room. Upon entering from the outside hallway, you saw tables and shelves filled with the press's books and back issues of the magazine. I was secretly pleased to see my own books and journals with articles I had written. I was even more delighted when the mail brought a fan letter.

WORK: ACT TWO, TOILING IN THE CAPITAL OF CAPITALISM

Manhattan is the center of world commerce, banking, finance, and deal-making. Most of us have romantic notions of the "Big Apple," the product of hundreds of films and plays like *When Harry Met Sally* and *A Walk in the Park,* and television shows like *Friends* and *Sex in the City*. We think of the Empire State Building, the Statue of Liberty, the christmas tree and skating rink in Rockefeller Center, Central Park, Radio City Music Hall, Forty-second Street, and Times Square. We imagine bohemians sacrificing everything for their art and immigrants on the Lower East Side preparing their children to live the American Dream. "If I can make it there, I'll make it anywhere." Everything seems possible in New York City, larger than life.

The reality is somewhat different. It is said that money makes the world go round, and nowhere in the United States is this more true than in Manhattan. Even the current mayor is a billionaire. The money men—and a few women—control the city; they make the deals and the rest of us bear the consequences. And underneath it all is an enormous mass of human labor, working harder than in any place we have lived, hour after hour, day after day, year after year, to produce the output that makes all the money. As in Yellowstone, it is labor most visitors seldom notice.

Manhattan's labor is sharply divided: by the level of wages and by race, ethnicity, and gender. It is not easy to find a white person fluent in English loading trucks in the garment or flower districts, driving a cab, prepping food in the basement of a Korean-owned greengrocery, washing dishes in the back of a restaurant, toiling in one of the city's numerous garment sweatshops, driving a limousine service car, caring for someone's children on the Upper East Side, operating a food pushcart, clerking in a bodega, bussing tables, selling knock-offs on the sidewalk, washing, ironing, and folding clothes in a laudromat, or doing orderly or cafeteria work in a hospital. Not all of these workers will be persons of color; in our neighborhood in the East Village, there were hundreds of workers recently arrived from Eastern Europe. In all of these jobs, wages will be low, though sometimes higher than in many parts of the country, but this is because housing and other necessities are expensive.

As we move toward the middle segments of the workforce, skin color whitens and men predominate. Construction workers, mid-level managers, real estate agents, waiters, police, firefighters, bus drivers, and subway conductors, with some exceptions, earn decent wages and are more likely to be white males. Racial minorities are more common in public employment than a generation ago (there are many black subway conductors, for example) but the shares of black and Hispanic workers, especially in the protective services, are lower than the shares these groups comprise of the entire population.

At the top of the wage hierarchy, the workforce is much / homogeneous, nearly all male and white. Real estate brokers Street analysts and operators, upper management in most cor/

Broadway producers and directors, symphony musicians, and the like are good examples. Exceptions are professional athletes and some others in the entertainment industry.

To give readers an idea of the gap between the top and the bottom of the labor force (I am not counting what Marx called "the Lazarus layers of the working class"—those who are unemployed, homeless, or severely disabled), consider some data. In 2005, the average weekly wage in the leisure and hospitality industry in Manhattan, where men and women of color and immigrants predominate, was $678. In the financial industry, the province of white men, it was $6,199. These averages are means; they are affected by both very high and very low wages in each sector.

Overall income inequality in Manhattan is greater than almost anywhere else in the United States, and this helps shape the distribution of jobs. Tens of thousands of them have as their main component serving those with high incomes: dog walkers, workers in expensive restaurants (nowhere else in the nation will you find as many of these as here), limousine service drivers, grocery deliverers, manicurists, and clerks in high-end stores. The labor of these workers is only necessary because the division of income is so lopsided.

During a visit to the city a few years before we moved there, I got a taste of the social chasm between poor and well-off workers. I was invited by a friend, a former assistant editor of *Monthly Review*, to visit the Chinese Staff and Workers Association (CSWA) in Manhattan's Chinatown. The CSWA is a Workers' Center, a place where residents can go and an organization they can join, to win justice in their workplaces and neighborhoods—unpaid wages, overtime, minimum wage, unjust evictions. The Director of this center was Wing Lam. Wing showed Karen and me around the office, which had recently been firebombed, no doubt by angry employers. The center's members and those it helped were mainly undocumented Chinese immigrants, who, after paying as much as $25,000 to secure passage from Asia to the United States, were put to work in Chinatown's restaurants and garment sweatshops. Wing's organizing philosophy was that grievants could use the Center only if they became actively involved in prosecuting their own cases and also helped others do the same. The need for such an organization was obvious. Wing told us that restaurant employees typically labored 100 hours a week, for a wage of $2.00 an hour. Organized labor had done little to aid them; even in unionized workplaces, employers sometimes paid below minimum wage. Out of their paltry income they had to repay their passage debt and meet their daily expenses. As many as fifteen might share a one-bedroom apartment, divided by thin wooden partitions into several bedrooms. In such a space the only privacy people had was their thoughts.

After telling us about the Center, Wing took us to lunch at a nearby restaurant. He insisted on picking up the check.

I had come to Manhattan to give a talk at one of Columbia University's ongoing seminars. Faculty and outside scholars have organized these on a wide variety of subjects; the same one might run for many years. I was to speak to the Seminar on Full Employment. I walked through the great university's gate at Broadway and 116th Street with some trepidation. I had never spoken at an Ivy League university, and I wondered if the group's participants would be as brilliant as I sometimes imagined people at such schools were. We found our way to Faculty House, where we were to have dinner and where the meeting was to be held. We met the person who had invited me, a friendly elderly man of some renown. The first thing he did was inform me that I would have to pay for my wife's dinner. I was astounded. I should have refused, but I gave him the money. Dinner was a lavish affair, with fine food and table settings. The dining room overlooked the slums of East Harlem. Everyone was white except the servers. The conversation revolved around trips these elite academics had taken and the research they were doing. When the talk turned to children, we silenced the polite chatter when we said that our three sons were cooks. Apparently no one could believe that a college professor had children who did such work. After dinner I gave my talk. It went well, but the questions were abstrusely academic and trivial. Later we were dragooned into going to a professor's apartment, which overlooked Central Park, to watch a television show about the overboard spending of American consumers. The host served cheap beer; I got a half a glass. When the show ended we had to go around the room in order and make comments. These were so convoluted, egotistic, and laden with academic jargon that Karen and I wondered what we would say. I was glad her turn came first. She stated that the show was shallow and again that pretty much stopped the discussion. Thankfully, we left soon after. As we walked out the door, we heard one person remind another that she owed a dollar for the short cab ride from the college to the apartment.

WALKING THE CITY'S STREETS

We hiked Manhattan from Battery Park to 125th Street—the main street of Harlem—and from the Hudson to the East River. We did all of the things tourists do and enjoyed every one. With our daughter we circumnavigated the island on a fast boat, up the Hudson, across the Harlem, down the East River to Battery Park, and back to the dock. I am not ashamed to say that I was thrilled to see Yankee Stadium for the first time; as we passed it, I became a child of ten pretending I was sick and getting to see Don Larsen pitch the only perfect game ever thrown in the World Series.

Karen and I rode the ferries to the Statue of Liberty, Ellis Island, and Staten Island. The day we went to Ellis Island, we were tired of the noise of the city. It was an unseasonably warm, sunny day in early spring. We explored the museum and looked up relatives who came to the island from Italy and the Ukraine. We admired the fine collection of shipping line posters, and lolled about in the sunshine, happy for the quiet.

Another day, we went on one of our favorite hikes. We walked southwest from our apartment to Washington Square Park, where there was always something interesting to see, whether it be street musicians, art exhibits, or Jews setting up their sukkahs to celebrate Sukkot, the Feast of Tabernacles, a kind of post-harvest festival. The sukkahs, or "shacks," which many Jews build in their own yards, are temporary shelters, lived in during the holiday to remind the faithful that this life is transitory. We had seen these in Pittsburgh but never knew what they were. From the park we wound our way into Greenwich Village and stopped to buy salami sandwiches at Zito's Bakery on Bleecker Street—now sadly gone—and the famous cupcakes at Magnolia Bakery. We continued west and south, winding our way through the narrow old streets of the West Village, to Hudson Street, one of our favorites. We went south on Hudson through rich and quiet TriBeCa, where we would measure how large the apartments were by how many windows had the same drapes or curtains. This is where luminaries like the late John Kennedy, Jr. and Martin Scorsese lived. Next, west toward the river and then along the river's promenade south through Battery Park City, to the Battery itself at the southern tip of the island. It was a wonderful walk, and I always hated to head back home. But this day, Karen rushed me to the Staten Island ferry terminal. We ran under the gate and got on the boat just before it left. We stood at the back of the ferry and watched Manhattan disappear as the captain set his course amidst the lesser boats in the harbor. As we got toward more open water, we saw gigantic container ships and the outline of Governor's Island. The ferry landed and we waited onboard for the return trip. It is surprising to remember now how excited I was to be away from my Manhattan island home, if only by a few miles.

We took a different route on our return trip, sticking east up the off-grid streets of lower Manhattan, hitting Broadway, the only thoroughfare that traverses the entire length of Manhattan, into the financial district and going north, past the ruins of the World Trade Center, until we could walk east to Little Italy and Chinatown. Not many Italians live in Little Italy; Chinese is more likely to be spoken there than Italian. It's mainly for tourists, who are badgered by the hosts, hustling them like street hawkers, to eat in one of the second-rate pasta joints lining Mulberry Street. The festival of San Gennaro, patron saint of Naples, brings crowds of *paisanos* back to their old neighborhood in September, but except for the scores of hot sausage stands, I found it to be a pretty ersatz affair. Chinatown, on the other hand, is full of excitement. People packed together, haggling with shopkeepers, eating everywhere, and selling everything from exotic sweets to phone cards. We often ate at a Vietnamese restaurant, aptly named Vietnam Restaurant, on tiny, semi-circular Doyers Street, which even a beat cop couldn't give us directions to. We always bought roast pork, which you wrapped inside lettuce leaves, along with mint, cilantro, and rice noodles, and dipped in a tasty sauce. From Little Italy and Chinatown we marched into Soho. We stopped at the Dean & DeLuca grocery store to snag free samples and to watch the patrons spend hundreds of dollars on the gorgeous but overpriced produce, meat, fish, cheese, and desserts. We looked for celebrities and headed home.

We took many hikes like this one. I took my children to the top of the Empire State Building whenever one of them visited. I never tired of looking at this marvelous building, built in thirteen months during the Great Depression, with steel from the mills of Pittsburgh that arrived so fast by train that the metal was still warm. We discovered that it was visible from hundreds of spots on our walks around the city. From the visitors' deck near the top, the city spreads out below in all its glory; you could even see the roof of our apartment building. You could feel the winds blowing wildly and imagine what it would be like to have been one of the construction workers who built it, walking on narrow beams high above the ground. To earn some extra money, I got a job teaching worker-students in the Labor Studies program at Cornell University's Manhattan campus, located on East 34th Street, between Fifth and Madison Avenues. It was exciting to think that I taught in the shadow of the world's most famous skyscraper.

There are parts of the city where it is unpleasant to walk. A stroll up Seventh Avenue in midtown will find you shouting over the street clamor. We couldn't go by Grand Central Station because the air was so foul it made us cough. Even the more charming walks were sometimes crowded and noisy. Every now and then it was necessary to find a retreat. We found two that we especially liked. The first took us downtown and across the Brooklyn Bridge. Hiking on the bridge above the traffic and the East River is something every visitor should do. The views north and south are spectacular. On nice days, pedestrians and bikers abound; someone will probably say, "Can you take my picture?" If you watch the traffic, you might notice that no buses cross the bridge; this is forbidden. (By the way, you can go under the East River to Brooklyn, on a subway, and travel to the end of the line at Coney Island and Brighton Beach. The latter is home to thousands of Russian immigrants; you can buy cheap, filling Russian food in restaurants with cafeteria seating. Or you can visit a Russian banquet hall, cavernous ornately decorated places filled at night with locals and tourists dancing, stuffing themselves, and drinking copious quantities of vodka.)

Brooklyn Heights is a short distance from the bridge. There is a small business district, but the main attractions are the quiet streets—lined with trees and classic New York City brownstones—and the Promenade. There are signs promising stiff fines to motorists who honk their horns. Karen and I drifted along the streets as if in a dream. You could hear neighbors talking. A scream or a cry or someone bellowing, "Please help the homeless," as happened all day long in Union Square, seemed inconceivable here. A short detour down one of the side streets brought us to the Promenade, a long wide walkway, bordered by leafy parks and large-windowed and expensive apartments. It overlooked the river, and across the water, resplendent, was lower Manhattan, looking abnormally still and calm. Mothers and nannies strolled with their children and charges; old folks read papers; and lovers held hands by the railing. Sometimes in our tiny and loud apartment, I longed to be in Brooklyn Heights.

Millions of words have been written about our second retreat, Central Park, and with good reason. This oasis in the city is a grand place to be. We usually took the subway to the northern end of the park in Spanish Harlem at 110th Street and hiked south to our apartment, a distance of 100 blocks, about five miles. Nearly everyone at the northern end was brown-skinned, but skin colors lightened as you walked south. I loved everything about the park: artists, street musicians, clowns, ball players, swimmers, joggers running around the reservoir, people fishing, picnicking, acting out, rowing boats, eating hot dogs, playing softball, the zoo and the nearby mechanical clock, the skating rink, the amphitheaters, skateboarders, poets' walk, concerts, operas, protesters, parades, a telescope set up so you could see the red-tailed hawks nesting on the roof of an apartment building, the remote control boats, everything, every time I went there. There is no competition; it's the greatest park in the United States. We'd stop at the southern end, at 59th Street, to visit the Plaza Hotel, watch the moneyed crowd have brunch, and use the restrooms, figuring that the tip you gave the attendant was a small price to pay for a day of free entertainment.

INEQUALITY: ACT TWO, STREETS OF MILLIONAIRES, STREETS OF PAUPERS

If I walked to work up Broadway from Union Square, I passed a homeless man sleeping in the doorway of a closed building, across the street from the ABC Carpet & Home store. This is a favorite of comedian Jerry Seinfeld, who has used some of his great wealth to build a garage on the Upper West Side to house his collection of antique cars. The homeless man almost certainly never shopped at the ABC store or any of Manhattan's elite emporiums. He was a middle-aged white man, and if he happened to be awake I would give him some money. He didn't thank me or say anything; he just took the cash. I usually saw him about seven in the morning, just as the produce, poultry, fish, flower, and other vendors were setting up for the farmers' market on Union Square. This market offers a cornucopia of high-quality food. You often see chefs shopping there for the items needed for their daily specials: heirloom tomatoes, organic micro greens, chicken, eggs, fresh fish, and many culinary exotica. Karen and I once saw a woman step out of a private limousine to shop there. The market surrounds the park in the square. The benches are always crowded in warm weather, and up and down the sidewalks hucksters try to make a few bucks selling cheap goods. A young black man sold batteries for a dollar a package, urging the bench warmers, *sotto voce*, "Don't be afraid of me."

If anyplace in the United States defines economic inequality it is Manhattan. It is possible to find in close proximity an apartment selling for $10 million and a homeless person using a garbage can as a urinal. Where some workers must make due with less than $10,000 a year, financier George Soros once "earned" a billion dollars—in one year. A gourmet hamburger might sell for $40 and have no shortage of buyers. In a June 2003 article in the *Gotham Gazette*, Andrew Beveridge tells us that according to 2000 census data, "Manhattan is now the U.S. county with the highest disparity of income, surpassing the only county ahead of it in 1989, a former leper colony in Hawaii." "The top fifth of Manhattan households received more than fifty times as much income in 1999 as the bottom fifth, according to analyses based upon Census 2000 data. Those in the top 20 percent averaged $366,000, those in the bottom 20 percent, $7,054. Those in the top group saw their average income increase $140,000, while those in the bottom group moved up only seven dollars." Beveridge goes on to say that if you walk up Fifth Avenue from 49th to 96th Street, "every census tract through which one passes had an average income above $200,000 in 1999. This area of Manhattan contains one of the highest concentrations of the truly affluent in the United States. The co-ops along Fifth Avenue often sell for more than $20 million each. This is the neighborhood where a double-sized townhouse reportedly sold for more than $30 million; some of the doormen wear ermine collars in the winter. Elite boutiques and other specialty stores dot Madison Avenue, where an appointment is preferred and one must "ring [a] bell to be admitted." In the economic downturn that began in late 2000 and was exacerbated by the events of September 11, 2001, the rich suffered considerable losses. However, these have been made up and then some in the years since.

In this richest of cities, one-seventh of all households and one-eleventh of all families had yearly incomes less than $10,000 in 2003 (families by definition are more likely to have more than one income earner than are households, which might contain just a single person). Eighteen percent of families and 19.6 percent of individuals lived in poverty in 2003, as did 31.5 percent of related children under eighteen years old. The poverty level of income for a family of four in the United States in 2003 was $18,660, before taxes. It is difficult to imagine a family living in Manhattan at less than the poverty level of income, and unimaginable to live on less than $10,000, in a city where 27 percent of all renters pay at least 35 percent of their incomes on rent.

DINNER PARTY

The following story describes some remarkable behavior. It is not typical, but it is reflective of certain attitudes common enough among those we met in Manhattan. It marked a turning point in our New York life and greatly sped up our decision to leave.

Karen and I invited a noted left-wing writer and her husband to dinner. I had met her a few years earlier and we had some correspondence after that. I used one of her books in a class I taught. Her book voice was that of a person sympathetic to the plight of ordinary people caught in the capitalist rat race. She got paid to write, and I was hoping that she could give me some tips on getting an agent and maybe introduce me to other writers. We began to read her latest book—Karen read the whole thing—so we would have something to talk about if the conversation lagged. I planned to tell her I would review it for the magazine. We spent half a day shopping for food and drink, settling on fresh wild salmon, fingerling potatoes, field greens, and haricots verts, with homemade olive hummus, roasted red peppers, and crostini for appetizers, and cheesecake from the famous Veniero's Bakery on 11th Street and First Avenue for dessert. We bought several bottles of good wine.

Our guests arrived on time. They handed me a jar of homemade quince jelly, and I walked them up our stairs. As we made introductions, the writer said she had been under the impression that we had given our possessions away, yet here we had a couch and a chair. We said that we had had to buy some things to live in the apartment. I had the feeling that the fact that we weren't living on the floor disappointed her. She didn't sit down but instead began to inspect the living room, raising and lowering our window blinds, looking at our pictures, books, and photographs. She opened our bedroom door and checked out this room. Karen went into the kitchen to do some food preparation, and the woman followed her, picked up the wrapped fish, and smelled the package. Karen and I finished the first of many glasses of wine.

I don't think people get home-cooked meals much anymore. Every time we cook for guests, they eat as if it were their last meal. These two were no exception. They greedily devoured the appetizers and ravenously ate dinner. The writer cleaned her plate, got up, found the salad bowl, returned to the table, and began to eat straight from the bowl. She did the same thing with the cheesecake, except that she didn't bother to come back to the table. She just ate from the pie plate at the kitchen counter. She managed to get in a dig about our dinnerware, suggesting that the English version was much nicer than our American brand.

While we were eating, we learned that the two of them maintained separate apartments (though they had been married for years), both of which were rent-controlled. Between them they also owned three cars. No doubt they could pay for the cars with the money they saved each month. New York City has a complex, nearly impenetrable, rent control law, in effect for more than fifty years. Nothing excites New Yorkers like rents; they love to talk about how much who is paying for what. We had come to hate these controls, so we picked up on their comments on their housing deals. She lived in a building that contained units originally meant for struggling artists. The subsidies were a way for the city to attract young writers, musicians, painters, and the like, who would otherwise not be able to afford a place to live in the nation's cultural center. Just as originally, controls were meant to make apartments in the city affordable to those of modest means.

It is difficult to make price controls work in a capitalist economy. Unless the government is vigilant and willing to punish transgressors, unless it allows rents to rise as a renter's income rises, and unless it builds decent and cheap housing itself, controls will tend to devolve into a system subsidizing those who don't need the benefits. And if they are not universal, enormous inequities will develop. In our apartment building, a couple living directly underneath us was charged one-fifth the rent we were paying for a unit the same size as ours. Theirs was controlled; ours was not. In the city as a whole, the greatest subsidies go to stable households living in desirable apartment buildings and neighborhoods, a class composed mainly of affluent whites, usually singles or couples, often elderly. At the same time, most poor and minority families, especially large households with children, don't benefit in the least from rent controls.

A number of studies have tried to figure out the full extent of this inequity, calculating the subsidy—that is, the difference between the maximum rent for a regulated apartment and the actual rent for a comparable unregulated unit—enjoyed by New Yorkers of different neighborhoods, races, and household sizes. Harvard's Joint Center for Housing Studies discovered that Manhattan's high-income neighborhoods and a few wealthier areas in Queens won the lion's share of New York's rent subsidies. In 1989, the typical discount on the Upper East Side, for example, was $432 a month, while in East New York and most of the Bronx and Brooklyn, the discount was actually *negative*, meaning that landlords were unable to find tenants willing to pay the maximum allowable rent. The consulting firm Arthur D. Little Associates estimated in 1986 that rent regulation in New York amounted to an annual subsidy of $754 million. White households received 95 percent of that sum, though they constituted only 56 percent of tenants; black and Hispanic households received just 2 percent. The study also found that one- and two-person households received 74 percent of the rent-regulation subsidy, while families with children got under 1 percent.

A recent column by John Tierney, aptly titled "Delusions of the Rich and Rent-Controlled" (*New York Times*, June 3, 2006), perfectly describes the attitudes of our guests and some of the high-income leftists we met in Manhattan. Tierney tells of the *mea culpas* now being uttered by film director and writer Nora Ephron, who "bribed her way into an eight-room apartment for $1,500 a month at the Apthorp, the palatial building at Broadway and West 79th Street." Ephron's apartment had a market rental value of $10,000 a month, but she recalls being indignant when "a new law stripped away her rent protection because her household income was more than $250,000 per year." Tierney really hits the nail on the head when he observes:

> Like European nobles in crumbling castles, rentocrats are
> above money grubbing. They deserve their homes because of
> their longevity and their virtues. They compare rent controls
> to Fulbright scholarships—a stipend wisely provided to

worthy intellectuals and artists. They will announce, with a
straight face, that they're entitled to keep their apartments
because of the extensive "emotional investment" they have
made in their building.

In any event, Karen said that she had seen an item in that day's
New York Times about a regulated apartment in which the owner had
hired thugs to harass tenants to move out. A few diehards had remained
and were still paying absurdly low rents. This article so excited our
guests that they asked us to retrieve it immediately. Karen fished it out of
the trash can, and they proceeded to read it and make comments at the
table, while we were still eating. He got up so he could get a better grip
on the newspaper. Minutes later, the writer asked if we had the Sunday
magazine's crossword puzzle. Karen duly fetched this, and our erstwhile
artist immediately retired to the bathroom. We went into the living room
and sat around trying to act as if nothing crazy was happening. She
remained on the toilet for thirty minutes, working the crossword puzzle
and yelling out responses to our conversation.

After she rejoined us things really deteriorated. She kept going
into the kitchen to gobble up whatever scraps of food remained. When
she went into our bedroom again and we heard her opening our closet
doors, we glanced at each other as if to say, "Keep calm." We somehow
kept the conversation going until they mercifully left around midnight.
She never talked about writing or offered me any encouragement. They
never called or sent a note to thank us for the dinner, and they didn't
reciprocate. I vowed never to review her book, or any book she might
write. In fact, I threw the book away.

LEAVING MANHATTAN

Manhattan was an exciting place to live, and *Monthly Review* was an
interesting place to work. However, many places are exciting and, in the
end, a job is a job. The city assaults a person's physical and mental health.
The racket is relentless, making it difficult to concentrate and to sleep.
A woman who owns several clubs in the trendy meatpacking district

around West 14th Street has had built a casket-like, high-tech "pod" bed that blots out all sound, just so she can get a good night's rest. Not only does constant noise disrupt normal daily rhythms, it also, according to the results of a recent study by German scientists, greatly raises the risk of heart attack. Manhattan may be the city that never sleeps, but sleep deprivation and other similar losses caused by noise exact a price.

Another harmful aspect of modern urban life is too much light. It never gets dark in many parts of a large city. You can't see the stars, and again, you can't sleep properly. Our street was a well-known location for films and television shows. The directors would often shoot after dark, using bright lights placed on rooftops by large cranes. In the middle of the night, sleep would be broken by the noise of the film crew and the piercing brightness of the lights, which made it appear as if it were the middle of the day. If light from cars can harm animals in a place as remote as Joshua Tree National Park in southern California, imagine the damage done by the lights of Manhattan to all forms of life.

There are thousands of taxicabs and tens of thousands of cars, trucks, and buses scurrying around Manhattan day and night. They make noise and give off light, and they also pollute the air. There is no comparison between the pure air of Yellowstone and that of New York City. We were there in the wake of September 11, and the pollution was especially noxious around Ground Zero; several months after the terrorist attacks it was impossible not to notice the odors. The health impacts of the explosions are still being studied, but there is little doubt that they were, and will be considerable. Even if 9/11 had never happened, those who live in Manhattan surely suffer an array of respiratory illnesses caused by the particulate matter there all the time. Asthma is epidemic among black children in the city, and the culprit is most likely this everyday contamination. We were in good physical condition when we left Yellowstone, and at my mother's we easily made an eleven-mile hike. We walked constantly in the city, but we never felt the kind of bodily euphoria exercise normally brings. After every walk we took, we were wheezing and out of breath when we got to our apartment door. We had scratchy throats and chronic sinusitis. We wondered if we were damaging our lungs.

A final thing that upset me was the constant in-your-face reminder that the city is too big and impersonal for people to care about one another. There are thousands of acts of individual kindness done every day, and Manhattanites don't often fit the stereotype of the callous urban dweller. But tens of thousands of them are locked into their own tiny worlds and too beset by worries large and small to have much time or energy to devote to the more fundamental matters of human existence. Karen and I expected to be drawn into a circle of left-wing intellectuals and activists, but we soon realized that this wasn't going to happen. There was a lot of pretending otherwise, but we knew after a month that we were not in the New York of the romantic imagination but in a place where no one much cared if we lived or died. The only time residents in our apartment building spoke at any length with us was when we were moving out, probably to gather information about a now empty unit. Everyone was working so hard just to pay rent and meet other expenses that they had no time for the neighborly give-and-take familiar to me as a child. Working too many hours for not enough pay while living in a tiny apartment in a nerve-jangling city is not a recipe for the building of solid social relationships. We invited a young couple to dinner. The man was the son of my friend Bruce, who died the month before I retired. He was a musician, and for him New York was heaven. It stirred his creative juices. But his girlfriend worked as a hostess in a small restaurant close by our apartment, on Second Avenue. She and her co-workers labored such long and stressful hours that they had no time for friendships. She had to make an appointment with another worker just to have a coffee at the nearest Starbucks. The life of my friend's son is the stuff of New York legend—the bohemian artist come to the city to make his name. But even should he succeed, his story is the exception today; hers is the rule.

I enjoyed the camaraderie I had with my workmates, and I liked reading submissions, editing, corresponding with writers, and helping with office projects. But I wasn't used to doing a desk job and keeping regular hours. My back and tailbone ached from long hours of sitting in an uncomfortable chair. The office was stifling in winter. Everyone else kept what to me were ridiculously long hours, and I felt guilty that I wasn't willing to do the same.

I had come to Manhattan not just because it was a fabulous city; It was also the center of progressive politics and thinking, the kind that aim to end every type of inequality, to liberate working men and women and encourage all people to fully develop their capacities, and to create livable spaces for everyone. I wanted to be a part of this creative ferment. Yet the intellectuals I met there often didn't match my expectations. They had a disconcerting way of dismissing the rest of the country and assuming that what their friends in the city were thinking and doing was what everyone else was thinking and doing. Their circles were remarkably well off, insular, and egotistic.

I can't say that I was unhappy to end my first six-month stint in May of 2002. I hadn't found what I wanted there. When I was a young teacher and a few of us were trying to unionize the campus and make the students think about society critically, life was exciting. Time on and off campus blended together, and life was whole, as it should be. During a sabbatical in 1976 I went to California to work for the United Farm Workers and experienced the same thing: a common purpose with thousands of migrant farm workers. I went to their meetings, their parties, and their houses. I was inside something grand. Even at the hotel in Yellowstone, I was part of a collective enterprise, the other clerks and I pulled together everyday, eating and living together. Most of the time it felt right. But here in New York, I felt alone and small. If left-wingers could make me feel like that, if radicals could act like the writer and her husband, I wondered what kind of good society we might make.

We had dreamed for so long of living in Manhattan, but we soon knew that things weren't quite right there. To continue to pay the exorbitant rent, we would have to find additional employment. But it struck us that first summer that we didn't have to work more. We could move to a cheaper, cleaner, less hectic place. Why had we quit the workaday life in Pittsburgh just to continue a new one in Manhattan? We had a fine summer; we saw everything in the city we had ever wanted to see. We had survived a tough place, and this gave us confidence that we could live anywhere. We devised a plan. I would ask the magazine to keep me on as Associate Editor and I would give the Board of Directors a group of tasks for which I would be responsible. I would do this work from wherever we happened to be. In return the magazine would pay for our health insurance. I would receive no salary. My request came as a surprise to everyone at *MR*, but they accepted my proposal. They gained a competent and dedicated worker and gave up a small amount of money in exchange. I would probably give more than I got, but we would soon be free again. Before I had made the decision to leave, I wrote a short article for the magazine's newsletter. Here is what I said:

> So, now here I am in Manhattan, working for *Monthly Review*. It is more pleasant and stimulating work than being a clerk. I have met interesting people, solicited good articles for the magazine, edited some bad articles into good ones, almost completed a draft of a new book, and enjoyed living in one of the world's great cities and working for the world's finest radical journal and press. I have even gotten a new teaching gig, at Cornell's Labor Center, near the Empire State Building. But still, when I walk down the harsh and impersonal streets, breathe in the foul air, and daily confront the greatest inequality I have ever seen in the United States, I long for the West. For the streams rushing down the mountains and the eagles flying free. And I miss my fellow clerks too!

Maybe I already knew. Right before we left the city, two of my office mates and I went to a nearby restaurant for drinks. Why hadn't we done this more often?

THE ENVIRONMENT: ACT TWO, THE FIREFIGHTERS

In the spring of 2002 I taught a class in Cornell's Labor Studies program to a group of New York City public employees. One of my students was a city firefighter and officer of the Firefighters Union. We often spoke during breaks about what the workers he represented were facing in the aftermath of September 11. He sometimes had to leave class early to attend a funeral. He told me that he didn't think any of the firefighters who had been in the thick of things at Ground Zero would be alive in ten years. He described a fire a few years earlier at a power plant, where poisonous chemicals had been released. Not one of the firefighters who fought that blaze was alive in 2002. Now the federal government would not even pay the money necessary to completely clean and disinfect the fire trucks used after September 11. The city government asked the union for concessions not long afterward. The workers were praised as heroes by the media and justifiably so. But heroism wasn't enough to keep federal and state governments from treating workers as commodities whose costs had to be contained.

In a report from the Government Accountability Office (GAO), the impact of 9/11 on firefighters is described as follows:

> Almost all of the FDNY firefighters who had responded to the attack experienced respiratory effects, and hundreds had to end their firefighting careers due to WTC-related respiratory illness. Within 48 hours of the attack, FDNY found that about 90 percent of its 10,116 firefighters and EMS workers who were evaluated at the WTC site reported an acute cough. The FDNY Bureau of Health Services also noted wheezing, sinusitis, sore throats, asthma, and GERD [gastroesophageal reflux disease, highly correlated with chronic respiratory problems] among firefighters who had been on the scene. During the first 6 months after the attack, FDNY observed that of the 9,914 firefighters who were present at the WTC site within 7 days of the collapse, 332 firefighters had WTC cough. Eighty-seven percent of the firefighters with WTC cough reported symptoms of GERD. According to the FDNY Bureau of Health Services, symptoms of GERD are typically reported by less than 25 percent of patients with chronic cough. Some FDNY firefighters exhibited WTC cough that was severe enough for them to require at least 4 weeks of medical leave. Despite

treatment of all symptoms, 173 of the 332 firefighters and one EMS technician with WTC cough showed only partial improvement. FDNY also found that the risk of reactive airway dysfunction syndrome, or irritant-induced asthma, and WTC cough was associated with intensity of the exposure, defined as the time of arrival at the site. In addition, FDNY reports that one firefighter who worked 16-hour days for 13 days and did not use respiratory protection during the first 7 to 10 days was diagnosed with a rare form of pneumonia that results from acute high dust exposure. According to an official from the FDNY Bureau of Health Services, because one of the criteria for being a firefighter is having no respiratory illness, about 380 firefighters were no longer able to serve as firefighters as of March 2004 as a consequence of respiratory illnesses they developed after WTC exposure.

The GAO report notes that many other workers suffered physical and mental illnesses as a result of their work cleaning up the mess caused by the collapse of the twin towers. The irony is that the federal government used the crisis to put into practice laws and policies that have hurt working people. What has happened in New York City and in the nation since September 11, 2001, is paradigmatic for what we have observed in our travels: working people losing ground, while those with money get even more.

The move from Manhattan in late October was as bad as the one to it. After months of weather so dry that the city turned off all its fountains, it began to rain every day. On moving day, we arose at five o'clock and began hauling boxes down the three flights of stairs. Then I took a cab across town to get the moving truck we rented. Things started smoothly, but I smacked the side mirror into a street sign on the way back to our apartment. I just kept moving. I illegally parked in front of St. Mark's Church, and we began to lug our possessions from the hallway to the truck and to our Dodge van. It was drizzling and cold. One of the Polish workmen who had gotten our apartment ready agreed to help us move, for $50 an hour. He never showed. About an hour into the move, Karen asked me why the emergency lights had stopped blinking. I jumped in and saw that I had left the lights on. The battery was dead. We called the U-Haul emergency number, and a repair person was dispatched. It took him an hour and a half to get to 10th Street. There was a long delay caused by a parade honoring the firefighters who died in the 9/11 rescue. Someone had to sit in the truck with a foot on the gas pedal while the battery charged. So only one of us moved boxes. An Asian man gathering ginkgo nuts kept getting in our way. A driver asked us to move the truck so he could fit his car into a tiny space. We glared at him so intently that he drove away.

We had sold our living room furniture to the new tenant, so we didn't have many large, heavy items. We managed to get the bed, mattress, and box springs into the truck, and all that was left was the television set. It was too heavy for us to carry, so we dragged and slid it across the floor to the edge of the stairs. From there we jockeyed it down a step at a time. At the bottom, our energy flagged completely. We couldn't budge the damned thing. Karen walked out to the sidewalk, hailed the first large man she saw, and told him we'd pay him $20 if he would help us put our television set into the moving van. He readily agreed. It took us about thirty seconds to move it. When I gave him the money, he said, "You're good people."

Once packed, Karen drove the truck, and I drove the van. I was to follow her. We immediately got separated, and I feverishly drove twenty miles into New Jersey before I caught her. We ate at an A&W Root Beer stand and slogged on another eight hours to my mother's house. We got there late at night. I kept awake on the lonely roads of Pennsylvania by listening to a Penn State football game and wondering what would happen next.

SUGGESTED READINGS

For some New York City history, see the masterful account of Edwin G. Burrows and Mike Wallace, *Gotham: A History of New York City to 1898*

(New York: Oxford University Press, 2000). For a sense of the older working-class culture in the city, see Joshua Freeman, *Working Class New York: Life and Labor since World War II* (New York: New Press, 2001). The new immigrant workers are described in Immanuel Ness, *Immigrants, Unions, and the New U.S. Labor Market* (Philadelphia: Temple University Press, 2005). To get around Manhattan peruse John Tauranac's wonderful *Manhattan Block by Block: A Street Atlas*, 3rd edition (New York: Tauranac Maps, 2004). The long quote on the inequity of rent controls is from Peter B. Salins, "Rent Control's Last Gasp," *City Journal*, Winter 1997, available at *http://www.city-journal. org/html/7_1_rent_controls.html*.

CHAPTER FOUR

PORTLAND AND THE PACIFIC NORTHWEST

PORTLAND

Population in 2003 538,544
Population in 2000
    White 77.9%
    Black 6.6%
    Asian 6.3%
    Hispanic (all races) 6.8%

Median household income in 2000 .... $40,146
People below poverty level of income 13.1%
Median rent in 2000 .... $562
Median mortgage, including associated costs $1,158

Portland's farmers' market is outstanding. The main location is on the South Park blocks at Portland State University. Website: *www. portlandfarmersmarket.org*. To see a cross-section of city life, visit the city's main public space, Pioneer Courthouse Square, in the heart of the downtown. For a spectacular view of Mt. Hood, visit the Pittock Mansion at 3229 NW Pittock Drive, 97210, (503) 823-3624.

FLORENCE, OREGON

Population in 2003 7,583
Population in 2000
    White 95.9%
    Black 0.3%
    American Indian 0.9%
    Hispanic (all races) 2.4%

Median household income in 2000 .... $30,505
People below poverty level of income 14.4%
Median rent in 2000 .... $456
Median mortgage, including associated costs $821

The Old Town is full of flowers and worth a visit. It is off Highway 101, just before the classic bridge. Ten miles or so south of town, again off Highway 101, is the Oregon Dunes Overlook. Walk to the top of the paved trail and then head down the high dunes to the sea. You can take the Tahkenitch Creek Loop Trail, from the Overlook to the ocean, then south on the beach, and then east and back to the Overlook. Be careful and follow the long wooden stakes over the dunes. It is easy to get lost.

WE TAKE ON COMPANY

When we decided to leave Manhattan, we agreed that we would go somewhere warm for a vacation. From 10th Street, we rented an apartment, sight unseen, in Miami Beach. We had been there before, once enjoying a romantic Christmas in one of the art deco hotels on Ocean Drive. On the way to south Florida, we stopped for two days in Savannah, Georgia. Some say that Savannah is the most European-looking city in the United States. We enjoyed the nineteen parks in the downtown. Most of these are surrounded by old churches and historic houses, many contain heroic statues, and all are shaded by tall old trees. We learned that there have been efforts to destroy these parks and "develop" the land. This would be a calamity. As we walked the old Savannah streets, I was glad that General Sherman had given the intact city to President Lincoln for a Christmas gift.

I will have much to say about Miami Beach and Florida in another chapter. After the year in Manhattan it was a joy to be there, seven weeks in an apartment with a balcony overlooking the ocean. We took long walks on the wide beach and enjoyed the crowds on the Lincoln Road Mall. Across the street from our building, the Ritz Carlton hotel, designed by famed Miami Beach architect Morris Lapidus, was under reconstruction after having been closed for several years, and this made for much noise in the daytime. We insisted on a price break from our realtor, and after some haggling we got it. Three of our children visited, and we showed them the sights. Almost every day was warm and sunny; I never tired of going out on the balcony in the middle of the night and seeing from the large clock/thermometer atop a neighboring building that it was over seventy degrees. In December.

Where to live next? We narrowed our choices to three: Missoula, Montana; Pacific Grove, California; and Portland, Oregon. Missoula is a university town and in one of those mountain-surrounded bowls that moderates winter temperatures. It had a laid-back, "sixties" reputation and was getting favorable press in the travel sections of city newspapers. We had visited Pacific Grove, a small town abutting Monterrey on the Pacific Ocean, south of San Francisco on half-moon Monterrey Bay. Like its sister town on the Atlantic Ocean, Rehoboth Beach in Delaware, Pacific Grove began as a Methodist retreat. Some of the streets are lined with the tiny houses first built by the faithful; their names are on historic door markers. We had stayed at the Bide-A-Wee motel, a quaint little place within earshot of the ocean. There were no phones in the rooms, and I once did a radio interview with a Cleveland station from the pay phone outside our room at 4:30 a.m. Pacific Coast time. I told the envious host that I was listening to the ocean while we talked.

Portland used to be the West Coast's forgotten city, an industrial center and port of no particular distinction. But rising home prices and population densities in California, along with the high-tech boom of the 1970s, made the city a desirable place. City leaders wisely kept the downtown clean and attractive for urban living, with cheap public transportation and manageable car traffic. Strict rules were enacted to prevent suburban sprawl; there is a large green belt of forests at the edge of town, with many hiking and biking trails. There are fine parks and trees everywhere. There are some first-growth "heritage" trees in residential areas. When we read about a "free" bicycle program, in which a pedestrian could pick up a bike at a designated stall, use it, and return it to this or another stall, we were sold. Portland, we hoped, would be a good place to live and a convenient base from which to explore and learn about the Pacific Northwest.

Our youngest children are twin sons. When we were in Miami Beach, they were living and working in Pittsburgh, but we had been encouraging them to leave. They had lived in the city for fifteen years, and their job horizons were narrowing. Pittsburgh is not a place where young people flourish. It is a run-down old mill town, always in fiscal trouble. The much-vaunted high-tech renaissance of the 1990s failed to bring it back to life. Within the last five years, city services and public employment have been severely cut. The population is one of the oldest and least mobile in the nation. The death rate exceeds the birth rate. So the number of people would have declined even if people hadn't been moving away. Without manufacturing, there are few decent work opportunities for young people, especially those without a college education. As with much of western Pennsylvania, adult children rely on their parents for economic support. Our twins had jobs and had worked steadily for many years. They were living in a dangerous old neighborhood, a place where there were pockets of gentrification, but still too many mean streets. In December they told us that they were ready to leave and wanted to go with us to Portland.

The logistics were now more complicated. Before driving to Florida, we had put our belongings in storage in my hometown. When we left Florida, we went to Amherst, Massachusetts, where we spent a cold and dreary two weeks while I taught a class to union staff persons. Then we traveled back to my mother's and made moving arrangements. We rented a large U-Haul, and by telephone, secured a furnished extended-stay apartment in Beaverton, a suburb near Portland. Early on a late-January morning, we took the U-Haul to Pittsburgh and maneuvered it up the steep snow-covered street on which our son's house was located. It was about ten degrees outside, and the sidewalk was icy. The boys hadn't prepared much for the move, so we spent the next few hours frantically packing their things and putting them into the truck. Next we drove the forty-five miles back to the storage place to get our possessions. It was so cold that my body gave up the ghost after an hour and the boys had to do most of the work. We spent the night at my mother's; after doing the laundry we had beers and some hot sausage sandwiches at a bar I hadn't been to for thirty years. We spoke with an old man who knew my father and whose son had played basketball at the college where I taught.

It took us five days to cross the country from Pittsburgh to Portland, two of us in the truck and two in our van. It was winter, but we were lucky. We were beset by high winds in southern Wyoming, a tennis-ball-sized bubble on a rear tire in Utah, and heavy rains in Portland, but we made it. Throughout the trip, I continued to teach a web-based college course I had begun in Miami, logging in at the motel where we stayed each night. I wondered what my students would think if they knew where I was when I answered their questions: Peru, Illinois; Kearney, Nebraska; Rock Springs, Wyoming; Boise, Idaho; and Hillsboro, Oregon. We moved into our temporary quarters and stored our gear in a U-Haul facility. The boys began to look for work, and we began to search for a new home.

IT'S RAINING

Portland is situated between two mountain ranges, the Coast Range to the west and the Cascades to the east. The eastern mountains are punctuated by a rare east-west gorge, the Columbia Gorge, which runs along the once wild but now much-dammed Columbia River, the last path taken by Lewis and Clark on their way to the sea. Portland weather is relatively mild despite its northern location. Ferns stay green in the woods year-round, and roses bloom in the famous Rose Garden from May to November. We met a woman who had a eucalyptus tree growing in her front yard. There hadn't been a hard freeze in four years, and it was more than thirty feet tall. Sadly this tree snapped and died during the second winter we were there. It snowed heavily in January 2004, and there was more sleet and ice than the tree could bear. The city was so

unprepared for this bad weather that streets were impassable for days.
Businesses didn't bother to clean the sidewalks in front of their shops,
and homeowners didn't clear their driveways. Everything, including the
airport and the professional basketball team, ceased to function during a
storm that would have been a minor inconvenience in Pittsburgh.

But if winters are seldom bitterly cold, they are rainy. It rains hard,
and it rains all the time. We had some good weather during our first
weeks, in February, warm and sunny enough to sit outside at a café.
We took the boys to the ocean so they could see the Pacific for the first
time. We stopped at the town of Oceanside, on Cape Meares, just west
of the cheese-making town of Tillamook, and walked in the bright sun
along the beach in light jackets, among seagulls much larger than those
in Miami Beach. We began to anticipate the greater warmth bound to
come in spring.

On March 5, 2003, we moved into an eighth-floor apartment just
blocks west of downtown Portland. It was window-filled, and from our
living room we could see, on clear days, Mt. Hood (Oregon's highest
point), Mt. Adams, Mt. St. Helen's, and Mt. Rainier. The last three
peaks are in Washington State. Portland is just south of the Washington
border; the boundary is at the middle of a bridge that crosses the
Columbia River from Oregon into Washington. All of the mountains are
volcanic peaks, part of a chain of volcanoes—a "ring of fire"—stretching
far out into the Pacific. Our sons had yet to find work, so they moved in
with us. Somewhat tight quarters, but we figured they would be with us
for just a few days.

We seldom saw the mountains in March or April. It rained for
twenty-seven consecutive days in March and for twenty-five in April.
Not just showers but deluges. The skies turned from blue to gray in
seconds. There was a small air conditioner in our bedroom, and torrents
beat down on it and against the windows. It woke us every night, with
a sound that made us feel that we were in a car wash. We despaired
that it would never stop. We cursed our decision to come here and
the locals who disdained umbrellas. We wanted to shower insults on
our neighbors who said that they loved the rain, that it was liquid
sunshine, that it was good for your skin, and that there was nothing

better than staying in pajamas and getting cozy in your apartment. We noticed that more than a few of our neighbors drank a lot to while away the depressing days.

The rains ended in May, and the gloom gave way to the finest summer weather we ever experienced. The sun shone every day and the temperatures climbed, by June often reaching ninety degrees. Remarkably, it was a dry heat. Warm weather in Portland is driven by winds from the east, through the Columbia Gorge. Once you get about a hundred miles east of the city along the gorge, the terrain becomes desert-like, and it is the wind from this area that warms and dries out the city.

Portland is laid out for walking. Anything we needed we could get on foot. The city is a haven for those who want fresh, healthy food. In addition to the many good grocery stores, there is a farmers' market, perhaps the best in the country, open from early May until late November. The stalls in the market (120 vendors that year) are heaped high with vegetables, fruits, nuts, mushrooms, and fish. You name it; it's probably there. Every imaginable type of berry is sold: blackberries, many varieties of blueberries, raspberries (two crops of them), red and black currants, huckleberries, marionberries, strawberries, elderberries, and probably a few I have forgotten. The market is in the "Park Blocks," a long stretch of streets made into a park, shaded with large trees, nearby Portland State University. Not far from the market is the Willamette— accent on "am"—River, and we enjoyed the River Walk, basking in the sun and watching the crowds of joggers, bikers, and boaters. From our apartment it was a short stroll to the Rose Garden and a maze of paths, playgrounds, picnic areas, amphitheaters, and the city zoo. There was a large authentic Japanese Garden, complete with a pond full of koi. Abutting this area are hills through which run miles of hiking trails. We took scores of fine walks on these, observing the flora and fauna, alert for the occasional coyote that sometimes wandered into the gardens, to the chagrin of the ravens who cawed in irritation at this interloper.

A longer hike takes you to the Pittock Mansion, an old home built by a Portland industrialist and now a museum. The view of Mt. Hood on a clear day is outstanding, and the mansion grounds are beautiful. One day as we were returning home from the Pittock, we saw a peacock in someone's yard. When it saw us, it spread its wings. We thought it was a pet until we talked to a neighbor. Apparently these fowl escape from the zoo and make nuisances of themselves, ruining gardens and lawns. As long as they keep away from predators, they survive the moderate winters. Not long after we saw the bird, we read an article in the local newspaper about a neighborhood's problems with peacocks. They not only damaged people's property, they had a penchant for bashing into cars, ruining them too. The insurance companies are probably still sorting out claims.

THE PACIFIC NORTHWEST

The best thing about Portland was its proximity to scenic places. Once the weather broke, we began to make excursions throughout the Pacific Northwest. The Columbia Gorge is walled in to the south by hills and cliffs, through which run streams and rivers, punctuated by more waterfalls than anywhere else in the country. Some of the waterfalls, including the dazzling Multnomah Falls (recently replaced by a casino as Oregon's most visited tourist attraction), can be seen along the historic Columbia Gorge Highway. The first hike we took in the gorge was in April, and on the Washington side of the river. We wanted to escape the rain, so we drove more than eighty miles east along the river, crossed a bridge, and wound our way up narrow dry hills to the trailhead. Already, wild flowers were blossoming. We took the hike to see them, happy to be in a dry climate and not worried about getting wet and muddy. A howling wind greeted us as we gained elevation. We were freezing but delighted when, at the top of a hill, we got a clear view of snow-covered Mt. Adams.

Throughout our stay in Portland, the Columbia Gorge remained a special place. Along the gorge, our favorite hike was at Eagle Creek, just west of the Bonneville Dam, one of many built in the West for cheap electricity during the New Deal of the 1930s. Woody Guthrie sang, "Roll On, Columbia, Roll On," but the dams along this great river have slowed the roll considerably. Eagle Creek flows through a deep north-south gorge before emptying into the Columbia. Along the trail we marveled at the rushing water, enormous pine trees, the sharp drop-offs, the rock formations, the flowers and moss growing out of the seeps in the rocks, and the waterfalls. One day we watched in horror and fascination as a group of teenage boys first threw over their sleeping bags, and then leapt off a cliff next to a waterfall and dove into the roiling waters beneath the falls, a jump of at least forty feet. We were happy to see each of them rise from the deep and swim joyfully away.

The Northwest is mountainous, with steep forested slopes running down to the sea and with volcanic peaks almost always in sight. There are so many dazzling things to see that it is hard to know where to begin. While we had begun to appreciate our nation's natural beauty at Yellowstone, it was in Portland that we came to love it and make it an integral part of our lives. Our weeks were filled with planning, preparing for, and taking trips—to the gorge, to national parks, to the Oregon coast. We never imagined that packing lunches and spending a day in the woods could be such a fine thing to do. We'd pick a destination, read everything we could find about it, plot out the driving directions, and go. Everything was new and amazing. Transforming too. I had let work dominate much of my life for so many years. Taking time to see, much less contemplate and enjoy, the beauty around me had little place in my life. During our fourteen months in Portland, I saw the error of my ways. Beauty, contemplation, enjoyment—these weren't something to feel guilty about, mere adjuncts of life. They were life.

Here are some places we loved and that no visitor should miss.

The Lodge at Mt. Hood: Mt. Hood, an hour's drive east, overlooks the city of Portland, although it is often hidden behind the area's infamous cloudy skies. People say, "The mountain is out today." It was somehow comforting to see the lone volcanic peak from the city, as if the mountain were a protector—ironic, since if it exploded, it would be a destroyer. Mt. Hood has many areas for hiking, and it is a great skiing venue. Skiers can find slopes to use well into summer; Mt. Hood has the only year-round ski runs in the country. For us, the main attraction was the stone ski lodge. It was built by the Civilian Conservation Corps (CCC) during the Great Depression. The builders, ordinary workers, were trained in the wide variety of skills needed to make this fine structure. I could feel their pride as I went from room to room in the great lodge, admiring the stone fireplaces and intricate metalwork. I was proud that this work had been done by ordinary people like me. Throughout the West, CCC works abound (roads, trails, buildings, bridges), and their craftsmanship shows what could be done even today through public initiative if only the will were there.

Crater Lake: This National Park in southern Oregon is about three hours inland from the coast. The result of an enormous volcanic eruption, Crater Lake is 2,000 feet deep and as beautifully blue as you will ever see. It is impossible to forget the wonder you feel when you initially come upon it. I remembered my first time, in 1971, and I had been telling Karen about this since we met. I was thrilled that she was getting to see it too. To local Indians the lake was a sacred site, and they kept its existence secret from the white settlers for fifty years; then whites discovered it by accident. It is especially stunning when the rims are snow-covered, which can be well into summer. There is a small attractive lodge, one of many similar structures in the Northwest, managed by the same company, Xanterra, that ran Yellowstone. One of the concessions at the park is a boat ride from the lake shore—accessible only by foot down a treacherous path—to a small island. Xanterra made a big deal about its decision to replace the tour boats with less polluting models. By chance, we were there the day of the exchange. We wondered why there were film crews with cameras on tripods present. We watched as the boats were hauled over the lake by helicopter and dropped down into the water. We were told that the same pilots had worked on the movie *Jurassic Park*. The old boats were then flown out. We took a hike up to a fire tower. It was unusually hot, ninety degrees, but at the top there was shade and a breeze. Snow still covered the hillside below us, and we spent an hour observing a natural spectacle—ravens devouring the dragonflies that come every year. We spent two days at the park, with an overnight stay in the forgettable town of Klamath Falls. Karen asked the motel desk clerk for directions to the falls, but we learned that the falls no longer exist. From the park we drove west, down the resplendent canyon formed by the North Umpqua River, to the windy coastal town of Bandon.

Mt. St. Helen's: We first saw this mountain up close twenty-three years after it erupted. It is in Washington, about two-and-a-half hours northeast of Portland. Evidence of devastation was everywhere, as were signs of life's renewal. The drive to the main observation sight is marked by road signs telling you where to evacuate if there is an eruption. We took hikes—alone and with our children. One of our sons became so fearful of falling rocks as we made our way along a narrow ledge that he turned back. Karen and I continued around the topless mountain, climbing to a vantage point above the log-sotted lake where eighty-year-old innkeeper Harry Truman made his last stand, deciding to die in his home when he knew that the volcano was going to blow. We were imbued with both a sense of doom—from the bleakness of the landscape (burned trees can be seen seventeen miles from the eruption, and a stream, much altered from its original course, flows through volcanic waste)—and of hope, as you see elk grazing in the valley and wildflowers and some small trees growing once again.

Mt. Rainier: This is another national park, in Washington, three hours from Portland. Mt. Rainier stands stark and alone, some 14,000 feet tall, completely covered by glaciers, almost glowing, most spectacularly in the light of a full moon. We saw one during a glorious late October visit. We spent a night at the Longmire Lodge inside the park and another in the nearby town of Packwood. This tiny village has refused to become a typical gateway to a national park. There are only a few motels (our favorite is the super-clean Crest Trail Lodge—highly recommended and inexpensive), even fewer restaurants, and no laundromat. Locals have to drive more than an hour over windy mountainous roads to Yakima to shop. Near the lodge at Paradise, twelve incredible miles from Longmire, we walked among the most beautiful array of wildflowers in the country. The ground cover turned into a quilt of reds, browns, and yellows, rivaling the colors of New England's autumn leaves. We hiked up steep steps and onto a trail that is the jumping-off point for those more intrepid souls who come to climb Rainier. When we came to the park a year later, in August 2004, we watched climbers training for the ascent, practicing in the snow what they would do if they began to fall. There is a second lodge at Sunrise without guest rooms and from there we took the Burroughs Trail to a view of Emmons Glacier, which, when you are close up, gives off a blue glow. Through a gap in the mountains,

Mount Rainier National Park, Washington.

we saw Seattle and Tacoma in the distance, some sixty miles away. We watched a herd of shaggy-haired mountain goats grazing in the sun as we wound our way up the rocky path, through tundra, to the lookout point. Although we had been sweating, we put on our coats to protect ourselves from the biting cold winds at the top. Chipmunks harassed us as we tried to eat our lunch on a chair made from stone.

Olympic National Park: This park in northwestern Washington has it all: snow-covered mountains along Hurricane Ridge, near the town of Port Angeles; true rain forests on the western side of the park; and miles of unspoiled coastline, with gigantic haystack rocks and tide pools filled with starfish and anemones of purple, blue, orange, green, and yellow. Our favorite beach, one on which you can camp overnight, was Shi Shi Beach, which we first learned about on the Travel Channel (it rated Shi Shi as one of the country's ten best beaches), reached by going through the reservation of the Makah Indians. At the end of a narrow road close to the beach trailhead, is the house of Tillie Flynn, who has converted her front yard into a parking lot. She will assure the safety of your car for a small fee (five dollars when we were there), which you place in an envelope she provides and then put in a drop box. You never get to meet Tillie. Also on the Makah reservation is Cape Flattery, the northwesternmost point in the continental United States. The waters around this cape are rough and the land is undermined by water caves. As we stood on the platform the Makahs built and looked out toward Vancouver Island, we could imagine the Indians hunting for whales, standing in their wooden boats. Today the impoverished tribe has reinstated its hunt (which, given that their production has always been for use and attuned to the rhythms of the natural world, has never threatened the existence of the whales), in part as a way to inculcate its culture in the young. This has caused an outcry among some (white) environmentalists, most of whom have shed precious few tears for the devastation of Indian society and culture by their white ancestors.

Another unique place in Olympic is the Hoh rainforest. It is south of the logging town of Forks (one of the few towns besides Port Angeles where you can get a motel), reached after a nineteen-mile drive from U.S. Highway 101. We took two short hikes, marveling at the ancient moss-covered trees and the translucent waters of the streams that empty from the rainforest into the Hoh River. Elk munched leaves along the muddy banks. We scooped up some "glacier flour," rocks ground up by the force of the nearby glaciers from the still icy water. Karen thought we might be able to market it as a facial exfoliant. On our way back to Forks, we gathered wild blackberries from the laden bushes on both sides of the road. That evening we bought vanilla ice cream and stuffed ourselves on blackberry sundaes.

Olympic is not contiguous; it has been pieced together as individual holdings and became available as the government usurped Indian lands. There are large swatches of private property among the public lands that comprise the park. These parcels have been despoiled by clear-cut logging, all of the trees in an area torn up, with the use of explosives, and the land left to its own devices. As you drive south from Forks, you leave and re-enter Olympic at various points. It is easy to tell when you are in the park and when you are not. Outside, the land is a wasted expanse of tree stumps, scrub, and mud. It is a startling juxtaposition and an indication of just how ruthless companies can be in the pursuit of profits. The towns dependent on logging are similar in appearance—dirty, grimy, polluted, and poor—to the mining towns I knew as a boy. Washington is the most ecologically devastated state I have seen, except perhaps for West Virginia, and, as we shall see, Florida.

The Oregon coast: Highway 101 traverses the entire Oregon coast, from Astoria in the north to Brookings in the south. Although the road gets crowded in summer, it is not as congested as its California counterpart. Oregon's coastal weather is often rainy and cool, and there are few sand beaches; both features have inhibited the growth of large beach communities. The towns that dot the coast tend to be small and not particularly attractive. Seaside, a few miles south of Astoria, has sand, but it is a poor cousin of towns like Wildwood, New Jersey, full of taffy and fudge shops and garish antique stores. People seemed to have fun though, strolling along the boardwalk, careening down the streets in bicycles-built-for-eight, and eating junk food. It was amusing to see them "sunning" themselves in sweat pants and shirts. Oregon's beaches are more suited to kite-flying than traditional ocean pursuits. Cannon Beach, about ten minutes south of Seaside, has bed-and-breakfast lodges and (high-priced) motel rooms. The beach is wide and sandy, and the rock formations offshore are awe-inspiring. But the overlooking cliffs have been ruined by garish, oversized houses, with fences and rickety steps going down to the shore.

The Oregon coast is public property, and it is rare for houses to be built on the beach. There are dozens of accessible and well-maintained state parks; many are free and the rest require a small fee or an inexpensive yearly pass. It is not difficult to find a spot where you can pull off the highway, have a picnic lunch, and enjoy a view of seabirds flying and waves splashing on the cliffs. You can hike along the rocky coast or on the mountains above. If you are lucky you might see whales making their annual migrations north or south. During the spring volunteers are stationed along the highway with whale viewing information. We marched to Cape Lookout, two miles around a headland, to try to spot them, but had no luck. This was a hike we took often. It juts you far out into the ocean to a perch where, if it is sunny, is a perfect spot to eat and take a nap. We sat for an hour watching the small fishing boats, the water's color changing from blue to green, the storms coming ashore, and just daydreaming.

There are three connected state parks near Bandon (Cape Arago, Shore Acres, and Sunset Bay) that can only be described as glorious. We usually started at the southernmost park and hiked north through thick shady forests and on the cliffs above the sea. At one lookout we watched seals and sea lions growling and yowling noisily on small offshore rock islands. All along the coast you had to be careful not to walk on land edges where harsh weather had eroded the underlying soil. The winds and rain create all sorts of marvelous tree formations. We saw a tree growing from a cliff straight out toward the ocean. We were always struck by how it mattered whether you were on the north or south side of a head land. On the northern exposure, the gale-like winds made you shiver as you trekked along. Once the winds were so strong we had to hold onto our glasses. But on the southern side, it was always sweetness and light.

We always anticipated with excitement a visit to the sand dunes, which stretch south for fifty miles, beginning at the town of Florence on the central Oregon coast. This is one of the few places along the coast where mountains don't extend to the sea. The dunes were formed as a result of the volcanic explosion that created Crater Lake. Some are over 500 feet tall. You can rent dune buggies and ride over and around the dunes, though this seemed too dangerous for us. Every year a few riders wreck and die or suffer severe injuries. What we loved best was to tramp through the dunes to the beach and hike for miles along the ocean. We seldom saw another person, though we did see dozens of seals peeking their heads above the water, looking like living periscopes watching us. And here too, after watching the waves month after month, we finally spotted a whale.

The dunes are a good place to let your inner thoughts flow freely. On another day, as we walked south along the beach at Florence, tall sand dunes flanked our left, the Pacific Ocean our right. Dark clouds raced toward us from the north. A fine mist began to fall and we became engulfed in fog. The wind pushed us along and compounded the noise made by the waves rolling without end toward the shore. Conversation became impossible and I was drawn inward. Thoughts ran randomly through my mind. It seemed as though I were going to have some profound insight. Then the ocean and sand and the tiny plovers scurrying away from the waves when they hit the shore reminded me of the insignificance of my thoughts. The immenseness and indifference of nature filled me with dread. I remembered a poem by A. E. Housman:

Stars, I have seen them fall,
But when they drop and die
No star is lost at all
From all the star-sown sky.

The toil of all that be
Helps not the primal fault;
It rains into the sea,
And still the sea is salt.

Somehow this gave me comfort as we turned around and began the long walk back, the wind whipping against us while the rain pelted our faces. It seemed we would never get to the opening in the dunes from which we had begun.

THE ENVIRONMENT: ACT THREE, THE BISCUIT FIRE

At the Portland farmers' market we bought mushrooms from a vendor who gathered wild varieties in Oregon's forests. One of the places where he collected his exotic and expensive fare was in the Siskiyou National Forest, located in the southwest corner of the state. In 2002 the "Biscuit

Fire" (named for Biscuit Creek) burned more than a half-million acres, and this greatly encouraged the growth of wild mushrooms.

The Siskiyou Forest is, according to University of Oregon sociologist Richard York, "one of the few areas in the lower 48 states that still contains extensive roadless wild forests and healthy salmon runs, and it is the most biologically diverse ecosystem on the West Coast." However, the fire gave the Bush administration ammunition for environmentally destructive but timber-industry-friendly policies. Timber companies wanted to "salvage" the lumber from the dead trees, and the government was only too happy to oblige corporations that gave politicians millions of campaign dollars. Bush argued that removing the dead wood from the forest would prevent future fires. This is not true. In fact, as a study cited by Professor York made clear, "data show that postfire logging, by removing naturally seeded conifers and increasing surface fuel loads, can be counter-productive to goals of forest regeneration and fuel reduction." The government ignored this evidence and approved a large timber sale, including not just the dead wood but many live trees that survived the fire. The researchers who advised against the sales were harassed by departmental colleagues at Oregon State University who, in league with Forest Service officials, tried to suppress their study.

What happened in the wake of the Biscuit fire will not surprise those who know about the cozy relationship between the Forest Service and corporate America. Our public lands are exploited by corporations such as timber and cattle companies, who are given cheap access to the land while the taxpayers foot the bill. An article in the *Denver Post* (November 1, 2005) noted that:

> In 2004, the Bureau of Land Management [BLM], the Forest Service and other agencies spent $144 million and generated just $21 million from grazing fees. Ranchers who hold public lands grazing permits pay as little as $1.43 per animal unit per month—the amount of forage a cow and her calf can eat in a month. But the BLM and Forest Service would have had to charge $7.64 and $12.26 per unit, respectively, to

cover their expenses, according to the GAO [Government Accounting Office].

The same kind of subsidization benefits the timber industry. Not only do sales to timber companies pay for only a fraction of the costs of planning, designing, building, and maintaining forest roads (the vast majority of which are not even accessible to the public, only to the loggers), but the government sells the timber at discount prices. The Forest Service's accounting practices are so shoddy that it cannot even say how much of its costs are recovered by the sales. Independent researchers, however, assess the subsidies to timber interests at hundreds of millions of dollars in the past decade alone.

Meanwhile the Bush administration wants to build new roads, solely for the timber industry's benefit, while refusing to ask Congress for money to repair badly deteriorating old ones. And it continues to strip the national parks of the funds needed to keep them the public jewels they were meant to be.

WORK VICARIOUSLY

I didn't have a regular job while we lived in Portland. I taught a weekend seminar to a group of Portland-area workers, and I did a web-based class for the University of Indiana. But neither of these gave me insight into the region's world of work. However, I learned a great deal about work in Portland through the experiences of my sons. My wife and I were soon embarrassed by our failure to investigate the job markets in Oregon and Portland. The state's unemployment rate was one of the highest in the nation, and the city's economy was in the doldrums. If we had checked, we would have known that Portland had lost much of its manufacturing base, and the job growth created by the high-tech boom of the 1980s and 1990s had ended even before the dot-com bust, with little chance of returning.

Both sons were restaurant workers, and we naively believed that, given their experience, they would have no trouble finding work quickly.

They began to answer help-wanted ads and went from restaurant to restaurant handing out resumés. We were frustrated that they didn't get jobs immediately and told them they weren't trying hard enough. But it became apparent that the restaurant market wasn't offering many jobs. Some days there would be fewer than ten openings in the newspapers. They did get phone calls and interviews, but there was always something not quite right about the situation. The wage was ridiculously low, or the position was far below what they were qualified to do, or the job didn't start for several months. It turned out that the market was saturated with chefs seeking work. No one wanted to leave a position, no matter how bad it was. A person I met told me that during the high-tech frenzy, Japanese businessmen with large expense accounts filled many restaurants, but they were gone now. The chef of a well-known restaurant called one of the boys, but we were upset that our son decided against an interview. However, within a month, this chef had been unceremoniously fired, for no apparent reason, and within another month prominent chefs in the city were holding a benefit dinner for him. We wondered why this established chef had no money. A few months later he opened a sandwich shop which, despite newspaper stories extolling it as the city's first authentic purveyor of French sandwiches and French-fried potatoes, was still a sandwich shop. As the days passed, expectations began to diminish; any job would do.

It took nearly three months for our sons to find work. I saw an advertisement on a street near our apartment for the opening of a new pizza shop and sent one son's resumé to the address listed. He got a call, trained at a sister parlor out of town, and when the store opened, he went to work. It was a poorly run operation from the beginning, but he was able to supplement his meager pay with the generous tips customers left in the tip jar on the counter. A homeless person stole the jar one day, and our son chased him down the street and recovered the money. Not a smart thing to do, but the money represented a significant part of his earnings. It was easy to see from this experience how working people might develop hostility toward those without work. Competition for a small pool of money doesn't make for relationships of worker solidarity.

You might think one way in the abstract, but reality checks these thoughts and makes for cutthroat competition.

Soon after one son found work, the other twin did as well. In Pittsburgh, he had been a sous-chef at one of the city's top restaurants. In Portland, the best he could get was a line-cook job in a seedy complex of four restaurants, each serviced from the same tiny kitchen. He spent his nights making bar food, kebabs, and fried fish. He soon was coming home, late at night, nearly in tears at how his craft had been debased. When the chef tried to upgrade the food in one of the places, he played dumb and pretended that he didn't know how to do simple things, to avoid having work heaped upon him. He couldn't make crêpes; he knew nothing about desserts; he couldn't do sauces. One night the cooks noticed a foul odor in the kitchen. As it worsened, the management worried that it would drive away the customers. When they discovered that liquid was oozing from the ceiling, someone called the police. There was a transient hotel above the restaurants, and the police found a dead and deteriorating body in a room. The manager told the cooks to burn wood chips in the grill to cover the smell.

Downtown Portland's fabulous farmers' market.

Our son kept this job for three months and then quit. Through a waiter he knew, he contacted a supervisor at another restaurant. She had worked with our son and knew he was talented. She helped him get the new job. This second place was well known in Portland; the chef had been featured in a national food magazine. The pay was slightly higher, though still well below Eastern norms. But the work arrangements weren't much better. A skilled sous-chef with many years experience at the restaurant was earning less than $30,000 a year. He was asked to leave because the employer said that it wasn't possible to continue increasing his salary. The head chef routinely appropriated the other chefs' recipes. Worst of all, the general manager stole hours from the kitchen staff. Each day workers had to clock in electronically. They got a daily receipt of their hours, but most of them didn't keep these. The manager logged onto the computer and simply keyed in a smaller number of hours for each worker. If the worker kept the daily slips and confronted the manager, an adjustment would be made. If not, the employer pocketed the money. One day our son logged in with seventy-two hours total for the two-week pay period and ended the day, after nine hours' labor, with seventy-four hours, cheated out of seven hours. He had his daily slip, but on another day he did not. Not surprisingly, theft was rampant there, the employees trying to get back what they were losing by stealing food, wine, linens, and dinnerware.

The son in the pizza shop was content for a few months, but as the shop failed to grow, due mainly to the owners' poor management, employee hours were cut. One manager was fired during her pregnancy. The young man who replaced her was under pressure to lower costs, so he cut hours and did some of the work himself. But when things got hectic, he demanded that the workers on short hours come in and work for as long as he thought necessary. When our son told him once that he couldn't come to work because of a prior commitment, his hours were cut so severely that he had to quit. Repeated calls to corporate headquarters yielded promises but no actions. The only consolation my son had was learning a year later that his former boss had been canned.

After a year, we knew that Portland was not a good place to earn a living. Unless you were willing to work more than one job (local writer Chuck Palahniuk says everyone in Portland has three jobs), double and triple up in tiny apartments, shop in thrift stores, eat generic food, and drink the cheapest beer, you couldn't make it there in the blue-collar job world. That year, our chef son earned 60 percent less than he had in Pittsburgh. We made arrangements for them to move to Virginia and stay with their sister until they got jobs. Sadly we helped the boys pack, shipped their things from the Greyhound station, and said goodbye.

WORK: ACT THREE, PICKETS AT POWELL'S

One of Portland's most famous landmarks is Powell's City of Books, whose main store is located in a building that takes up an entire block at Tenth Avenue and West Burnside Street, not far from the downtown. Portlanders like books nearly as much as they like movies (films often opened in New York City, Los Angeles, and Portland), and the store is always crowded. The rooms are color-coded: the Red Room, the Purple Room, and so on, in a maze-like pattern in which it is easy to lose yourself. There is a café in the store, filled with avid readers drinking coffee, which next to beer is the favorite drink of city residents. Powell's is a great place to while away a rainy afternoon.

Powell's was founded by Michael Powell, who opened his first bookstore as a graduate student in Chicago in 1970. The company's website tells us that Michael was encouraged by no less a literary luminary than Saul Bellow. Michael's father, Walter, spent a year in Chicago working at his son's store and then returned to Portland where he opened a used bookstore. He had a large inventory, and his business was a great success. It must have tickled the fancy of the city's thrifty inhabitants. Walter soon moved into a larger space, and his son joined him in 1979. Powell's has been expanding ever since. In addition to the original location, there is Powell's Technical Books, Powell's Books for Cooks and Gardeners, an outlet dedicated to travel, and several more, including a huge warehouse. What makes them all unique is that new and used hardcovers and paperbacks are stacked together on the shelves. This makes for a browsing paradise. The selections are better and more diverse than in any Barnes & Noble or Borders, and where normally you would have to buy a new book, at Powell's you might be able to purchase a discounted but clean used copy, available on the same shelf as the new one. If you can't find an item, Powell's will either get it from the warehouse or order it. Now it has a profitable online store too. On the first floor, there is a long counter where people can sell their used volumes. Given what I was learning about Portland's economy, it didn't surprise me to see that this counter was usually marked by long lines of sellers with stacks in their arms and in carts and boxes. The buyers were not particularly friendly, and they didn't pay very high prices, reflecting the economic necessity that pushed people to sell. (A few blocks west of Powell's there is a Fred Meyer grocery store—the name of the Kroger company stores in the Northwest. Underneath a parking lot ramp close to the main entrance, there is a machine in which old bottles can be deposited for money. The bottle returners get a receipt and they can then redeem it for cash in the store. This space was always jammed with poor people trying to put together a little money.)

Good bookstores have knowledgeable workers, and Powell's prided itself on its well-read and well-versed staff. The company promotes a cooperative, family-like environment. It is a paternalistic arrangement with Michael Powell as the father. Sometimes this is enough for workers; in some ways it is better than the impersonal employment relationships typical of so many workplaces. We might prefer to be sons and daughters than what the economists call "human capital." But paternalism can wear thin, especially if wages and benefits are not satisfactory and discipline is arbitrary. In the late 1990s Powell's workers began a union-organizing drive—I remember sending them money from Pittsburgh. Powell reacted like a rejected parent, and a protracted struggle ensued. In April 1999 the workers won a union representation election, and the union was recognized by Powell as the bargaining agent. However, the employer refused to sign a collective bargaining agreement, forcing the union to strike and picket. The union was the legendary International Longshore and Warehouse Union (ILWU) founded by the Australian immigrant Harry Bridges, who led the famous general strike that unionized San Francisco's docks in 1934. Finally, in August 2000, Powell's employees won their first contract, and Powell's became one of the few unionized bookstores in the country.

When unions were stronger in the United States, in the 1950s and 1960s for example, once a new contract was signed, the two parties entered into an implicit agreement that they would have an indefinite relationship. When a contract expired, negotiations for a new one might be intense and there could even be a strike. But the employer did not see each expired contract as an opportunity to break its opponent. Today, however, less than 13 percent of employed workers are union members. In the private sector of the economy the number is less than 10 percent, as low as it was at the onset of the Great Depression in 1929. So every new negotiation puts the union's life on the line. The employer smells blood and dreams of being union-free once again.

While we lived in Portland, a fierce battle was underway between Powell and the ILWU local. Powell wanted give-backs on health insurance and more arbitrary management power. Despite high profits, the employer's wage offer was minimal. Months went by without a new agreement. Many workers wore buttons to work urging Powell to negotiate. They spoke openly to me about their grievances. They began to organize job actions to pressure the employer. Always militant—a Portland labor person told me that whenever a supervisor harassed a worker, a steward would get on a phone and say, "Harry Bridges to the Red Room" (or whatever room the hassle was in)—the union started a series of informational pickets. Workers and supporters walked with signs and passed out leaflets to potential customers. This is legal and can be done without a strike being called. Today strikes are risky because most employers are willing to hire scabs (replacements), and the law offers no guarantee that the strikers will get their jobs back. Informational picketers cannot legally block entrances to the workplace, nor can they intimidate potential customers.

I joined the picket lines on two occasions. We had at least one hundred people, and we marched around the block, which comprised the perimeter of the store. Quite a few of us congregated at the two entrances, where we handed out leaflets. Customers were urged not to enter the store and, in fact, we were probably a bit intimidating to some people. Most didn't go in, but some did. I have never crossed a picket line, and I don't understand why people do. A worker's livelihood should not be taken lightly. But for a shopper, a trip to a bookstore can't be a critical event. I was surprised that the police never came around. Powell's is a high-profile business in Portland, and I thought that the police would order the pickets to disburse or at least stay away from the entrances. Though I saw some patrol cars, the cops never showed. I learned later that the ILWU locals in Portland (it is a port city and the longshore workers are ILWU members) had a good relationship with the police, having supported them in previous labor disputes. I expected that the job actions, which eventually paved the way for a new agreement, would get prominent coverage in Portland's major newspaper, *The Oregonian*, but they weren't mentioned.

It makes a difference which union organizes a workplace. There used to be militant left-leaning unions in the United States, but they and their members were purged from the ranks of organized labor during the anti-communist witch hunts of the late 1940s and early 1950s. This was the single worst thing that ever happened to the country's labor movement. The unions kicked out of the Congress of Industrial Organizations (CIO) were among the best: they were the most democratic and least racist and they negotiated exceptional contracts. The ILWU was evicted from the CIO, but it managed to survive. It kept its progressive character. It knows how to represent workers, and it knows how to educate them. I don't think the Powell's local would have survived had another more docile union been their bargaining agent.

A LIBERAL CITY

Portland has a national reputation as a liberal city. There is a strong environmental movement, and the city is a hotbed of the organic food movement. Even those who think we should eat only raw food find a welcoming home there. Residents are proud of how green the city is, and the greenery isn't just due to the heavy rain. The environment is taken seriously; and it is the only place we have lived where it is possible to find hiking trails in thick woods within the city. Portland is inordinately clean too; you don't find litter covering the streets as you do in Pittsburgh or

Philadelphia. Portlanders are famously tolerant of homeless persons and panhandlers. They have a laid-back attitude toward work, refreshing after the workaholic frenzy of so many New Yorkers. (My sons, who have the masochistic worldview of many kitchen workers, complained incessantly about how lazy their co-workers were). When the record-breaking storm hit Portland in January 2004, Portland came to a standstill. But nobody did anything to dig it out. Sidewalks were left snow-and-ice covered. I was away at the time, but Karen told me that the manager of our apartment building made no effort to clear the ramp to the parking garage. When she asked her what she was supposed to do if she wanted to use the car, the manager said calmly, "Well, if you have an emergency, call 911." When some zealous Eastern transplants were seen shoveling their driveways, passersby aggressively mocked them. No one seemed to mind missing work, even though they didn't get paid.

There is a significant gay presence in Portland—the city made headlines around the country when gay partners were permitted to get marriage licenses. Hundreds of couples lined up at City Hall to get married, and while the right-wing talk show hosts ran amok and there were letters sent to the editor, most people didn't seem particularly upset about this. Men and women weren't as openly gay in Portland as they were in San Francisco or Manhattan, but it seemed that they felt comfortable living there.

But Portland's progressiveness was superficial. Liberal politics were channeled through the Democratic Party; there was no organized alternative politics. As is true everywhere, business interests operated in the background and were the powers behind the throne. And when it came to two critical issues, labor and race, Portland was the very opposite of liberal, it was backward and oppressive. Everywhere, wages and working conditions were abominable. There were many anarchists in Portland and this was good for anti-globalization and anti-war protests, both common occurrences. A countercultural milieu made for an alternative music scene and a healthy nonmaterialistic outlook on life. However, this didn't translate into a working-class perspective. A well-known and respected anarchist, notorious among the city's business elite for his bold environmental initiatives, opened an organic food restaurant with some fanfare and talk about collectivity. It wasn't long before he began to act like a typical employer, interested in cutting costs and controlling the workers. When the staff affiliated with the Industrial Workers of the World, still in existence many years after it led the famous strikes at Lawrence, Massachusetts and Patterson, New Jersey, the owner denounced his former comrades as selfish and not interested in building an alternative community. I thought that if an environmentalist/anarchist wouldn't champion workers, who would?

The Oregonian, a liberal paper by U.S. standards, almost never covered unions and labor struggles. There were heart-wrenching personal stories about workers, usually from high-tech, who had lost their jobs and were struggling mightily to survive. But the city's lower-than-average wages were ignored, and it was never suggested that laborers should organize to address their difficulties. When the city's gangs of homeless street kids—there were more homeless children in Portland than any city we have visited—committed a particularly egregious crime, the papers gave it prominent coverage. But no one wondered why the city had so few job opportunities for youth. After my son's boss stole hours from him, I read an article about how widespread this practice was—in the *New York Times*. To make matters worse, the city's labor unions seemed to make little effort to organize workers or to actively publicize their plight. There is a mismatch between the city's image and working-class reality.

Portland's liberal image was also belied by the open inequality of wealth. If you walked the few blocks from our apartment to the downtown, you would be assailed by panhandlers. Even on trendy Twenty-third Avenue, hustlers stood on corners or roamed around the tables at outdoor cafés asking for money. We saw an elderly Asian woman doing this, something we never witnessed in all our travels in the United States. Nowhere else in the country are there so many thrift shops, and all were busy everyday. We also saw open hard drug sales and use, always in poor parts of town. Yet near our apartment tower were enormous houses, all with well-kept grounds maintained by Hispanic gardeners and caretakers. New apartments and houses were being constructed everywhere, with price tags worthy of more renowned

cities. Nonunion labor was the norm, again Hispanic. For a city with so
many poor people, there were an inordinate number of elite retail stores:
Tiffany's, Kiehl's, Nordstrom's, Lucky Jeans, Diesel, and pricey local
shops like Moonstruck Chocolates.

INEQUALITY: ACT THREE, DINNER AT HURLEY'S

For Christmas, our twins gave us a gift certificate of $120 to a restaurant
that had recently opened to great excitement. The boys were irreverently
critical of Portland's eateries. Caprial's Bistro and Wine Bar is in the
southeast section of town. Caprial has her own television show and is
the author of popular cookbooks. I drove one of the twins there to apply
for a job. He took one look at the menu and dismissed the fare as "diner
food." My son's views were confirmed when I ate with a visitor from
Germany at a Vietnamese bistro, well regarded and reviewed. I charitably
described the food as slop. In any event, the boys were excited, sure they
had found a winner. The new place, Hurley's, was owned by the chef,
a former New York City firefighter. It had received rave reviews for its
uniquely composed dishes.

We didn't get to use our present until the day before we were to leave
Portland, in late April 2004. Tired from emptying our apartment, selling
more furniture, and planning a long road trip, we were excited about a
night out. We seldom eat in restaurants. The food isn't usually healthy,
and the prices are high. We know too much about how their kitchens
function. We prefer to cook for ourselves. But this one looked good; the
menu in the window promised the kind of food even our chef son might
approve. We missed the boys, and this would remind us of them.

We have never had an eating experience like the one we had that
evening. We were led by the host to a small table with sharply angular
and uncomfortable chairs. Karen had injured her left foot in a bizarre
accident and by night's end, the seat had made her entire leg numb.
An overly attentive waiter soon appeared and began to advise us about
the menu. I had already looked at it, and my heart was set on the
lobster paella. It was $30, but we were feeling extravagant with our gift

certificate. However, the waiter soon disabused me of my choice. This was a restaurant that served "small plates," a culinary euphemism for high-priced small portions. It was necessary, he said, to order at least three, and better yet four, courses. He showed us with his hand that the dish I wanted would never satisfy my appetite. Later as we watched with amusement—the only enjoyment we had that night—customers at other tables do double-takes when their tiny servings arrived, we marveled at the calm way the waiters led us down the garden path with a patter of gibberish about the dishes. When a woman insisted on having but a single course, her waiter gave her a look of disgust as if to say, "You'll see."

We took the waiter at his word and ordered three plates each. He thought we should have a soup too, but at $8 for six ounces, we decided to pass. We thought that surely we would get enough to eat and even be able to share each other's dishes. I ordered a Caesar salad, an elaborate sea scallop dish, and a chicken entrée. It is difficult to describe our shock and that of the other patrons when the food arrived. There was a television commercial a few years ago for Wendy's that featured the company's owner, Dave Thomas. A haughty waiter brings a dish to Dave's table and removes the silver cover. Dave looks at the plate and can barely see the entree because it is so tiny. The waiter says, "Enjoy." An amusing commercial matched exactly by our dinner at Hurley's.

The Caesar salad came on a small plate and consisted of lettuce chopped into a slaw-like mess in a Caesar dressing. I liked its taste, but I had to take elaborately slow bites to make it last more than a couple of minutes. I nostalgically remembered the large, traditional Caesar salad I used to eat at Putanesca's on Ninth Avenue in Manhattan—lots of real anchovies and beautiful romaine lettuce leaves. Good Italian bread. None of this was present at Hurley's, not even bread. I guess I was supposed to appreciate the composition of the dish on the plate and not notice the price or the skimpiness of the portion. Despite my best effort, it disappeared all too soon but just in time for the sea scallops. These were priced at $20. There were two of them, about three bites and thirty seconds worth of eating. When I told a friend of mine about our dining experience, he asked what would have happened if I had dropped one of the scallops on the floor. Ten dollars down the drain.

We finished the third "course," feeling like we hadn't eaten more than a snack, but entertained by the astonishment of the woman at the next table when she got her single course, the paella I had originally lusted for. Our calculating waiter brazenly told us that dessert for the two of us would take the bill to exactly $120, the amount of our certificate. We had thought about asking for cash back but decided to play out the game and have dessert. These were good but the most expensive we had ever eaten.

The total bill, including tip, came to $140; we didn't give our usual 20 percent gratuity, a feeble protest I admit, but at least it was something. We should have stormed into the kitchen and told the chef that he was perpetrating one of the most remarkable frauds we had witnessed, that our sons had to work for more than twelve hours in hot and dangerous kitchens to pay for our dinner, that none of Hurley's kitchen laborers could afford to eat in his restaurant. But had we done so, Chef Hurley could have put us in our place by asking if we had noticed that the restaurant was packed with patrons, each spending a small fortune for their food and drink, and on a Thursday evening.

Our dinner at Hurley's told us something important about Portland, and about the United States itself. An abiding inequality haunts this city and every city in the country. It strikes you like a hammer. In a city with one of the nation's highest unemployment rates, with homeless children on every street corner, with adult beggars at every highway entrance ramp, diners were packed cheek by jowl in a restaurant whose prices were surely among the highest in the nation.

The most distressing thing about Portland, and the fact that most belied its liberal image, was its racism. A writer once called Portland the "last bastion of Caucasian culture." It is certainly a white town; less than 7 percent of the population is African-American. Even the city's homeless are nearly all white, as are all the young people asking for money. Blacks who gravitated to Portland to work in the wartime shipyards were housed in a floodplain of the Columbia River and were soon enough driven out by high waters. The ghettoes where they were next allowed to live were destroyed by highway construction. Today the tiny black community is scattered over several mostly poor neighborhoods.

Despite the small number of black residents, whites were inordinately hostile to them. While we lived in Portland, there were several highly publicized and completely unjustified police shootings of black people; in the six months before we left, they shot and killed a black woman and a black man. The woman and her male companion were stopped. The man, a suspected drug dealer, was taken from the car and confronted by the cops. The woman moved from the back seat to the front and got behind the steering wheel. She started the engine and was probably about to flee. She was unarmed, and the police knew who she was and where she lived. One of them tried to prevent her from leaving. He claimed that, as he put his arm in the window, he felt his life threatened. So he simply pulled out his gun and shot the woman, leaving her children without a mother. A few months later, two cops, including one who was clearly a psychopath (though presented later as an upstanding Christian by the minister of his fundamentalist church), stopped a black man for failure to use his turn signal when pulling into a strip mall. The man was apparently high on cocaine, but was unarmed and offered no resistance. Within twenty-four seconds from the time he was motioned over by the officers, he was shot dead. Most white people acted as if these killings were justified. The radio talk show hosts ranted that when a person showed anything but complete obedience to police commands, he or she deserved to get killed. And if he or she had had any previous run-ins with the law, something hard for a black person to avoid in this country, then the shooting was not only justified but a positive benefit to society. Letters to the editors of local newspapers made the same arguments.

But it wasn't only police confrontations that got folks riled up about race. Portland has a professional basketball team. Their best player was Rasheed Wallace, an outspoken black man who led the league in technical fouls, seldom spoke with reporters, never dressed up, and made pointed remarks about racism in the National Basketball

Association. When he declared in a rare interview that the league loved to recruit unsophisticated black players just out of high school because they were easier to exploit, the media went wild. How could a rich athlete make such comments? Didn't Portland treat him and the other players like royalty? And now he spits on them. Editorialists, including former white Portland star Bill Walton, condemned him, and the sports show hosts suggested none too subtly that he be driven out of town on a rail. Interestingly, he was eventually traded to the Detroit team, and ever since has been a model citizen. It is hard to imagine two more different cities, in terms of racial mix and attitudes, than Portland and Detroit.

In our large apartment building there was one black person. Karen was talking to him and two white women on the rooftop deck of the complex. She asked him what his experiences had been being a black person in a town with such a small minority population. He answered the question matter-of-factly, but one of the women exploded. How could Karen ask this man such a question? When Karen pointed out that Portland seemed to be a city devoid of black people and was generally lacking in diversity, the irate woman said vehemently that this was not true. It was Karen who was the racist for saying this. "Why," the woman said, "if you want to see diversity, come clubbing with me some night at four a.m. There are all kinds of people out then." It was difficult to respond to such a ridiculous assertion, but the woman kept up her harangue. The other woman, who had worked in customer service for the phone company for twenty years and was now retired, expressed wonder that she had never noticed what Karen was talking about. She was genuinely surprised that almost everyone in our building was white.

There is a growing Hispanic community in both Portland and the rest of Oregon. But this community goes largely unnoticed, unless you are observant enough to see that nearly all the motel and hotel cleaners, yard-care workers, nannies, and lower-level kitchen staff in restaurants have brown faces. The odious local and now national talk show host, Lars Larson, like CNN commentator Lou Dobbs, is obsessed with these Hispanic immigrants. Larson sponsored a contest for listeners to submit a new state slogan. Among his favorites were: "Welcome to Mexico," and "Oregon: Habla Español?" Not surprisingly, anti-immigrant sentiment resonates in Portland. A history of racism—Oregon had anti-miscegenation laws until the Supreme Court overturned these in the late 1960s—and high unemployment made workers susceptible to immigrant-bashing. The absence of a strong and progressive labor movement denied working people the education needed to defeat this.

WANDERLUST

We were ready to leave Portland after a year, but we stayed an extra two months to accommodate our sons' apartment lease. My mother says we aren't happy no matter where we live. Friends wonder where we will eventually "settle down." The fact is, this is a big country. We didn't get to see it when we were young, so we were going to explore it now.

We had dreamed of abandoning any permanent residence and just living on the road. We decided to do it. Get rid of the new possessions we had accumulated, store a few things, pack the van with what was left, and drive away. We devised a rough itinerary centered around the national parks of the West. We'd see the sights and maybe find that perfect town where we'd live happily ever after.

SUGGESTED READINGS

Novelist Chuck Palahniuk is something of a cult hero in his hometown of Portland. He has written a quirky guide to the city: *Fugitives and Refugees: A Walk in Portland, Oregon* (New York, NY: Crown Journeys/ Random House, 2003). An insider's look at restaurant kitchen work, highly recommended by our son, is Anthony Bourdain, *Kitchen Confidential: Adventures in the Culinary Underbelly* (New York, NY: Harper Perennial, 2001). A standard but useful guide to the national parks of the West is *Fodor's National Parks of the West* (New York: Fodor's Travel Publications, 2004). On the "Biscuit Fire," see Richard York, "Corporate Forestry and Academic Freedom," available at *http:// mrzine.monthlyreview.org/york240106.html*. On public subsidies to the timber industry, see Taxpayers for Common Sense, *Lost in the Forest: How the Forest Service's Misdirection, Mismanagement, and Mischief*

Squanders Your Tax Dollars, available at *http://www.forestcouncil.org/
pdf/lostintheforest.pdf*.

CHAPTER FIVE

CHEAP MOTELS AND A HOT PLATE I

FLAGSTAFF, ARIZONA

Population in 2003 55,893
Population in 2000
    White 77.9%
    Black 1.8%
    American Indian 10.0%
    Hispanic (all races) 16.1%

Median household income in 2000 .... $37,146
People below poverty level of income 17.4%
Median rent in 2000 .... $607
Median mortgage, including associated costs $1,168

The planet Pluto was discovered at the Lowell Observatory. Look through its large telescopes at 1400 West Mars Hill Road, 86001, (928) 774-3358. Don't miss the Museum of Northern Arizona, 3101 N. Ft. Valley Road, 86001, (928) 774-5213. An excellent place to buy fresh organic food, including cheap baked goods, is New Frontiers Market, 1000 S. Milton Road, 86001, (928) 774-5747.

SEDONA, ARIZONA

Population in 2003 10,905
Population in 2000
    White 92.2%
    Black 0.5%
    American Indian 0.5%
    Hispanic (all races) 8.9%

Median household income in 2000 .... $44,042
People below poverty level of income 12.4%
Median rent in 2000 .... $810
Median mortgage, including associated costs $1,427

There is no town in the United States located in a more beautiful setting. Skip the shopping and take a hike.

ALBUQUERQUE, NEW MEXICO

Population in 2003 471,856
Population in 2000
    White 71.6%
    Black 3.1%
    American Indian 3.9%
    Hispanic (all races) 39.9%

Median household income in 2000 .... $38,272
People below poverty level of income 13.5%
Median rent in 2000 .... $501
Median mortgage, including associated costs $1,034

The University of New Mexico is one of the most beautiful colleges in the country. It's in the center of the city, on Route 66 (Central Avenue), the town's main street. It is a great place to catch some shade in the summer. Learn about the Pueblo Indians at the Indian Pueblo Cultural Center at 2401 12th Street N.W., 87104, (505) 843-7270. The museum contains a significant collection of Pueblo pottery.

MOAB, UTAH

Population in 2000 4,779
　White 90.4%
　Black 0.4%
　American Indian 5.5%
　Hispanic (all races) 6.4%

Median household income in 2000 .... $32,620
People below poverty level of income 15.7%
Median rent in 2000 .... $420
Median mortgage, including associated costs $753

Loved by Edward Abbey, Moab perfectly embodies the beauty of Utah's canyon country. Arches and Canyonlands National Parks are close by, as are the La Sal Mountains. Spacious, clean, and inexpensive rooms can be found at Big Horn Lodge, 550 S. Main St. 84532, (435) 259-6171.

DO THEY STILL MAKE HOT PLATES?

We left our apartment in Portland, Oregon, sold or gave away our furniture, stored our personal possessions in a five-by-ten-foot storage space, and began our next odyssey on April 30, 2004.

We discussed our trip for weeks before leaving. We wanted to make an open-ended, spontaneous journey; our only goal was to be in Miami Beach for the winter. But there were many questions we had to answer. What would it feel like not to have a home—no house, no apartment, no condo, just our Dodge Caravan and each other? We swore never again to sign a lease of more than six months or to buy and then sell or give away furniture, something we did in both Manhattan and Portland. We bought three couches in three years! From now on we would just stay on the road, and when we found a place we liked, we might rent a furnished apartment for a few months at most.

It is one thing to make a decision, but the devil is in the details. We couldn't see ourselves camping; we had no idea how to pitch a tent and we wanted a shower and a bed every night. We couldn't imagine buying, much less driving, an RV and towing our car. We had seen too many people, some of them aged, careening down mountain highways in bus-sized vehicles, some towing a car and a boat. So, we decided that we would stay in motels. We had been on cross-country excursions before, first for a month and then for five weeks, and we never minded motel rooms, although we have learned to be aggressive about rates and to look at a room before taking one.

What about food? Eating every meal in a restaurant was not an option. We estimated that it would cost at least $6,000 to do so for four months, and that is assuming that we each spent just $25 per day for meals. The food would be abysmal. For us, fast food is a gastronomic nightmare, and the cuisine served at the diners and eateries that dot the local landscape is hardly conducive to long hours behind the wheel, much less strenuous hikes. How could we eat in restaurants, with their propensity to overuse grease, salt, and flour and to serve the large portions so loved by our fellow citizens, and not gain weight or have chronic indigestion? Complicating matters was our desire to continue the healthier habits we had refined in Portland. We had stopped eating beef after the recent mad cow scare. The cow was from a farm in nearby Washington, and the company that processed the meat was in Portland. We decided to forgo all foods containing corn syrup, trans fats, and artificial colors or flavors. We began to use organic foods whenever possible and consumed smaller portions, for both better health and economy. But would we be able to continue our new food regimen on the road?

We talked about this nonstop—over coffee in the morning, on hikes in the hills surrounding Portland, and while we did daily chores. Sometimes we would get mad at each other when one of us made a particularly silly suggestion or said, "Don't worry. It'll all work out." We kept hoping to get a sudden flash of insight, and for a while, we stopped discussing it and made other preparations.

Three weeks before our departure date, we still hadn't solved our food problem. We had rejected a diet of snacks and cold food bought along the way—adequate for short excursions but not for an extended trip. We were about to give up when I said to Karen, "I wonder if they

still make hot plates? Maybe we could cook our meals on one of those."
At first, this sounded ridiculous. We both imagined some down-and-out
drifter in a transient hotel heating a can of Campbell's soup. But then
we asked ourselves how a plate with two burners is any different than an
electric stove. We stopped at the local hardware store and found a hot
plate, a two-burner model with adjustable heat, made by Toastmaster
and priced at $40. (Later we noticed that these were sold in many places,
including drugstores. Now, however, manufacturers call them "electric
buffet ranges" and "table stoves.") Before we bought it, we began to
figure out what kind of meals we could cook on it and what types of food
might be available, since we would be in small towns as well as cities. We
soon had an extensive list of possible menu items. We could cook soup,
pasta, rice, oatmeal, noodles, fresh, frozen, or canned vegetables, and
the like. We could make spaghetti sauce and prepare eggs, fish, chicken,
and pork. We bought the hot plate. We would prepare our own meals, in
motel rooms.

What kitchen equipment, staple foodstuffs, and food-related
supplies would we take? We kept going through our cupboards,
tentatively agreeing to take this or that, then changing our minds, until
finally we decided on only those things that were absolutely essential. We
were mindful of the fact that our van had just so much space. We agreed
on this: two coffee makers, one that made two cups and a larger one with
a built-in grinder (a gift from our sons), two small All-Clad Limited pots
and lids (good pots would be best for hot plate burners, which might not
be easy to regulate), a frying pan, two china plates, two bowls, two cups,
two forks, two knives, a strainer, a few utensils, our miniature Peugeot
pepper mill (a gift from our daughter), a sixteen-quart cooler (since we
would probably be without a refrigerator in most motel rooms), and, of
course, the hot plate.

Portland is a haven for health-conscious food shoppers, with several
organic food aisles even in chain supermarkets. Our favorite store is
Trader Joe's, where you can get everything from organic soups to nuts.
At Joe's, Whole Foods, the Food Front, Fred Meyer, and several other
stores, we hoarded staples for the trip: organic chips, nuts, trail mix; and
cookies, noodles, olive oil, balsamic vinegar, a few spices, peppercorns,

kosher salt, sugar, garlic, peanut butter, granola, oatmeal, raisins, mustard, canned salmon; cans of organic beans, vegetables, and chili; boxes of organic soups; a ten-pound bag of basmati rice; and as much water, beer (Portland markets also have the best beer selections in the country), and Starbucks coffee beans as we could reasonably pack. At Portland's farmers' market we had met a fisherman from Newport, a town along the Oregon coast. We bought fresh salmon from him every week for six months. He also canned his own top-grade tuna fish. We purchased a case of twenty-four cans. Using coupons at local markets and drug stores, we stocked paper towels, foil, plastic wrap, dishwashing liquid, and coffee filters. We would get other supplies, including fresh bread, butter, eggs, yogurt, fruit, fish, meat, and vegetables, and replenish our inventory while on the road.

Our preparations were in high gear. The next question was how to pack our van efficiently. It needed to be a combination of larder, closet, and office. We divided the space into three parts: one for food and food-related equipment and supplies; one for clothes; and one for laptop computers, books, office supplies, and personal papers.

We bought four plastic rectangular laundry baskets at a local department store. One of these we reserved for snacks such as pretzels, chips, cookies, and nuts. In the second we stored staple foods such as soups, chili, oatmeal, and spices. The third basket held kitchen utensils, pots, and pans, and in the fourth we put cleaning supplies, paper towels, plastic storage bags, tissues, and such.

The blue and yellow plastic shopping totes used by customers at IKEA home furnishing stores provided a second storage device. These durable and flexible bags measure approximately twenty-one-by-fourteen inches on the bottom and are fourteen inches deep. They are convenient for packing just about anything. We have used them as suitcases and have had several for at least ten years. We allowed ourselves one IKEA bag each for stored clothes, and two others were used to transport clothes and cooking materials from the van into motel rooms. We kept office supplies, computers, books, and maps in canvas briefcases and heavy-duty paper bags. Our storage and retrieval system worked amazingly well, and our van's interior always looked neat and trim.

For the first three days of our trip, we subsisted on fruit, soups, sandwiches, and pizza. Our "home cooking on the road" began in earnest on the fourth day, in Twentynine Palms, California, our base for exploring Joshua Tree National Park. Just before we got to town, we stopped at a grocery store along Route 62 to buy bread, lettuce, butter, eggs, and vegetables. The perishables we kept on ice in our cooler. We checked into an enormous Motel 6, using a coupon clipped from one of the motel discount books. We got a room on the top floor, figuring that our cooking would be least intrusive there and hauled our equipment, food, and clothes up the elevator in our trusty IKEA bags.

The room, like most of those in which we stayed, did not have a refrigerator. So we relied on our cooler to keep food from spoiling. We became experts on the idiosyncrasies of motel ice machines, quick to complain if they didn't work and adept at filling our cooler without taking more than our fair share—it held three ice buckets. The ice lasted all day; we drained the melted ice in the bathtub each evening and refilled the cooler in the morning. During our entire trip, we never lacked ice and nothing spoiled.

After settling in, we made an auto tour of the park to get our bearings, admiring the unusual land formations, "jumbo rocks," and the Joshua Trees. The last are neither trees nor cacti but a species of yucca plant. We returned to our room, exhausted from the triple-digit heat and the thousand miles we had already traveled, and prepared our first dinner.

Cooking on an "electric buffet range" was simpler than we thought; it was just like using an electric stove. A hot plate plugs into any standard outlet, and usually we just placed it on a dresser or desk. But sometimes motel outlets are in awkward locations, and we used any available surface, including the floor. Fortunately, the body of the hotplate stayed cool, so we never had to worry about scorching a rug or countertop. The one tricky part was temperature control. Once a burner is turned on, it tends to get hot quickly. We dealt with this problem by turning a burner on and then off as we cooked; this proved to be an effective way to adjust the heat. Cooking rice is an example of this technique. We couldn't bring rice and water to a boil, put a lid on the pot, and then simmer, because the mixture would boil over. Instead we added more water to the rice (two cups of water for one cup of rice instead of one and one-half cups as is recommended for the basmati rice we used), brought the rice to a boil, left the pan uncovered, and turned the heat off and on until the rice had just about absorbed the water. Then we placed a lid on the pan and let the rice stand for about ten minutes. A bit more labor intensive, but it came out perfect every time. A similar technique worked for our morning oatmeal. To cook chicken or a thicker cut of meat or fish, we first cooked it in water (as you might cook sausage). Then when the liquid evaporated, we added olive oil to the pan and browned the meat or fish. Of course, some things just had to be heated, like canned soup and chili.

We dubbed our dinner "Twentynine Palms Salad." It is a variation of "Salad Niçoise." For our first meal we used the traditional tuna fish. However, we made several versions of it during our trip, using chicken, sliced pork, salmon, and salmon patties, and whatever vegetables were available. If local cucumbers were in season, we added them. If we found canned organic beets, in they went. We made a vegetarian salad by substituting garbanzo or black beans for the meat or fish. All proved delicious. After we ate, we washed the few dishes and pans in the bathroom sink, using a hand towel to dry them.

When hearing about our hot plate use, friends and family asked about cooking odors. Before our first meal, we decided that we would scratch the whole arrangement if the smells proved overpowering. Remarkably, they were no different than those in our Portland kitchen, dissipating quickly when we switched on the air conditioning and opened a window. Also, we always disposed of food scraps outside. The only food that we did smell was that emanating from other rooms: microwave popcorn, delivered pizza, Chinese takeout, and fast food leftovers. Or from those with kitchenettes.

We perfected our cooking arrangements over the next few weeks, especially during a twenty-one-day stay at a Ramada Limited in Flagstaff, Arizona. Flagstaff is a great place for an extended stay. The town boasts the fine Museum of Northern Arizona and the Lowell Observatory. It is close to the south rim of the Grand Canyon, ancient Indian ruins, and amazing hiking around Sedona. We found an excellent food store—New Frontiers—and adequate chain groceries. Actually, many towns in the West have organic food stores, such as Wild Oats, Whole Foods, and New Frontiers, and even small towns like Moab, Utah; Glenwood Springs, Colorado; Taos, New Mexico; and Bozeman and Missoula, Montana, have local independent stores. The chain stores—Albertson's, Smith's, City Market, and Safeway—usually have a few organic items. In some towns, especially those with high concentrations of immigrants, we shopped at ethnic markets; at a Hispanic market in Taos, New Mexico, we got avocados for a dime apiece, as well as decent quality fruit. We noticed that in the ethnic stores, many types of cookies and other snacks contained no undesirable ingredients, in marked contrast to the foods in the snack aisles of the supermarkets.

In Flagstaff, we developed a routine that we followed throughout our journey. In a new town, we found a motel as close to the town's business district as possible, settled in, and then spent some time driving or walking around, locating points of interest. We like to know as much about the area as possible: demographics, architecture, history, economics, employment, and land formations. Often on this initial excursion, we bought whatever food we needed. One of us would start shopping, while the other would apply for the discount card most stores require for sale items (we have quite a collection of these). We made the look around town and the shopping integral parts of our travel, to understand quickly as much as we could about each place we visited. We returned to our motel, storing perishables in either our cooler or, when we were lucky, the room refrigerator. If it was still early we took a hike or did some sightseeing. If it was late, we made dinner, checked email, and watched television, being sure to take in the local news and weather report. We always read the local newspapers, including the free weeklies found in most towns. We usually fell asleep plotting our next day's activities.

In the morning, while the coffee was brewing, we showered and then prepared breakfast. Most often we ate fruit and oatmeal. Organic rolled oats are both nutritious and cheap (fifty cents for two servings), and they take just ten minutes or so to prepare—bring water to boil, cook oats for four minutes, remove from heat, cover and let sit for four minutes. They can be eaten with fruit, milk, and sugar or any combination of these. We used a mixture of sugar and cinnamon, tastier than plain sugar and good for digestion.

After breakfast and cleanup, we prepared the lunch for our daily hike. We bought a baguette or some other type of bread, including bagels and whole wheat pita, and made sandwiches. We used hard-boiled eggs, cheese, leftovers from the previous evening's supper (chicken, pork, salmon), pork salami, or peanut butter. The first four we combined with salad greens, onions, tomatoes, cucumbers, cilantro, hot peppers, whatever was available. Our only condiment was mustard, which we got in small squeeze bottles convenient for our cooler. For variety, we used large lettuce leaves as sandwich wraps, something we learned about in the Vietnamese restaurant in Manhattan's Chinatown. Some combination of fruit, raw carrots, pretzels, chips, cookies, and chocolate bars completed the meal. We put our prepared lunch into our ice-filled cooler, drove to the hike trailhead, and stowed our food and water in our backpacks.

SOUTH ON INTERSTATE 5

Interstate 5 can be driven from Vancouver, Canada, to San Diego, California, more than one thousand miles. This is the road we took out of Portland, on our way to the deserts of southern California. About an hour or so south of the city, the Willamette Valley widens into farm country. Oregon is a major agricultural state, with large production of wheat (during the U.S. invasion of Iraq, the local newspapers featured stories about the export of wheat to Iraq; apparently Oregon's hard wheat is perfect for the making of pita bread, a staple of the Iraqi diet), grass seed, berries, currants, apples, grapes, peaches, nectarines, plums, cherries, mushrooms (including most of the culinary favorites such as morels), artichokes, most other common vegetables, cut flowers of all types, potatoes, and every type of seafood, including oysters and, of course, salmon.

Much of Oregon's farming is big business, as it is in California, the nation's most important agricultural producer, with all of the accoutrements of such farming: subsidized water and land, heavy use of pesticides, complex mechanization, use of animal feed with various kinds of contamination in it, and almost universal hiring of immigrant labor from Mexico and Latin America. But there is also smaller scale, organic farming. The produce and meat of such farms is relatively expensive, but they would not have to be if such production were the focus of our public policy.

The landscape changed dramatically as we continued south. Closer to the California border, the elevation increased, and the terrain became more rugged approaching Grant and Siskiyou Passes. We spent a night in Ashland, one of Oregon's prettiest towns, just fifteen miles from the border and home to Southern Oregon University and a year-round Shakespeare festival. Unfortunately, my computer stopped working in the motel's office, and I tried to get it fixed locally. I ended up with a machine more badly broken than when I brought it to the repair shop. I bought a cheap replacement in the hot and dry town of Medford, but it became immediately infected with the Sasser worm, as did my backup. It took me a week to fix them, as I frantically wrote down instructions from Microsoft's website before the worm kicked me off the Internet. Later, I mailed the broken computer to the store in Pittsburgh where I bought it. The Post Office damaged it, and I battled the postal bureaucrats for nearly a year before collecting the $1,000 insurance.

We drove through mountains in northern California and took a room in the poor town of Redding. It was here we first saw people living in cheap motels. Probably folks had to move for economic reasons, but when they got to a town to look for work, they couldn't afford any other place to stay. In her exceptional book, *Nickel and Dimed*, Barbara Ehrenreich tells us that she had to live in motels to make ends meet on her meager paycheck. And many of her co-workers lived in motels more or less full-time. The monthly rent wasn't cheap, but it was lower than anything else available, and no first and last month rent and security deposits were necessary as with apartments.

Many small motels, including the one in Redding, are owned or managed by families from India. Invariably their name is "Patel." A week later we learned from the managers of a place we stayed in Williams, Arizona (also named Patel), that Patel is a common name in western India. Family members come here and use the money of relatives to buy or lease buildings, and then they send for other members. Numerous gas stations and convenience stores in remote places are also run by immigrants from India. Sometimes, once they are established, they open an Indian restaurant. I have spoken to several Patel managers. They hope to earn enough money to move to a larger city and make a better life for their children. When we first noticed this phenomenon several years ago, we found these motels to be especially clean and cheap. Such is no longer the case, as the new arrivals have quickly learned more "American" ways of doing business. The manager in Williams told me that some townsfolk are hostile to the Indians. Large signs tell the traveler that a particular motor inn is "American owned." The Patel enterprises have been quick to assimilate and often fly U.S. flags and post pro-U.S. slogans ("We support our troops") on their properties.

South of Redding we came upon California's great central valleys, which would be deserts except for water diverted from distant rivers. The West is full of dammed waterways, and their accompanying reservoirs and irrigation channels are often monumental in size. The history of capitalism in the West is in large part the history of the commodification of water. Many of Los Angeles's early fortunes, for example, were made through various shady deals and outright thefts involving this precious resource. Today California's central valleys are the breadbaskets of the nation. In the Sacramento and San Joaquin valleys we were amazed that there was desert to the west of Interstate 5 and green irrigated fields to the east. Among many other crops, we identified huge fields and groves of olives, almonds, plums, cotton, pistachios, cashews, apricots, and wine grapes. Name the crop or food product, and chances are California produces it. Eggs, beef, wheat, mushrooms, oranges, lemons, beans, peas, carrots, lettuce (the biggest cash crop), tomatoes, avocados, and brussel sprouts, all are big business in California. When we saw surface water on hundreds of acres of land, Karen said, "I think that's rice."

Neither of us had ever seen rice paddies before. She didn't know this was grown in the United States. We stopped at a roadside marker and learned that the crop was seeded by planes using laser technology so that the planted rows are super-straight.

We said as we drove on a dusty backroad that every person in the United States should travel to the California valleys and see how our food is produced. The late and great editor of *The Nation* magazine, Carey McWilliams, called the farms of California "factories in the fields." This is an apt description. A trip through the central valleys quickly dispels nostalgic notions of family farms. Instead of trim green plots, we saw fields of thousands of acres, so large that named roads go through them. These fields are alive with poorly paid and badly treated Mexican labor during the planting and harvesting seasons, but otherwise not many workers are needed. Every manner of invention is employed to raise productivity. Shaking devices remove nuts from trees. Special seeds are developed to ensure that citrus trees and grapevines grow to the same height for mechanical harvesting. New strains of tomatoes are developed and land patterns changed (larger, flatter land areas) so that tomatoes used for items such as tomato sauce can be machine picked, with the fruit—hard so as to be resistant to bruising by the equipment—moved directly to attached refrigeration cars. Much of the research for agribusiness is carried out in public universities, most notably the University of California at Davis. This research benefits mainly the big corporate farmers that help fund it. In California, the growers are kings, and a politician confronts them (and anything to do with a more rational use of water) at great risk. Over the past century there have been many attempts to organize the farm laborers. Workers have been murdered in these struggles by the growers and their hired guns and goons. Yet it is rare for anyone to be prosecuted for the death of a *campesino*.

California's agriculture, like Iowa's cornfields, exacts a heavy toll. A haze of pesticide poison hangs over the fields of the central valley. You can see it as you drive down the mountain on Route 58 west toward Bakersfield (Country-and-Western capital of California and home of Merle Haggard but also the carrot capital of the world). Near Bakersfield is the King Ranch, a major cattle company. Ranchers graze cattle on public lands. This government largesse has exacerbated the destruction of the region's natural habitat for which cattle are notorious. From a purely economic standpoint, beef production in the West is extraordinarily inefficient, made profitable for the cow capitalists only by public subsidy.

Both ranchers and farmers are publicly funded, not just by university research, but more directly through cheap water. It is grossly overused from a social point of view. Everywhere in the West water tables are falling, rivers are being ruined by dams, and there is increasing evaporation from reservoirs (Lake Powell, the result of the flooding of the wondrous Glen Canyon, is rapidly filling with silt and is at record low level). Cities such as Los Angeles, Phoenix, Tucson, and Las Vegas—dependent on diversions from the Colorado and other rivers—are becoming urban sprawls polluting the landscape even further. Water woes will soon be one of our most serious political problems.

THE ENVIRONMENT AND WORK: ACT FOUR, WHAT AGRICULTURE HAS WROUGHT

For most of our time on earth, humans have lived as hunters and gatherers. In the main, we have been healthy, and kept ourselves in relative harmony with the world around us, seldom putting too much pressure on the land's productivity, either by overpopulating an area or destroying the environment. We divided our output in an egalitarian manner; there were neither rich nor poor. We were remarkably observant, and this acuity led to major technological and social achievements, as well as a connection to the natural world unknown today. All was not peace and light, of course, but compared to the disasters that befell us afterward, the world of the hunters and gatherers seems almost paradisiacal.

The invention of agriculture about ten thousand years ago brought with it an end to the universal egalitarianism of the original humans. This was because farming went hand-in-hand with the rise of class society. From here on, each system of production would be marked by a grotesque inequality in which a small minority in each society used force and violence to extract a surplus from the majority of workers, whether they be slaves, serfs, or wage laborers. Agriculture was a great success in terms of the growth of human populations, and all future class societies allowed a few to live in splendor. But for the many, life became harsher than gatherers and hunters could have imagined. Life expectancies fell, physical stature diminished, and diseases became rampant. Richard Manning, in his book *Against the Grain: How Agriculture Has Hijacked Civilization*, tells us:

> Summarizing evidence from around the world, researcher Mark Cohen ticks off a list of diseases and conditions evident in skeletal remains of early farmers but absent among hunter-gatherers. The list includes malnutrition, osteomyelitis and periostitis (bone infections), intestinal parasites, yaws, syphilis, leprosy, tuberculosis, anemia (from poor diet as well as from hookworms), rickets in children, osteomalaria in adults, retarded childhood growth, and short stature among adults.

Agriculture and the attendant class society were also ruinous of the environment. As populations grew, less viable lands were brought into cultivation, gradually eroding the soil and facilitating periodic catastrophes whenever the rains failed to come.

With capitalism, agricultural problems took on new and more ominous dimensions. Capitalism converts the land and the food supply into commodities, things to be bought and sold in the ceaseless pursuit of profits. Peasants were (and are still being) forced from their lands so that large-scale, highly mechanized farms could produce crops and meat for export: sugar, tobacco, cotton, coffee, beef, pork, and chicken. To counter the lack of large expanses of new lands for cultivation, farming became increasingly intensive, with more machines and chemical agents used to raise yields per acre. The consequences were growing pollution of our soils, water, air, and bodies, outputs not factored into the calculation of farm productivity. Enormous quantities of food were produced, and yet hundreds of millions of people still went hungry and farmers were strapped economically as high outputs drove prices ever downward.

Corn provides a good example of the pitfalls of modern capitalist farming. A drive through Iowa takes you past picturesque villages with neat white churches and red dirt roads leading into the countryside. But there are no longer the mixed crop farms of yore. Instead, for miles in every direction, there are unbroken fields of corn. Iowa farmers produce more than their fair share of the nation's 80,000,000 acres and 125,000 square miles of corn. Production began to rise dramatically with the invention of hybrid seeds. Farmers who planted such seeds gained an economic advantage over other farmers and used this to buy the fields of those farmers who failed. Farm size also grew to take advantage of economies of scale. Large farms needed machinery, and corn farms became highly mechanized; the high costs of machines further spurred the concentration of holdings. Hybrid seeds have to be bought anew each year, so a seed-producing industry developed. Large-scale farming and hybrid corn also brought with them massive doses of chemical fertilizer and pesticides. Again quoting Manning, " . . . corn farming accounts for 57 percent of all herbicides and 45 percent (by pound of active ingredients) of all insecticides applied on all U.S. crops."

Corn production in the United States is enormous, but little of the corn grown is for direct human consumption. Some is exported, ruining the corn farmers of countries like Mexico, who have higher costs. Much of it is fed to meat-producing animals, themselves produced in assembly-line fashion in huge mechanized hog and cattle "factories." A good deal of it is processed into corn syrup, which has become ubiquitous in our food. Check the ingredients of what you buy at the grocery store. Corn syrup is in everything:

> Since the 1980s's most soft drink manufacturers have switched from sugar to corn sweeteners, as have most snack makers. Nearly 10 percent of the calories Americans consume now come from corn sweeteners; the figure is 20 percent for many children. Add to that all the corn-based animal protein (corn-fed beef, chicken, and pork) and the corn qua corn

(chips, muffins, and sweet corn) and you have a plant that has
become one of nature's greatest success stories, by turning us
(along with several other equally unwitting species) into an
expanding race of corn eaters.

The environmental consequences of all this grain production are
considerable and negative. Two examples will suffice. First, the nitrogen
used in fertilizer eventually finds its way into our rivers. It depletes
the oxygen in water and kills plants and animals. Nitrogen from the
corn belt flows down the Mississippi River and creates a "dead zone"
of 12,000 square miles in the Gulf of Mexico. The high-protein fish
and shellfish of the Gulf have died so that a "low-quality, high-input,
subsidized source of protein can blanket the Upper Midwest." Second,
the corn-infused food we eat is not so good for us. It may be partly
responsible for the great increase in obesity since the 1980s, when food
manufacturers switched to corn sweeteners. And a recent study at the
University of Minnesota found that a diet high in fructose (as compared
to glucose) elevates triglyceride levels in men shortly after eating, a
phenomenon that has been linked to an increased risk of obesity and
heart disease. Little is known about the health effects of eating animals
that have themselves eaten so much corn, but in the case of cattle,
researchers have found that corn-fed beef is higher in saturated fats than
grass-fed beef.

The great irony of corn production is that its explosion has pushed
prices sharply downward, so much so that the cost per bushel of corn
produced is much higher than the price. The government makes up
the difference with a generous subsidy. The more corn produced, the
more acreage devoted to it, the greater the gift. More marginal lands
are brought into cultivation and more fields are devoted to one crop,
compounding the environmental damage.

Then there is the cost of agribusiness to the workers. The life
expectancy of a farm worker in California is still forty-nine years, the
same as it was in 1960 when Edward R. Murrow narrated the famous
documentary, *Harvest of Shame*. Most farm workers in California come
from Mexico; for 81 percent of them, Spanish is the native language.

More than half are men who come to the United States alone, though nearly a third have families who remain in Mexico. They are relatively young and uneducated; the average amount of schooling is seven years. A large number are here without immigration documents. Wherever we have traveled in the West, there has been a growing hysteria about "illegals," with right-wingers, egged on by demagogic and racist talk show hosts, calling for increasingly stringent measures against them. In all the states adjoining Mexico, vigilante groups have formed to patrol the border. States are enacting legislation denying health care and other benefits to the undocumented. Draconian laws are now before the U.S. Congress, one proposing to make the absence of appropriate papers or giving aid to a person without them a felony. In March and April of 2006, undocumented immigrants and supporters took to the streets by the millions to protest and demand that they be treated like human beings.

It is remarkable that immigrant workers are subject to such hostility. They are usually the poorest of the poor. Nationwide, 30 percent of farm worker families live in poverty. Their mean individual yearly income is between $10,000 and $13,000; for families it is between $15,000 and $17,500. A mere 13 percent earn more than $20,000 per year. Fewer than half own a car or truck. The mean wage is $7.25, and 19 percent make less than $6 an hour. Almost none have benefits like health care, pensions, vacations, and the like. 22 percent live in trailers, dormitories, barracks, conjoined multi-family structures, or motels. 20 percent have no access to drinking water in the fields. All of this for the worst, most physically demanding labor—stooping over short-handled hoes, often with their kids working too, all breathing poisonous pesticides. And yet, contrary to what we hear from the likes of CNN's Lou Dobbs, these poor people seldom get social security (just 2 percent), disability insurance (1 percent), Medicaid (15 percent), WIC (11 percent), food stamps (8 percent), or public housing (1 percent). But they do pay taxes, including social security. And they generate profits for their employers.

Suppose that the government subsidized organic farms, which are growing in popularity around the country. Suppose we promoted smaller farms, manure fertilizers, natural pest controls, organic urban farms on vacant lots and rooftops (as have been promoted successfully in Havana—an effort to break down the divorce of countryside and city that generated factory farming in the first place). Suppose we made sure that those who labored on farms had rights and were paid decent wages and guaranteed safe conditions? Suppose we embraced the kind of massive propaganda campaign about healthy food, diet, exercise, and workers' rights that we successfully waged against cigarettes? Wouldn't everybody's health and well-being improve dramatically?

JOSHUA TREE, WILLIAMS, FLAGSTAFF, SEDONA

Our trip south through California ended at Joshua Tree National Park. On the way, we passed the famous resort town of Palm Springs. There are more than one hundred golf courses there, striking testimony to the irrationality of our economic system. In a land devoid of water, rich people ride golf carts, enjoying a leisure sport on green grass. Not many miles west and south, future farm workers live in miserable makeshift camps, getting ready to find employment in our water- and human-wasteful agricultural system.

Joshua Tree National Park is in southern California, east of Palm Springs and just south of the small desert town of Twentynine Palms. The park, which was nearly empty during our visit, perhaps due to the extreme heat (one hundred degrees in early May), sits on the boundary between the Colorado and Mojave deserts. The former is at a somewhat lower elevation than the latter, and this makes a great difference in terms of terrain, plant life, and temperature. The Colorado is a classic barren-looking desert, hot and dry and seemingly inhospitable to life. However, there is life if you look for it. Besides the creosote bushes, there are gardens of cholla cactus, lying in wait to stick to the unwary visitor's skin, and patches of ocotillo plants, rising languidly and unsteadily toward the sky and tipped with red flowers in the spring. Other cactus plants, such as the beaver tail, also produce brilliant spring flowers. Some of these seem to have a sexual essence, alive and anomalous in such an arid country.

At the southern end of the park, the Colorado desert boasts an oasis with cottonwoods, palms, and many other trees and plants that are home to a large number of bird species. We took a hike here, scrambling up the rocks to Mastodon Peak and a view of the Salton Sea, California's largest body of water. Along the way, we looked for abandoned gold mines and saw holes bored in large rocks by ancient people who used them as mortars for grinding seeds and nuts. In the Mojave Desert, which traverses the eastern part of the park and is higher and slightly cooler, there are thousands of Joshua trees. They were named by

Joshua trees in Joshua Tree National Park, California.

Mormon pioneers who thought they looked like the prophet Joshua raising his arms up to heaven. (The modern history of the West cannot be understood without grasping the crucial role played by the Church of Jesus Christ of Latter-day Saints. Mormonism is perhaps the world's fastest growing religion, with more than 11 million members worldwide. Some scholars believe that it is on the cusp of becoming the first major world religion since Islam. If it does, it will be the first such religion to originate in the Americas. I will have more to say about the Mormons later.)

In the Mojave Desert region of the park, we drove to Keys View, the highest point in Joshua Tree accessible by car. From there the lights of Palm Springs were visible, as was the San Andreas Fault. On a clear day it is possible to see mountains in Mexico. One evening we sped there under a blood-red setting sun that illuminated the sky with an ethereal glow and gave the "jumbo rocks" and monoliths for which the park is famous an eerie look. Not long after the sun set over the San Bernardino Mountains, an enormous yellow full moon showed its face in the opposite direction, so bright that we drove on park roads without lights. Soon the sky was spattered with stars, showing off in a sky unblemished by city lights. The air was cool enough to make us don jackets when we got out of the car to look at a grove of Joshua trees silently praying in the moonlight.

The desert appears to be a lonely, peaceful, and natural place, somewhere to breathe clean air and forget about the "civilized" city world that seems a million miles away. Nearly all of the Southwest and much of the West as a whole are comprised of deserts, not particularly suitable for human habitation with their nearly waterless open wastelands, mesas, and canyons. In 2002, it rained less than two inches in much of Joshua Tree.

However, the desert's appearances are deceptive. There has been a human presence in these deserts for more than ten thousand years. And the peace can be shattered by flash floods. When rain comes, it does so in violent torrents, pushing walls of water, trees, and rocks down the washes. There are no "natural" places, even the most remote places on earth exist within a social context, one in which "nature" is perpetually being humanly altered. Even the impact of rain can change depending on the actions people take.

It is important to note that there are striking differences between modern and ancient human interactions with the desert. Ancient peoples and their contemporary descendants, such as the Navajo, have taken the desert as it was and tried to live in harmony with it. Here is how Willa Cather describes this relationship in *Death Comes for the Archbishop*:

> It was the Indian manner to vanish into the landscape, not to
> stand out against it. . . . [The Indians] seemed to have none

of the European's desire to "master" nature, to arrange and
re-create. They spent their ingenuity in the other direction;
in accommodating themselves to the scene in which they
found themselves. This was not so much from indolence. . .
as from an inherited caution and respect. It was as if the great
country were asleep, and they wished to carry on their lives
without awakening it; or as if the spirits of earth and air and
water were things not to antagonize and arouse. When they
hunted, it was with the same discretion; an Indian hunt was
never a slaughter. They ravaged neither the rivers nor the
forest, and if they irrigated, they took as little water as would
serve their needs. The land and all that it bore they treated
with consideration; not attempting to improve it, they never
desecrated it.

In capitalist society, nearly the exact opposite occurs. The deserts
and all that are in them are rapidly commodified; in two hundred
years, we have changed these barren lands more than the Indians did
in a hundred centuries. Lands were stolen from the Indians so that
they could be "improved" by inefficient and costly irrigated farming,
and by cattle ranching that polluted the water supply and denuded the
vegetation. Today superhighways crisscross the deserts; mines despoil
the mountains; dams flood the canyons; and military outposts and the
megalopolises of Phoenix, Las Vegas, and Los Angeles desecrate some
of the most beautiful places on earth. From Keys View in Joshua Tree,
we saw pollution from Los Angeles, brown and deadly, coming through
a pass in the mountains. Yet political leaders tell us that these cities must
continue to grow or they will die. The truth is that it will be the deserts
that die. And humanity will be the biggest loser.

We left Twentynine Palms after our visit to Joshua Tree, heading
north through the Mojave Desert on a two-lane highway. We wondered
what kind of people lived in the small and humble shacks we saw far out
in the empty landscape on both sides of the road. As we entered Arizona,
we saw a salt mine, and an abandoned town (Amboy) for sale. The
town's post office was still open, probably for the salt mine workers.

As we drove, I thought how lucky we were to be able to travel freely, with no particular destination and no timetable. Long road trips have an almost iconic significance in the United States. This is a large country with a diverse, and in many places, unique topography. To know it, we have to see it, and to see it, we have to get in our cars and on our feet and travel. And this is just what we were doing. I was glad that I had quit teaching in Johnstown. For how can going through the motions after thirty-two years of teaching students not particularly interested in learning compare with a crimson sun and a luminous moon hanging in the sky, almost close enough to touch, over the wondrous desert?

Williams, Arizona, is located on U.S. Highway 40, about 160 miles east of the California border town of Needles—where the Joads in *The Grapes of Wrath* first see the promised land of California and take a swim in the Colorado River—and about thirty-five miles west of Flagstaff, Arizona. It is the closest gateway town to the south rim of the Grand Canyon. We rented a motel room from Mr. Patel and spent four days there, restocking our larder and making the first of several visits to the "world's most beautiful scar." The drive from Williams to the south rim, on the gently sloping Coconino Plateau, gives no indication of the wonders you are about to see.

We had been to Williams before, but this time we noticed that it had changed for the worse. There was still a vintage train tourists rode to the Grand Canyon, and a number of old buildings typical of towns in the West. But the café we used to visit for good coffee and homemade sweet rolls, run by a motorcycle aficionado with a lust for the open road, was now a combination espresso bar and Chinese restaurant. Many other places were closed or were for sale, and most of the remaining businesses appeared to be counting on a continuation of the nostalgia for Route 66, the famed "mother road" where, as Nat King Cole sang, you could "get your kicks." The old highway, which began in Chicago, Illinois, and ended in Santa Monica, California, still goes through Williams, as it does through Gallup and Albuquerque, New Mexico, and Flagstaff, Arizona, all of whose main streets are the great road itself. Route 66 memorabilia shops abound but nowhere more than in Williams.

Like many other western towns, Williams trades on its past. Every evening in the summer there is a cowboy "shoot-out," complete with bank robbers and damsels in distress. As in Cody, Wyoming, the participants are often people who are down on their luck, heavy drinkers, trying to put a few dollars in their pockets. The only one of these events I saw that had any character was in Jackson, Wyoming, where there was a cowboy poet who read a clever poem. At that shoot-out, the dogs in the audience howled when the bandits started shooting and a young boy almost fell off his father's shoulders. In Williams, an entire "Wild West" village has been constructed for the edification of the tourists. When we were there, the employees were practicing various routines with lassos and guns, while two singers gave the worst rendition of "Tumblin' Tumbleweeds" I have ever heard. The Sons of the Pioneers must have cringed in their graves. There were only a few visitors in early May, most of them Japanese, who seemed fascinated with anything Western, no matter how pathetic. It is remarkable how towns try to capitalize on their histories, in a completely distorted way, after these have been destroyed. Jerome, Arizona, fifty miles south of Williams, used to be a copper-mining town controlled by the Phelps-Dodge company. It sits dramatically on a hill so steep that there is an elevation difference of one thousand feet between the beginning and end of town. Bitter and heroic struggles took place there when the miners tried to organize against the killing work regimen that is the lot of miners everywhere. Now there are mine tours, shops, and bed-and-breakfast inns. All-terrain vehicles ride the dizzying dirt road that used to be the route of the trains that hauled the copper out of the town (we drove this road from Williams to Jerome, the most harrowing drive of my life). Tourists are probably unaware that the beautiful rainbow of stripes that marks part of the mountain is the result of copper waste dripping from the mine. A few miles from town are ancient (reconstructed) Indian ruins at Tuzigoot National Monument. In front of the ruins there are what appear to be terraced dirt fields, seemingly indicating land that the Indians once planted. However, these are comprised of waste from the mines, piped from Jerome. They have to be watered down periodically to prevent poisonous dust from contaminating the surrounding townspeople.

We traveled from Williams, Arizona, to nearby Flagstaff, where we spent twenty-two days in a Ramada Limited motel, which we rented for the princely sum of $29.99 per night (plus tax). We hadn't planned to stay so long, maybe a day or two. As we entered town, a brake warning light flashed on our dashboard. We panicked but quickly found a Dodge garage and got the car repaired. The friendliness of the staff at the dealership—they drove us downtown, and returned our car to us when it was finished—gave us a good feeling about Flagstaff. The weather was fine, cool in the morning, dry, and never too hot. We were tired from the fifteen hundred miles we had traveled in just nine days. And it turned out that there were dozens of dramatic places to see and hikes to take. So our day or two turned into one week, then two, then the rest of May. I kept extending our stay at the motel and the taciturn but agreeable clerk kept giving us the coupon rate.

Not only did we refine our cooking routine in Flagstaff, we also sharpened our hiking skills and began to more systematically and objectively see the world around us. In fact, hiking and observing became our new "work." They became the foundations of our daily conversations, our reading and research, our "take" on life. They made us more than tourists on a long road trip.

We found especially fascinating the nearby town of Sedona, which came to encapsulate for us an important part of the meaning of our journey. Sedona is a small town about twenty-five miles south of Flagstaff in north central Arizona. *USA Weekend* recently voted it the "most beautiful place in America." Sedona's setting is stunning. To get there from Flagstaff, you drive down Oak Creek Canyon on a steep and heavily switchbacked road. As the canyon deepens, you are surrounded by rugged rock-cliffed walls, and as you get closer to the town, the canyon opens to vistas of red-rock sandstone buttes, mesas, monoliths, and pinnacles. Fantastic shapes abound: Coffeepot Rock, Cathedral Rock, and Bell Rock. The town used to be off the beaten path, known mainly as a setting for Western movies. But it has been discovered by wealthy tourists, sporting enthusiasts, and "new agers." This last group arrived in the 1980s, attracted by the "vortexes," magical and mystical places in the red rocks where electrical currents supposedly converge and in which, if you are in the right spot, you might have visions or even an out-of-body experience. Today Sedona is visited by four million people each year, and the town is filled with outsized mansions, resorts, hotels, gated condominium complexes, and smart shops.

Sedona is a hiking paradise, with trails crisscrossing the landscape in every direction. You can hike up Wilson Mountain and look down on the town from a perch high above the helicopters that take tourists sightseeing. You can stroll along the West Fork of Oak Creek, crossing the water several times on stepping stones and ending up in a canyon where you must wade and swim in the stream for miles to continue your hike. You can scamper up the slickrock—so named because it gets slippery when wet—in a hundred locations. If you're adventurous, you can take a hair-raising "Pink Jeep" ride over the seemingly impassable rock-stepped buttes.

In every beautiful town like Sedona there is a clash between public and private space. There are millions of rich people in the United States, and they want to own as much property as possible. The more desirable the place, the more they want to possess it. Most of Sedona's hiking trails are on publicly owned land, under the administration of the National Forest Service or the state's public land agency. However, public lands have always been available for private development in the United States. They have been used for animal grazing, mining, fishing, logging, and even ski resorts. On some public lands there are parking, picnic, and concession areas, and these are now routinely contracted out to private companies, which are responsible for maintaining trails, restrooms, and the like and which often charge a not insignificant entrance fee. This incensed us, since we had already purchased a pass giving us permission to use public lands.

We had a Sedona hiking guide, and one of the hikes that attracted us was the one through Boynton Canyon: "This scenic and most visited box canyon in Sedona is also a vortex site. Ruins dot the red sandstone canyon walls. Towering buttes, crimson cliffs, and a quiet trail on the cool canyon floor all add up to magic, vortex or no." Since this guide had never failed us, our excitement grew as we parked our car at the trailhead.

We decided to visit the vortex site first. We walked a short distance along the main path and took a spur trail up to the Boynton Spires and the Kachina Woman monument. It was a clear cool morning; the heat of the day had yet to set in; and the sky was the pure blue color you see only in the desert West. We were admiring the beauty of the rocks and wildflowers as we climbed up the slick surface toward the spires. A sign pointed to the end of this part of the trail, at the top of the boulders. We anticipated a spectacular view of the canyon. But at the crest, in the shade of the spires and monument and amidst the juniper trees, cacti, and wildflowers, we looked over the other side and saw a sprawling private resort, at the mouth of the canyon and privy to the best views. We sat and surveyed the scene for awhile, growing increasingly distressed. The resort consisted of many buildings spread out over one mile in length and taking nearly the entire width of the canyon. Cars and delivery trucks drove in and out; lawnmowers buzzed; women in tennis whites slapped balls over the net; and golf carts hauled players over manicured greens that contrasted sharply with the desert terrain all around. Besides the condominium apartments, there were lavish private homes, some built right into the hillsides. Construction workers mixed cement, carried lumber, pounded nails, and ran power tools, adding to the din. The Kachina Woman must weep every day to see the desecration of her sacred canyon.

We returned to the main trail and began to traverse the canyon. We had to walk alongside the resort, hard up against a tall and imposing boundary fence. We complained about it as we hiked past. How did this vacation spot gain control of so much of the canyon? Did the guests find it natural that they were behind locked gates and needed keys to access the trail? What was the fence protecting? Upset as we were by this intrusion into a dazzling natural landscape, we were taken aback by the sign posted at the spot where the resort buildings and the trail were closest to one another. There on the fence was posted the following:

PRIVATE PROPERTY

HIKERS NOTICE

YOU MUST EXIT BOYNTON
CANYON ON THIS TRAIL
HIKERS ARE NOT PERMITTED
TO EXIT THE CANYON THROUGH
RESORT PROPERTY

TRESPASSERS WILL BE PROSECUTED

ARMED PATROL ON DUTY 24 HOURS

VIDEO TAPING IN PROGRESS

Sign in Boynton Canyon, Sedona, Arizona.

Here the oppressiveness of private property revealed itself. We looked up at the surveillance camera and made obscene gestures.

The resort continued beyond the sign, finally ending nearly an hour after we had begun the hike. We walked up the canyon through the late-summer wildflowers and stands of tall ponderosa pines. On a hike in Bandelier National Monument in New Mexico, we learned that these trees are the source of the artificial-flavoring agent vanillin. If you come upon a ponderosa, stop and sniff the bark. It smells strongly of vanilla.

When it is hot, the trees perfume the air. Eventually the path slopes sharply upward through trees, rocks, and bushes, until you come to the end of the canyon. We climbed the slickrock to a spot under a juniper tree, ate lunch, and admired the subtly colored canyon walls, enclosing us all around. We enjoyed the solitude and after awhile began the steep descent back to the trail. We walked peacefully along it until we came again to the resort. We stopped to contemplate the sign and wished that some misfortune would erase this monument to excess forever.

We returned to Flagstaff and did some investigating. The name of the place is Enchantment Resort, and here is how it advertises itself: "Surrounded by the majestic red rock formations of Northern Arizona's Boynton Canyon, Enchantment Resort combines luxury with rugged grandeur inspired by Native American culture. The resort's adobe casita-style accommodations offer world-class comforts amid its pristine 70-acre setting." Nightly room rates run from $295 to a whopping $2,005. But you get a lot for your money. In addition to the three restaurants (the Tii Gavo "casual" restaurant features a "signature drink," a prickly pear margarita), guests can go on nature walks with a U.S. Forest Service ranger or take guided hikes, experience a "journey of teas," and attend gourd pottery art classes, wine tastings, vortex lectures, narrated star gazings, or Native American guest performances. There is golf, swimming, outdoor whirlpools, championship croquet, bocce ball, and ping pong. Best of all is the Mii amo spa, voted by readers of *Travel & Leisure* magazine as the number two destination spa in the world. Here for a modest fee of between $368.55 and $415.35, guests can buy a variety of day packages, including the Native Mii amo, advertised by the resort as follows:

Native Mii amo $415.35

The Native Americans used ground corn to cleanse and purify the skin. We blend our blue corn with mineral salt crystals and aloe vera to make a vigorous scrub, polishing your skin to perfection. Next indulge in a 'La Stone' massage, using hot, smooth river rocks to melt away tension. We recommend having lunch at the Mii amo Café before

completing your spa day with a custom facial. One of our
experienced aestheticians will evaluate your skin and design
a facial specifically for you.

The repeated referrals to American Indian cultures are both
inaccurate and typical. What does it mean to say that the "rugged
grandeur" of the place is "inspired by Native American culture"? The
Indians didn't build the canyon. The wealthy whites who come here
want to appropriate the Indians' culture just as they want to have the
canyon. This "affinity" with the Indians contrasts markedly with the
indifference or hostility to the poor Navajo and Zuni Indians who live a
short distance away.

The National Forest Service, which administers the Boynton
Canyon trail, controls millions of acres of public land. As we have seen,
the service routinely leases it to private businesses, often at rock-bottom
prices and for purposes that destroy the very grounds entrusted to this
government agency. So it is no wonder that private owners often come
to feel that what is ours is theirs to exploit. While Enchantment Resort
is private property, the canyon that makes it attractive is not. In Sedona,
as elsewhere in the country, the tension between private and public
domains is growing. Unfortunately, the public will likely not be much
enchanted by the outcome.

THE ENVIRONMENT: ACT FIVE, WHITHER
THE NATIONAL PARKS?

Between early May and late August, we visited Joshua Tree, Grand
Canyon, Petrified Forest/Painted Desert, Rocky Mountain, Arches,
Canyonlands, Zion, Bryce Canyon, Grand Tetons, Yellowstone,
Glacier, Mt. Rainier, Olympic National Park, Walnut Creek, Tuzigoot,
Sunset Crater Volcano, Wupatki, Bandelier, and the Colorado National
Monument. All are national treasures; each one has scenery as dramatic
as most people will ever see: natural bridges and arches, waterfalls,
fantastic canyons, buttes, monoliths, hoodoos, and astonishing rapids.

We were in these parks dozens of times. Seldom were we disappointed; almost always we were exhilarated. It is impossible to see the Balanced Rock and Delicate Arch in Arches, Grand View in Canyonlands, the sand beaches and lush foliage in the Narrows in Zion, the thousand-year-old trees in Rainier's Grove of the Patriarchs, or the eight-hundred-year-old petrified lava flows at Sunset Crater and not be mindful of the vast indifference of nature and our insignificant part in it. The human world, with its relentless injustices and inequalities, is put in sharp relief and made all the more intolerable. In the face of such beauty, it is surely an unforgivable crime for any society to let its people live in misery.

But if the parks are beautiful, they are also the products of the social structures that created them. Yellowstone was our first national park, established in 1872. Already when George Catlin was waxing eloquent about establishing "a magnificent park, where the world could see for ages to come, the native Indian in his classic attire, galloping his wild horse, with sinewy bow, and shield and lance, amid the fleeting herds of elks and buffaloes," white settlers and the government had begun brutal campaigns to remove the natives from their land. The history of the national parks is marked by systematic and, for the most part, successful efforts to remove indigenous people from them. In Yellowstone, for example, many Indians traversed what is today the park to hunt, but a cornerstone rule in the national parks is that there cannot be any hunting. In some cases the "treaties" entered into by the U.S. government guaranteed the Indian nations traditional hunting rights, but these agreements were routinely broken. (I put treaties in quotes because these treaties were ordinarily *faits accomplis* made after white settlers had entered and taken possession of land and the government stood ready to ratify this theft by force if necessary.)

Only one group of Indians lived in Yellowstone, the Sheepeater Shoshone, who managed to survive in this harsh wilderness, with its killing winters, by hunting and eating the mountain sheep native to the region. The tribe was physically removed from the park in 1879 (in that year fifty-two members of the tribe, mainly women and children, were hunted down and subdued by the U.S. Army after a three-month search). This process of removal from areas designated national parks was repeated again and again. Indians might be tolerated for awhile in the parks, either because they were too numerous to remove at once or because they could be utilized commercially, as hunting guides or performers for the rising number of tourists, but not because the parks had been their land.

Interestingly, the first rationalization for national parks was that they would serve as "monuments," signifying the grandness of the new nation, just as the human-made monuments of European countries denoted their majesty. They would mark the United States as a great nation, one whose very terrain was more magnificent than that of any other country in the world. That they were not human-made meant that God himself must have singled out this new nation as something special, one which, by its very nature (literally speaking), was Olympian. However, in a country founded upon the transcendence of commerce, it was not long before monetary interests came to the forefront. (Ironically, later rationalizations for the parks were rooted in the notion of communal property, that is, the national parks would belong to all of the people. But at the same time, the communal holding of land and the absence of any concept of private property in many Indian groups were condemned as unnatural, as communistic, and a sign of the Indians' primitive thinking. Many leaders argued that only when the Indians were forced to accept private ownership could they become productive citizens of the United States.)

Spurred on mainly by the burgeoning railroads, the government acquired, by bogus treaty or by force, more land for the national parks. (Constant conflicts occurred between the government and other commercial interests, such as timber and mining companies, and these were resolved in various ways. These commercial interests were not always satisfied, but neither were they ignored. For example, George W. Bush is not opposed to the mining of uranium on the south rim of the Grand Canyon.) Soon a variety of tourist attractions, run by private commercial interests, sprang up and began to make considerable sums of money.

We have given a lot of thought to national park reform. I offer some recommendations, with an acknowledgment to Edward Abbey, who has similar proposals in *Desert Solitaire*:

1. Sharply reduce the money spent on road construction. As soon as a park has been established, private interests, keen on the arrival of waves of money-bearing motorized tourists, begin petitioning Congress for funding and a frenzy of construction begins. As this process continues, traffic mounts and visitors are stalled for hours in traffic jams. Highways encourage the use of super-sized SUVs and RVs, which slow down traffic further, damage the roads (requiring more repairs), and make accidents more likely.

2. Stop building parking lots and paving trails. At Grand Canyon, a visitor can almost drive a car to the rim by the El Tovar Hotel (named after one of the Spanish imperialist Coronado's men, who came north aiming at conquest and were the first Europeans to see the Grand Canyon). Visitors walk from their vehicles or the hotel to an overlook, take a few pictures, and head back to the snack shop for ice cream. Parking lots and paved trails ruin much of the experience of seeing a natural wonder. On one such trail, built for persons with disabilities and from which there are no views of the canyon, workers have actually spray-painted rocks to look like the red earth of the canyon. At one visitor's center, signs give distances to various buildings in feet so as not to discourage the millions of sightseers who are too unfit to move on foot.

3. Build more trails, maintain existing trails, and encourage exploration. Rangers should lead more excursions into the parks, and they should be teaching us to survive in the wilderness: how to climb, find water, pitch tents, find and prepare food, use a compass, deal with bears and other dangerous animals, ford streams, walk on ice and snow, treat bug and snake bites, identify the things seen on the trails, and

dozens of other activities. The rangers should have better job protection and pay.

4. Eliminate the park hotels. The parks ought to be publicly operated, not run by profit-seeking corporations. Expensive private accommodations should be converted into cheap publicly owned hostels and more hostels built, with bunk beds and basic supplies provided. Campgrounds, with water for showers and drinking, should be expanded, and more should be built. Inexpensive nutritious food should be available for sale, and tents available for rent.

5. Working people, people of color, and young people should be actively encouraged to visit. Thousands of "scholarships" should be granted, maybe through a lottery, so that people without means can see their parks. They are supposed to be for everyone, but this is not the case. Their remote locations and commercial focus make them all but inaccessible to people without time and money. The proportion of park visitors who are people of color (except for Asian tourists) is very much less than the proportion of the population comprised of blacks, Hispanics, and Indians. It is possible to hike an entire day in Rocky Mountain National Park or Arches or even Yellowstone and not see a single person of color. And given the expenses associated with a park visit (gas, entrance fee, camping or motel fees, etc.), poor people are unlikely ever to come to a national park. Remember the activities I sold at the Lake Hotel. Their prices in 2006 are as follow: one- and two-hour horseback rides: $34.32 and $54.60; stage coach rides: $9.46; "authentic" Western cookouts: $53.04, extra if combined with a horse ride; guided fishing tours: $148.40 for two hours; several types of bus tours of the park: $26.50 to $58.24; and a photo "safari": $57.20. A family trip to Yellowstone for even a few days will cost a lot. This means that as economic inequality worsens in the United States, the

parks will become retreats for those in the top quintile of the income distribution.

6. Prohibit, wherever feasible, automobile traffic in the parks. Have a few large lots at the entrances and shuttles and bikes readily available. This is done now during the summer and fall at Zion National Park, and it works well.

7. In conjunction with number 5, forbid concessionaire activities, except perhaps for some cooperative ventures with small local enterprises to supplement the rangers. Examples are rafting, pack trips, and the like.

NEW MEXICO

From Flagstaff we went to New Mexico, where we spent the first three weeks of June in Albuquerque, Santa Fe, and Taos. Albuquerque's population has quadrupled since the 1950s, and it now spreads out interminably from the intersection of Interstates 15 and 40. There are nineteen Albuquerque freeway exits, and residents think still more are needed to accommodate the ceaseless traffic. It is difficult to go from one place to another in this city without getting on an interstate highway. What seems like an endless expanse of suburbs and exurbs crowds out the desert, filled with developments of cheaply built but expensive homes on treeless lots baking in the sun and spreading almost to Santa Fe, sixty miles north. Just west of the city is the Petroglyph National Monument. We took a hike there on a hot June morning. The rocks had been defaced with graffiti. We learned that there was a move afoot to build a highway through the monument, to accommodate the growing sprawl. We cynically wondered if real estate interests were encouraging the graffiti, to make the monument so degraded that it would not be worth saving.

The exurban growth we saw around Albuquerque is becoming the norm in the United States. Entire communities are being constructed in the open spaces beyond suburbia. To ensure tax revenues and attract residents, builders lock in (usually with the help of tax concessions) "big-box" stores like Lowe's, Home Depot, and Wal-Mart. The taxes are then used to finance schools, police, and other social necessities. *New York Times* columnist David Brooks has applauded the exurban explosion, arguing that they provide relatively cheap housing, decent schools, and safe streets for those who can't find such amenities in either cities or suburbs. He also says that the industrial parks in the exurbs have become centers for the development of exciting new scientific advances like nanotechnology. Perhaps Brooks is right, but we're skeptical.

Santa Fe is the state capital of New Mexico, with a reputation for sophistication that attracts thousands of visitors annually to its opera, Indian market, and museums. It is the second largest art market in the United States; only New York City's is larger. Along Canyon Road, there are more than one hundred art dealers. In the downtown, there are several excellent art museums, including one dedicated to the works of Georgia O'Keeffe, many fine restaurants, and numerous luxury hotels. The town's geographical setting is magnificent, with easily reachable mountains rising to over 13,000 feet to the north and east. Much of the year the weather is warm and sunny.

Not many people live in Santa Fe's downtown. But they do live in the surrounding hills, and in houses that can boggle the mind. One morning we began a hike at St. John's College, located east of downtown. This college is the sister school to the one of the same name in Annapolis, Maryland; both are famous for their focus on a "Great Books" curriculum. We parked in a college lot and after crossing two arroyos, we headed up a hill toward Atalaya Mountain. We came to a private road that entered a gated community, filled with large costly adobe-style houses. As we ascended the mountain, we came upon isolated homes, each more spectacular than the one before. These were gigantic adobe structures, containing thousands of square feet of living space plus various outbuildings, gardens, stables, and swimming pools. As we discovered in our travels, these "*haciendas*" are often not occupied year-round but are just one of several homes of the owners. And as a perusal of the real estate ads in the *New York Times Magazine* shows, such estates are ten million dollars, or more.

Santa Fe's famous square.

The southern entrance to Santa Fe is Cerillos Road, a congested ten-mile stretch of strip malls, motels, businesses, and retail stores. It is on the streets behind this road that one encounters the living quarters of the poorly paid workers who attend to tourists in downtown restaurants, hotels and shops. We learned this from a clerk in a bookstore who told us that many service-sector workers earned the minimum wage or slightly above and found it difficult to find adequate housing in Santa Fe. Still poorer abodes can be seen in the predominantly Indian villages close to the town.

The Native American presence is strong in New Mexico, and there are nineteen pueblos, which maintain a rare independence, the legacy of the successful pueblo revolt against the Spanish conquerors in 1680. The most famous (built in the fifteenth century) is in Taos, though the first thing you notice on the way into it is a casino. I lost fifty dollars there one afternoon during our three-day stay. Given its acclaim, we expected Taos to have a grander setting. It is surrounded by mountains, but there are large flat-and not particularly attractive-spaces between them and town. There is also a steady flow of traffic all day on its main highway. There is not much to remind a visitor that this is a sacred place to the Indians, and the same is true for the bohemian spirit brought by the counterculture in the 1960s (though we did see abandoned "hippie" buses at the end of a fine long loop drive through the mountains and valleys to the north and east). Tourism is king, and the second-homers are moving in, with all that this means in terms of inequality, work, and the environment.

Despite its shortcomings, we enjoyed Taos. The central square was more comfortable than Santa Fe's. The shopkeepers were friendly. We found a bakery that featured organic bread and lunches. The farmers' market was charming; a vendor split a carton of eggs in half and charged us a dollar for them. It was pleasant to wind our way through the narrow streets of the Old Town and the courtyards of shops behind many storefronts. It was in Taos that we learned what a "dew point" is (the temperature at which humidity is 100 percent). We looked it up the day it was minus six—the humidity was 3 percent! During this, our first time in Taos, we were given a good omen. On June 21 it rained, the first time for us in fifty-two days.

THE REST OF THE WEST

We left Taos and continued north into Colorado, detouring east for a day at the spectacular sand dunes that have built up over centuries against the Sangre de Cristo Mountains. It got dark at 3:30 that afternoon, and as we drove toward Colorado Springs, the skies let loose. The air cooled, and we were freezing when we stopped at a rest area. We had gotten used to ninety-degree weather. The next day found us in Estes Park. Our oldest son had been urging us to go there for five years. We stayed a week to hike and marvel at the high snowy peaks. We then backtracked south and west to Glenwood Springs, where we spent the Fourth of July and climbed up to the frigid waters of Hanging Lake from the trailhead along the Colorado River.

We were on our way to Zion National Park to meet this son, who had taken a job with our Yellowstone employer, Xanterra. In Utah, arguably our most beautiful state, we stayed in Moab, Springdale, and Panguitch, trekking in Arches, Canyonlands, Zion, and Bryce Canyon national parks. We left Utah in mid-July via Interstate 15, hugging the Utah-

Nevada border, first through desert and then up through long valleys made verdant by Mormon farmers, who gave their towns names like Nephi and Moroni, heroes of the Book of Mormon. Throughout the West it is common to find the Book of Mormon along with the Gideon Bible next to the beds in motel rooms. Approaching the bedrock Mormon city of Provo, home of Brigham Young University, billboards advertise stores and websites specializing in gear for Mormon missionaries. To the east, at the foot of the Wasatch Mountains, is the Dream Mine, where Mormon fundamentalists claim there are vast gold deposits that will be found when Christ comes again. The gold will be used by the Mormons to get them through the "Last Days." It is remarkable how many prominent Mormons have invested in this mine since the first revelation about it was made by the Mormon angel Moroni to John Koyle in 1894.

Sign near Moab, Utah.

INEQUALITY: ACT FOUR, THE MORMONS

Mormonism is both radically totalitarian and egalitarian. The religion's founder and prophet, Joseph Smith, envisioned a heaven on earth, made up of the "latter-day saints." The religion had a particularly American bent and attracted followers, especially the poor, immediately. It was a religion not just of thought but of action, demanding the whole of its adherents' lives. The Mormons were viciously persecuted; their early history is one of constant movement as Smith and then, after Smith's murder, Brigham Young tried to find the special place of Smith's visions where the faithful could establish their kingdom. The early years were ones of extraordinary heroism and hard work, and this period cemented the Saints to one another and to their faith, in ways difficult for us to imagine today. The long trek from Nauvoo, Illinois, where Smith was murdered and from which the Mormons were driven by their many enemies, to Utah is one of the most remarkable migrations in history. Saints from England actually hitched themselves to wagons and crossed the plains in winter. (Mormonism was famously proselytizing from the beginning. Everyone has probably had the experience of young Mormon men dressed in suits roaming the streets and knocking on doors looking for converts.)

Once settled in Utah, Mormons were routinely sent out by Brigham Young to settle areas in the West. Young had an idea of an empire spreading to the Pacific Ocean. But in the end, he had to settle for what is now Utah. Whenever "Gentiles" (all those who were not Mormons) threatened to settle any part of the state, he and his successors sent out colonizers. One group was sent to the empty and forbidding southeast corner of the state in 1880. They traveled with wagons and horses across the Escalante Desert, building a road as they went, in territory even Indians avoided. They suffered many travails but none so great as when they reached a nearly sheer cliff at what is called Hole in the Rock, about eighty miles west of the town of Bluff. Here they constructed a road that defies belief. With dynamite and drills, often hanging on ropes over the cliffs, they gouged a road over 2,000 feet straight down to the bottom. They cut "dugways" deep in the rock, so that wagon wheels would fit into them, and the wagons would not tip over. Then, as Wallace Stegner tells us in his moving book, *Mormon Country*:

> . . . when they came to a steep, smooth rock face, they were
> stumped. It was too abrupt for a dugway, and they had no
> powder to blast a ledge. . . . [So] . . . they suspended drillers

over the cliff and had them drill large deep holes on an even incline all the way to the bottom. Other men went out to the mountains and the river bottom and cut scrub oak stakes, and the stakes were pounded deep into the drilled rock. Across the stakes brush and driftwood were banked, and broken rock scattered on top of that. Give those Mormons credit. When they couldn't blast a road out of the cliff, they tacked one on as a carpenter might nail a staging under the eaves of a high house.

More than eighty wagons and hundreds of horses and cattle were safely hauled down this precipitous road.

Joseph Smith's vision for the Saints was that they establish a fully communitarian society in which everything would be owned and worked in common. But the reality of Mormon life made him hesitant to impose this on an already stratified society. Mormons did tithe, and the proceeds were used to advance the interests of the group and provide for the poorest among them. But in the 1870s, Brigham Young, in response to what he perceived as a weakening of the Mormons' millenarian spirit, began to urge his people to organize themselves into cooperative villages. Not many Mormons embraced the idea, especially those who had become richer than their fellow believers. But there were those willing, indeed keen, to fulfill the prophet's dream. Among those who were very poor and who had already uprooted themselves and colonized new places on orders from the leaders, several full-blown communist communities were established. The most famous one was at Orderville, at the southern end of Long Valley, today on Highway 89, between Zion and Bryce Canyon national parks. This is a beautiful place, made green by springs and the farming skills of the Mormons. For nearly a dozen years, the people of Orderville lived successfully and happily without private property. Every member put all of his and her property into a common pool; everyone shared equally the goods and services collectively produced; there was no money or debt. Again quoting Stegner:

[Orderville] eliminated completely the fear of poverty and want; it furnished to all its members the amplitude of food, shelter, and clothing whose possession, according to some ways of thinking, ought to remove every source of human quarrelsomeness. It managed to bring its several hundred members into a communion of goods, labor, religion, and recreation such as the world has seen only in a few places and for very short times, and to do it without loss of gaiety or good nature. The life was strenuous, but it was also wholesome; it brought content. The number of people from that town who lived past eighty is good statistical evidence that heaven-on-earth does not breed the will to die.

Events both external and internal eventually brought Orderville's communism to an end. It is probably impossible to have an eternal island of equality in a sea of capitalism.

The whole history of the Mormons made them steadfastly committed to one another, but their relationship to outsiders was one ranging from indifference to murderous hostility. Just as the Jews considered it no sin of usury to loan money at interest to Gentiles, so too the Mormons commit no sin when they shun nonbelievers. We met innkeepers in the town of Springdale, just outside Zion National Park, who were shunned so completely by Mormons in a town close to St. George (in that part of southwest Utah known as "Dixie" because Brigham Young sent settlers there to grow cotton) that they had to sell their newly built house and move. I got a haircut in the Long Valley town of Panguitch. The Mormon proprietors would not make small talk no matter how hard I tried. When Karen started talking to the young daughter of another customer, the mother looked at her as if she were insane. Things are changing in the bigger cities, such as Salt Lake City, but still Utah is a Mormon state, and non-Mormons are not treated as equals.

When those who are secular (and even religious) think of Utah and the Mormons, they are likely to think of fanatics: ultra-conservative, clannish, thoroughly oppressive to women, and secret polygamists. The image of Senator Orrin Hatch comes to mind. There is much truth to the negative stereotypes. They stole Indian land and forcibly separated Indian children from their parents and farmed them out to the faithful. They murdered Gentile settlers. They have spawned numerous cult-like sects. But there is much we can learn from this most remarkable group. Solidarity. Sacrifice for the common good. Belief in the possibility of a good life here on earth. Community. Self-sufficiency. At their best, they were most like that other group of outsiders—American Indians. The trick for radicals has been and will be to make of earth a heaven, but without blind faith.

We turned east at Salt Lake City on July 21 and drove to Wyoming. About twenty miles into the state on Interstate 80, we turned north along a desolate two-lane highway toward Jackson, the Teton Mountains, and Yellowstone National Park. The road was so straight and traffic-free that we drove our van at nearly ninety miles an hour. Then suddenly the road gave way to construction that reduced it to oil-slicked dirt in both directions, and we were lucky if we could go ten miles per hour. As we got closer to Jackson, the desert-like terrain changed to pine-covered hills and the Green River. In the nearby town of Green River, John Wesley Powell began his famous journey through the Grand Canyon, not imagining that the placid Green would soon become a foamy cauldron of deadly rapids. Snow-covered mountains loomed in the distance. There are so many beautiful rivers in the West, flowing down out of the mountains. They rush along, making twists and turns, convoluting into oxbows and other strange shapes, flowing clear and cold over the rocks, creating formidable rapids and carving out incredible shapes in canyon walls. The Gallatin, the Snake, the Gibbon, the Green, the mighty Colorado—it is difficult to tire of them. Like the stars in the open sky, the rivers of the West inspire sublime thoughts. They make you wish you could drive alongside them forever.

Jackson, Wyoming, despite its physical setting, was difficult to navigate, much more so than it was in 2001 when we were at the Lake Hotel. The surrounding Teton County is the richest in the United States in terms of per capita income, and, as noted in Chapter Two, Jackson is chock full of antique shops, upscale restaurants, art galleries, and expensive motels. But the traffic was unbearable. We had a hard time finding a room, settling finally on a motel we had stayed in before. The former owner had been married at the hotel we worked in at Yellowstone National Park, and she gave discounts to park employees. However, after marrying, she sold her motel to the owner of the one next door. The new proprietors, we later discovered, were planning to tear the old motel down and sell the property. But they didn't want to pass up the busy summer season and were still renting the old rooms to suckers who were desperate—like us. We piled our gear into the room and immediately left, not returning until near midnight. We went to see Michael Moore's *Fahrenheit 9/11*. When we returned to the motel, we were repelled by the stench of cigarette smoke, urine, and mold. We spent a restless night, and the next day vociferously complained. Half of the room charge (nearly one hundred dollars, the highest we paid during our entire trip) was immediately canceled. I complained to American Express and eventually got the rest of it dropped as well.

Mountain Goat on rock, Glacier National Park, Montana.

After our miserable night in Jackson, we went to Yellowstone for five days of hiking, sightseeing, and renewing old acquaintances. We stayed in a nicely remodeled cabin at Lake Lodge. It was good to be back. From there we drove through Montana, visiting Bozeman, Missoula, and Glacier National Park. In the park, we drove up the Going-to-the-Sun Road, an engineering marvel that affords stunning views of the glaciated mountains. At the summit of the highway, there are some fine trails. On one of them, we had to lean against the mountain while a troop of mountain goats demanded the right of way. On the other, we watched two photographers wait patiently next to a goat that was sleeping on a rock, looking for all the world like an animal just killed and ready to be slaughtered and roasted over a spit. The goat made a few feeble moves to get up and each time the men eagerly readied their cameras. But then the goat thought better of it and went back to dreamland.

From Glacier we drove west through Montana, the silver towns of the Idaho panhandle, and into the desolate wastelands of eastern Washington. Driving south toward Yakima, we were shadowed by what looked like a Blackhawk helicopter, probably on a practice run from the huge Air Force base nearby. This gave us an eerie feeling. We completed our grand loop by returning to two of our favorite parks, Mt. Rainier and Olympic, and stopping once again in Florence, Oregon, to enjoy the dunes.

We returned to Portland the last week in August to collect our belongings, stored at the U-Haul facility not far from the city. We rented a small trailer and had it attached to our van hitch. It took us less than an hour to load our possessions: some twenty-odd boxes (filled mainly with books, clothes, and kitchen equipment), two metal chairs, a small Moroccan inlaid tile table, two trunks, a fan, a space heater, an assortment of framed pictures, and the things we had been traveling with.

EASTWARD HO!

Back to Pennsylvania! It took us five days to reach my mother's home. We drove east on Interstate 84 through northern Oregon, past a dense, 7-mile by-7-mile-poplar farm (the trees are genetically engineered and grow more than ten feet per year), and into Idaho. The last town in Oregon along the highway is Ontario, and it is the home of the Ore-Ida potato company, named for its location on the Oregon-Idaho border. It smelled strongly of french fries. Interstate 84 turns south in eastern Oregon and continues south through Idaho and into Utah, ending where it connects to Interstate 80 at Echo, Utah, just west of Park City and not far from the Wyoming border. We drove across the arid and fantastic landscape of Wyoming into the high plains of Nebraska. Then came the cornfields of eastern Nebraska and all of Iowa. Iowa gave way to the boring turnpikes of Illinois, Indiana, Ohio, and Pennsylvania. Traffic came to a stop south of Chicago, as it always did, and we again noticed for the first time in months that the air was difficult to breathe.

We stayed with my mother for two weeks, and then with our daughter and twin sons in Arlington, Virginia, for almost three weeks. The days passed, full of events too personal to be of interest to readers, just family stuff. While we were in Arlington, we visited the National Cemetery, which is located close to the Iwo Jima Memorial and is dominated by a colonial house up on a hill with a striking view of Washington, D.C. One of the marines who hoisted the famous flag, Michael Strank, was from Johnstown, where I taught. His nephew and namesake was a student of mine. It galls me that the house on the hill above the cemetery, once the residence of Robert E. Lee, was ordered by the Supreme Court to be returned to the Lee family after the Civil War. Then Lee's son sold it to the United States government for $150,000, an enormous sum at the time. I think this is an outrage to every Union soldier and every former slave.

We said goodbye to our kids at the end of September and drove south on Interstate 95 toward Miami Beach.

SUGGESTED READINGS

On farming, farm workers, and related subjects, see Richard Manning, *Against the Grain* (New York, NY: North Point Press, 2004); Vandana Shiva, *Stolen Harvest: The Hijacking of the Global Food Supply* (Cambridge, MA: South End Press, 2000); Peter Matthiessen, *Sal Si Puedes: Cesar Chavez and the New American Revolution* (Berkeley, CA: University of California Press, 2000); Marcel Mazoyer and Laurence

Roudart, *A History of Agriculture: From the Neolithic Age to the Current Crisis* (New York, NY: Monthly Review Press, 2006); Marc Reisner, *Cadillac Desert: The American West and its Disappearing Water* (New York, NY: Penguin Books, 1987). The two quotations on the use of corn syrup in everything and the health impacts of corn are taken from Michael Pollan, "When a Crop Becomes King," *New York Times*, July 19, 2002. On the land and people of the Southwest, see W. L. Rusho, *Everett Ruess: A Vagabond for Beauty* (Layton, Utah: Gibbs Smith, Publisher, 2002); Edward Dolnick, *Down the Great Unknown: John Wesley Powell's* 1869 *Journey of Discovery and Tragedy through the Grand Canyon* (New York, NY: Perennial, 2002); Edward Abbey, *Desert Solitaire* (New York, NY: Ballantine Books, 1985); Edward Abbey, *The Monkey Wrench Gang* (New York, NY: Harper Perennial, 2000); Willa Cather, *Death Comes for the Archbishop* (New York, NY: Vintage Books, 1990); Robert Silverberg, *The Pueblo Revolt* (Lincoln, Nebraska: University of Nebraska Press, 1970); Raymond Friday Locke, *The Book of the Navajo* (Los Angeles, CA: Mankind Publishing Company, 2001); any novel by Tony Hillerman. The Edward Abbey quotation is from *The Journey Home: Some Words in Defense of the American West* (New York, NY: E. P. Dutton, 1977), 187. David Brooks's optimistic views of suburban/exurban America can be found in *On Paradise Drive* (New York, NY: Simon & Schuster, 2004). On the Mormons, see Wallace Stegner, *Mormon Country* (Lincoln, Nebraska: University of Nebraska Press, 1981); Jon Krakauer, *Under the Banner of Heaven: A Story of Violent Faith* (New York, NY: Anchor Books, 2004). On workers living in motels and other stories of low-wage work, see Barbara Ehrenreich, *Nickel and Dimed: On (Not) Getting By in America* (New York, NY: Owl Books, 2001).

CHAPTER SIX

MIAMI BEACH

MIAMI BEACH

Population in 2003 89,312
Population in 2000
    White 86.7%
    Black 4.0%
    Hispanic (all races) 53.4%

Median household income $27,322
People below poverty level of income 21.8%
Median rent $581
Median mortgage, including associated costs $2,555

Visit the moving Holocaust Memorial with the powerful raised hand sculpture at 1933-1945 Meridian Ave. 33139, (305) 538-1663. Enjoy a movie and the architecture at the Regal Cinema, 1100 Lincoln Road, 33139, (305) 674-6766. The third-floor deck gives a great view of the city.

KEY WEST

Population in 2004 24,768
Population in 2000
    White 84.9%
    Black 9.3%
    Hispanic (all races) 16.5%

Median household income $43,021
People below poverty level 10.2%
Median rent $822
Median mortgage, including associated costs $1,658

Rent a bicycle and tour the island from the good folks at Island Bicycles, 929 Truman Ave. (at Grinnell), 33040, (305) 292-9707. If you're from western Pennsylvania ask if they'll give you the Pittsburgh special discount!

WE LIVE AMONG THE BEAUTIFUL PEOPLE

We arrived in Miami Beach on September 30, 2004, after an unpleasant trip south on Interstate 95, a death trap of a road along which there is little of interest. During the weeks before we got there, three hurricanes had ripped through Florida, leaving paths of human and environmental devastation. Nearly all of eastern Florida stunk from the refuse the storms left behind; the air was dank and foul until just north of Miami Beach, which was spared the hurricanes' fury. From the highway we could see downed palm trees, power lines, light poles, bill boards, and hundred of blue roofs, tarp-covered in place of destroyed shingles. Drivers lined up for blocks at gas stations. Thousands were seeking shelter, food, and ice. Since the president's brother was the state's governor (Jeb Bush) and the president needed to win Florida in that year's election, federal aid was rushed there—in stark contrast to the federal response a year later in New Orleans. While it was still insufficient, especially for the poor, who somehow always seem to suffer the most in "natural" disasters, the aid came in fast enough and in large enough quantity to help many of those in need and to assure that the president didn't suffer a calamitous loss of popularity in the state.

The drive from Palm Beach to Miami is a nightmare of traffic, motorists speeding and lane changing, but it is exciting to cross the Julia Tuttle Causeway over Biscayne Bay and into Miami Beach. People we have talked to often confuse Miami, Miami Beach, and South Beach. Miami is the large city (population about 400,000) bordering Biscayne Bay. It does not abut the Atlantic Ocean. Miami Beach is an island east of Miami, across the bay. It is connected to Miami by a series of six bridges or causeways. South Beach is a part of Miami Beach; it doesn't have precise boundaries, but the consensus is that it extends from the southern tip of the island north to 21st Street.

Discount coupon in hand, we checked into a Best Western motel and gasped when we looked out the room's window and saw the turquoise tropical ocean. Somewhere along the Florida coastline the color of the sea changes, from the gloomy green-grey of the middle Atlantic to the blue-green of the tropics. We took a short stroll along the wooden boardwalk, which overlooks the beach for two miles, between 21st and 47th Streets. It is a nice place to take a walk, lined with trees, tourist hotels, and apartment buildings. After an hour, we went back to the room to watch the second debate between George W. Bush and John Kerry.

The next morning we went to South Beach, to the apartment building in which we had stayed two years before to meet our realtor. We had set up an appointment from Virginia. The building, constructed in the 1960s, had begun life as a hotel but had since been converted into condominiums. About half the owners rented their units. At first they were permitted to lease them for any period of time, even one day, but the condominium association has changed this to one month. During our stay we learned that there was a move afoot to raise the minimum lease period to six months. Some owners thought that this would limit their ability to rent. Who besides people like us could lease for at least half a year?

Our agent was a Peruvian who grew up near the ruins at Machu Picchu. When she came to the United States, she took advantage of whatever educational opportunities were available—learning English, taking college classes, and getting her real estate license. She had a furnished efficiency apartment for us; we later learned that it belonged to her. We decided to live in it for one month while we looked for a larger apartment. It was awkward to tell her that her efficiency wasn't much to our liking, but she gladly showed us several other apartments she had the listings for. We liked a one-bedroom that was directly beneath the apartment we had rented in 2002. It was too expensive, so we made an offer much below the asking price just to see what would happen. To our surprise, the owner accepted, with the proviso that we pay the entire six-month rental up-front. This put a strain on our finances, but with some creative use of our credit cards and a small withdrawal from our pension account, we managed. We would put the money back each month and by the end of our stay be about even. Our agent arranged the details, even successfully lobbying her client for a lower rent in exchange for our lump-sum payment. We never met our landlord.

In November we moved into our new apartment, on the north side of the building, again just across the street from the Ritz Carlton. But now their renovations were complete. The street (Lincoln Road) had been redone in multicolored bricks and lined with palm trees. It dead-ended in a turnaround at the beach, which made it a thoroughfare for beachgoers, who came and went at all hours. The street was also filled with cabs waiting to pick up hotel guests. They honked incessantly, vying for spaces and patrons, and a hotel valet hailed them with an

From our balcony: Lincoln Road and the Ocean.

obnoxiously loud whistle. Delivery trucks and buses roared up the street, idling their motors, sometimes for several hours. The apartment was spacious and well-appointed (we were pleased to have our first furnished home), but the noise generated by the hotel and beach access proved to be more than we had bargained for. We soon learned that living in a tourist town meant that we were always subjected to the bad behavior of people who were just visiting and need not be concerned about the feelings of others. One of the banes of a society enmeshed in extreme individualism is that every person acts as if his or her space is completely isolated from that of everyone else. People assume that whatever they do, no matter how annoying, is their business alone; the fact that it affects others eludes them. They throw garbage on the beach and on the street; they talk loudly in movie theaters; they take their pets on crowded sidewalks; they chatter on their cell phones while clerks are waiting on them.

After so much time on the road, it was good to have a more permanent place again. It was warm every day, and each week the humidity fell and temperatures moderated. From November through April, it seldom rose above eighty degrees or fell below the upper sixties. Around Christmas, the weather got rainy, chilly, and windy, but unlike the tourists whose holidays were ruined, we enjoyed the change. One storm so badly eroded the beach that the water nearly lapped the nearby boardwalk. In mid-spring, trucks began to bring in sand, repeating a routine common to Florida's beaches. Miami Beach was, like most of the islands along the Atlantic coast of Florida, a barrier island, covered with impenetrable foliage and "held down" at the shore by mangrove trees, critical to protect the land from severe storms, including hurricanes. Its conversion into a tropical "paradise" began in earnest when Carl Fisher, the owner of the Indianapolis Speedway and inventor of automobile head lamps, gained control of much of the island's land just before the First World War. Using cheap and exploited black labor, Fisher had the island cleared of nearly all its natural vegetation and then began a brazen advertising campaign to lure Northerners down to his new Shangri-la.

We quickly fell into a pleasant routine of tramping miles on the beach and learning as much as we could about our new home. Nearly every morning we took a long walk. We were always shocked to leave our air-conditioned building and go outside into the warm and sunny pool area. We usually said hello to the efficient attendant and to our friend

Marylou, a German who came every year. She had devised a rigorous exercise routine to which she was religiously devoted—laps in the pool, workout in the condo gym, and yoga on the beach—and in the two years we had known her had completely transformed her body. If he was there, we smiled at the old man who had been a snowbird for many years and was now confined to a wheelchair after a stroke. We put our shoes under a deck chair and looked out to sea.

We usually walked south to the pier where we could watch the cruise and container ships enter Government Cut to the harbor in Miami. Smaller fishing and speedboats trolled the waters too, trying to stay out of the wakes of the big ships. Sometimes kids jumped off the pier into the green water. Across the Cut was privately owned Fisher Island, accessible only by boat and home to the rich and famous. From the rocks along the walkway by the pier you can see Virginia Key, one of the few relatively unspoiled refuges left in this part of south Florida. It is about a thirty-minute drive from Miami Beach, well worth the traffic hassle. There are plenty of places to have a picnic; there is an interesting nature hike; and there is Jimbo's, a filthy-looking eatery that gets rave reviews for its smoked fish in all the guidebooks (the television series *Flipper* was filmed close by). When our oldest son visited, I said I would take him there for lunch. We never made it, and he's been reminding me about this ever since. The beaches at Virginia Key were the first ones black people had access to in Miami. Though it is an oasis of calm and beauty in a sea of urban sprawl and development, developers would love to build luxury condominiums there, and the city of Miami, which owns the island, stands to make a lot of money if it sells the land. A volunteer at the old lighthouse on Key Biscayne told us that a compromise was in the works. If history is any guide, the rich will soon have another place to live. Once capital gets its foot in the door, it seldom tolerates compromises.

On any given day, it is possible to run into a celebrity on the beach. Next to our neighbor, the Ritz Carlton, are the luxury hotels favored by the stars: the Delano, the Raleigh, the Sagamore, the Shelburne, and the Shore Club. Each hotel has an elaborate pool area facing the beach, with entrances that are always heavily guarded. But the VIPs must still walk in public spaces to get to the beach, so you might spot models, actors, musicians, and sports heroes leaving their poolside cabanas and tiki bars to mingle with the rest of us. Karen read all the papers and knew who was in town. So we'd be on the lookout, and her sharp eye identified quite a few famous people. We were hoping to see Ossie Davis the week he died in a Collins Avenue hotel. He was filming a movie on Ocean Drive with Peter Falk; I had my picture taken with this fine man at the fiftieth anniversary celebration of *Monthly Review*.

At most of these hotels, parties last long into the night, both inside and around the pools. One party blasted techno music so loud that for several hours it rattled our windows, more than a block away. Shaquille O'Neal rented one of the Collins Avenue hotels for his wife's surprise birthday party. In addition to flying guests in from overseas, Shaq had a baker make his wife a cake in the exact shape and size of her favorite dress; 2004 and 2005 seem to have been the years of the "exotic animal" party. Rap mogul Sean Combs had penguins brought in. Other parties featured leopards, tigers, and monkeys.

Posh bashes were mandatory whenever there was a special event, such as the pretentious Art Basel week in late fall, when celebrity artists pushed their latest creations to rich business men and women from around the world. The local newspapers were full of stories about who was where and who bought what at what price. The *Miami Herald*'s arts editor wrote a column mocking the uncool people who attended Art Basel events inappropriately dressed (complete with photos of the unsuspecting slobs), and made fun of the attire of the cab drivers and other service workers who attended to the needs of the art lovers. We were so outraged by the condescension that Karen wrote a letter to the paper, to which the editor responded with acid sarcasm. We got an anonymous email telling Karen to "get a life." Sometimes a star or entertainment mogul rented an entire hotel for the kind of over-the-top party we usually associate with the robber barons of the Gilded Age.

Miami Beach is a city of excess. Ordinary hotel rooms can sell for $1,000 a night, and they are booked solid. Stretch limousines, Bentleys, Rolls Royces, Escalades, Hummers, and Jaguars are everywhere. The

Miami Beach Polo Club holds matches on the beach. Couples have lavish weddings there too. We watched one from our balcony. An elaborate beach tent had been set up to hold hundreds of dinner guests, and after the ceremony there was a fireworks display larger than those of most towns. The final burst spelled out the couple's names. Hotels

Container ship at Government Cut, Miami Beach.

compete to show which has the most luxurious accoutrements. Several have outdoor disc jockeys; the Setai has one working the lunch crowd at its beachside grill.

The Hotel Victor, whose construction was completed while we lived in Miami Beach, sits next to Casa Casuarina, the former home of fashion designer Gianni Versace, who was murdered right in front of it by spree killer Andrew Cunanan in 1997. (Casuarina is the name of an Australian pine tree brought to Florida in 1860, which has since spread like a plague, destroying most other vegetation wherever it takes root. The Versace house is now a private club. Tourists have their pictures taken in front of it. Cunanan also killed Chicago real-estate developer Lee Miglin, husband of television beauty product promoter Marilyn Miglin.) Here is a description of the Victor from the *Miami Herald*:

Purple and green daybeds designed by French decorator Jacques Garcia dominate the lobby, where the iced vodka bar takes the place of the old reservation desk. The glowing jellyfish tank serves as the main theme, with beaded tentacle tassels appearing on lamps and furniture throughout the building.

Vibe Manager [to think I was amazed when a Manhattan hotel hired a water sommelier] Victoria Prado will supervise the rotation of scented oils wafting through the common areas and the set lists created by the hotel's resident disc jockeys....

Guests will choose from pillow menus, bath menus and a cigar menu with pre-embargo Cuban cigars selling for $1,500 a piece. The 6,000-square-foot basement spa includes a co-ed steam room, with only tile pillows for privacy.

It was at the grand opening of this hotel that Sean "P. Diddy" Combs had the penguins, although his publicist claimed that the rapper had nothing to do with bringing them there.

INEQUALITY: ACT FIVE, A FEW BLOCKS AWAY

You sense right away that there is something seamy and tawdry about Miami Beach. On the one hand, there is every kind of extravagance. Miami is home to a professional basketball team, the Miami Heat. The owner, Mickey Aronson; the president, legendary coach and fashion plate, Pat Riley; the star player, larger-than-life Shaquille O'Neal; and many of the players are millionaires many times over. All fit nicely into the Miami Beach "playground for the wealthy" atmosphere. In March, while I was in Pennsylvania visiting my mother, Karen regaled me with the story of the Heat's "Family Day." A small compound of tents was set up on the beach, presumably public property but treated as the private preserve of anyone with enough money to pay for its use. The big day was a Sunday. As the Heat "family" gathered, the kids were treated to a beach zoo, complete with camels, giraffes, and elephants cavorting in the sand. Adults enjoyed gourmet food and drink amidst lavish displays of flowers. Guards were stationed all around to keep the public out.

Such events were common and ranged from luxury automobile shows to the South Beach Wine and Food Festival. In every case, hordes of workers appeared in the morning, transporting by truck and by foot, pipes, tents, poles, flooring, air conditioners, and heaters. Then they built a tent city. Before the event, another crew of workers set up tables, place settings, glassware, flower arrangements, linens, and whatever else needed to be put in place. As the guests arrived, scores of waiters, bartenders, and hosts went into action. In late November of 2004, jewelry magnate David Yurman and his wife Sybil had a warehouse-sized tent, designed to look like a chic lounge, constructed on the beach, complete with several industrial air conditioners, to house a lavish dinner party in honor of the charitable work of the Cuban-born singer Gloria Estefan and her husband Emilio. The next morning the work crews reappeared and tore everything down. All that remained were thousands of cigarette butts and drink straws.

Much of the glitz in Miami Beach is along Ocean Drive, which runs from near the southern tip of the island to 15th Street in South Beach; on Collins Avenue, which travels the entire length of the town; and on Lincoln Road itself, which is between 16th and 17th Streets, goes from the beach to the bay, and includes a pedestrian walkway, along which are many shops, restaurants, and clubs.

Walk east on Lincoln Road and then south at the first cross street (Washington Avenue) and the glamour quickly ends amid fast food joints, cheap clothing and shoe stores, small Hispanic groceries, liquor stores, electronics outlets, and run-down apartment buildings. You see down-and-out people, panhandlers, drunks, prostitutes, drug dealers, and poorer working-class men and women. There is crime on these streets; a tropical city with plenty of wealthy tourists naturally attracts criminals, especially in winter. Robberies were common, even in daytime, but especially in the wee hours of the morning. Bars close at 5:00 a.m.; drunk tourists make good marks. On these streets, people look poor, and many are. According to the 2000 census, a quarter of all people under eighteen years old live below the official poverty level. The poor who live in Miami Beach are crowded into small, noisy, and hot one- and two-story apartments that look like cheap motels, and may have been at one time. As in Los Angeles, where tropical foliage and an absence of drab high-rise apartments give the appearance of middle-class prosperity, so too in Miami Beach do pastel colors, art deco facades, and sturdy shade trees. But the reality is that those who serve the tourists live in one world, and the visitors to the Hotel Victor live in another.

During our first week, we saw a homeless woman bathing herself with a bar of soap in the ocean. Every morning men would be curled up on the beach, warming their bodies in the bright sun. Outside the raucous party hosted by the Estefans, the homeless tried to sleep. Across the bay in Miami City, a woman in an expensive car hit a child in a poor neighborhood. Instead of stopping, she threw a fifty-dollar bill out the window.

We spent our afternoons and evenings enjoying movies, concerts, museums, and festivals. Also, doing chores, working (teaching my web classes, and writing and editing for *Monthly Review*), walking on the boardwalk, the beach—and Lincoln Road. Lincoln Road is a great place to watch tourists and locals mingle. It is always crowded, especially in the evening. While Morris Lapidus designed the traffic-free part of the street to be an urban area where people could stroll and sit leisurely under a canopy of trees amid sculptures and fountains, today the middle part of the pedestrian mall has been usurped by the restaurants lining Lincoln Road on both sides. Outdoor dining is popular, but the restaurants have made what should be public space into extensions of their kitchens and dining rooms. Most of them are second-rate and overpriced, with hosts begging you to take a seat. Actually it's more fun to watch the customers than to buy a meal. We often saw the comedian Jackie Mason holding court at one popular café, and we watched tennis star Anna Kournekova being harassed by a photographer. But our favorite place was the restaurant Nexxt. This eatery has an extensive outdoor seating area, and you can sit on a ledge across the sidewalk and marvel at the show. People go there for the enormous portions—not cheap, you can easily spend $30 for lunch—and to show off their pets. We felt sorry for the waiters. First they had to carry those large servings; the omelets must have had ten eggs in them, and many dishes were piled nearly a foot high. Then they had to cater to the customers' dogs, cats, and birds. It wasn't unusual for a server to be hailed with a request for water for a dog or cat. And it wasn't uncommon for pets to wander from table to table. Pedestrians walking by often had large dogs on leashes, and these would growl and try to get at the animals lurking under the tables. Other strollers would ooh and ah over the diners' pets, clogging foot traffic and adding further misery to the work of the waiters. One evening when our daughter was visiting we watched in amazement as a man sat down with his extended family. He had a large parrot on his shoulder, and the bird remained there the entire meal. He seldom spoke to his wife, parents, or children but kept up a running conversation with his friend, even when it pooped on his shirt.

At the end of Lincoln Road, on Alton Avenue, is a grocery store named Epicure. Here, the glitterati do their food shopping. We only bought sale items, usually day-old pastries or Italian sausages. The real fun, however, was spying on shoppers as they checked out to see how much they were paying. Prices were stratospheric, even higher than at Dean & De Luca's in Manhattan's Soho. A half-dozen small packages of meat and cheese might cost two hundred dollars. A woman checking out told us she was bringing a selection of deli items for her husband who couldn't stand the food in the hospital where he was a patient. She spent over a hundred dollars. On Thanksgiving Day we watched a woman ask the clerk in the meat department about a duck for dinner. He showed her one, a not particularly large or plump fowl. She took it without asking the price, but then remarked when she saw it that it seemed a bit expensive—$90. Haughty-looking men and women chatted breezily on their cell phones, ignoring the gracious and ever-patient cashiers who rang up the astronomical totals.

We shopped regularly at the Wild Oats market on 10th Street. We walked for a few blocks on Lincoln Road and then turned onto Meridian

Avenue. This is the prettiest street in South Beach, lined with large old shade trees. One day we stopped a dozen residents and asked each the name of the great trees. No one knew. I was surprised, but the experts at the Botanical Gardens nearby didn't know either. One person told me that they were a species of ficus tree, but she didn't know which. I found out later that they are weeping figs. Most of the trees in Florida's

Beautiful people on the beach.

cities, including these, are nonnative, the native trees having long ago been cut for commercial use or to make way for suburban subdivisions. So it is not that remarkable that no one could name the trees. There is a baseball park and playground on this street, and it was always nice to see locals playing ball with their kids—and as an old baseball player myself, it was interesting to see the game being played in winter on bright-green fields. In the park, we'd stop and watch the basketball players, often a group of young Jewish boys clad in white shirts and leather shoes, wearing the *peyos*, or sidelocks, of those studying at the nearby Orthodox school.

INEQUALITY: ACT SIX, THE JEWS

Miami Beach used to be a haven for the elderly, most notably Jews who flocked there after the Second World War, coming to retire and to die. Every Saturday after temple, we saw many orthodox jews strolling the boardwalk. I always remarked to Karen that I wondered how the strictest observers among them could bear the heavy clothing they wore, men in black suits, hats, and full beards, women in long skirts, shirts, and coats. Sometimes we saw Orthodox Jews in very un-tropical outfits sitting in chairs on the beach, their cell phones the only things reminding you that this was 2005 and not 1900. We were curious about the wire that was strung on poles along the boardwalk. A security guard told us that the wire, called an *eyruv*, marked a boundary, set by the rabbi, within which the Orthodox could do things on the Sabbath that they could not do otherwise, such as carrying objects or pushing a stroller.

Jews faced terrible discrimination in Miami Beach. There is a museum, the Jewish Museum of Florida, located in a former synagogue—it housed Miami Beach's first congregation—at 301 Washington Avenue, in a rapidly gentrifying area now known as SoFi (south of 5th Street), that traces the history of Jews in Florida. A docent at the museum told us that for many years Jews were confined to the area south of 5th Street and were denied admittance to most private clubs and vacation spots He showed us a hotel advertisement that said, "Always a view, never a Jew." Ironically, some of the island's most famous structures, including hotels, were designed by Jewish architects, sometimes without the knowledge of their financiers.

As the civil rights movement made progress, the Jewish presence in Miami Beach increased and expanded into all parts of the city. Elderly Jews (and, of course, many other retirees), filled the lovely art deco hotels along Ocean Drive and Collins Avenue. Large "Kosher" hotels lined the boardwalk, open between October and May and closed in the hot and humid summertime. Miami Beach deteriorated markedly in the 1980s, and many of the art deco edifices became more or less transient housing. Crime was rampant, and it was unsafe to be on the streets at night. However, the "Kosher" retreats continued to draw elderly Jews escaping from the harsh northern winters. Then in the 1990s, Miami Beach began a renaissance, becoming once again a favored destination for the rich. Soon the establishments that had catered to the elderly middle class were being bought by big real estate interests, and either demolished or converted into luxury accommodations. One by one the Jewish hotels came down or were closed for "renovations." When we were living in Miami Beach, there was one Kosher place left on the boardwalk. It was a curious and somehow moving sight to see the old folks sitting on their lounge chairs and swimming in the pool. The loudspeaker announced lunch and the events of the day, while in the shade, couples played cards, listening to a recorded band playing the hits of the 1930s. Toward the end of our stay, we learned that this venerable refuge would join the others and close for good at the end of the season. Maybe the guests will still come to the city, perhaps staying with their successful children, warm in the winter once again, but probably lonelier.

CALLE OCHO

The first time we stayed in Miami Beach, we were so stressed from our year in Manhattan that we never strayed more than a few miles from our apartment. So this time we were determined to explore south Florida. We had a Cuban-American friend who kept asking us if we had been to Calle Ocho, the famous main street of Miami's Little Havana. We went there, but it was a disappointment. The street is a major highway, that leads out of town eventually to the northern entrance of Everglades National Park. It was crowded and dirty, hot, and without many trees. There were small shops of various kinds but nothing very attractive. It has strong emotional significance for Cuban-Americans, but I knew too much about the history to feel this.

Cubans began migrating to Miami after the 1959 revolution that brought Fidel Castro to power. There have been several waves of immigrants from the island, but the first one, since it was dominated by those with the most resources, remains the most important. This elite was vehemently and violently opposed to Fidel and left with the aim of generating a revolt from abroad. Within a few years, they had mounted scores of terrorist attacks from their new home. The United States government itself-began to wage war against Cuba after the confiscation of some U.S. business properties and the beginning of Castro's friendship with the Soviet Union. The immigrants became fanatic supporters of the U.S. campaign, and both federal and state governments began to shower the new arrivals with money and privileges seldom accorded to exiles. As a result, Cuban-Americans soon came to dominate the economics and politics of south Florida, especially Miami.

The second and third waves consisted of not-so-well-to-do men and women. Some were at odds with the government and had spent time in its prisons, including people persecuted for their sexual orientation. But many others came for economic reasons, especially when the collapse of the Soviet Union and the end of its massive aid drove their homeland into a deep economic depression. Nearly all took great risks to leave and thousands arrived here on rafts and makeshift boats. These later arrivals, as well as the children and grandchildren of the original refugees, are not so uniformly antagonistic to Cuba, but it is fair to say that overall they are a bulwark of the most right-wing elements in U.S. politics. Any openly expressed pro-Castro or pro-détente sentiments still meet with extreme hostility, and few people are willing to risk expressing them. The furor over the return to his father of Elián Gonzalez—the child taken by his mother to Florida on a small aluminum boat in late November 1999, drifting ashore on an inner tube after the boat capsized and his mother died—gave good proof of this. As did the Miami School Board's withdrawal in 2006 of a textbook deemed too sympathetic to the revolution.

So, despite the heat of the day, Calle Ocho left me cold. Cuban-Americans have made good art, music, and literature, and they have helped regenerate the city of Miami. We found them friendly and caring. They look after their families and communities. When the city of Miami began to cut down large old-growth trees in Little Havana to make room for a pedestrian walkway, people protested so loudly that the city stopped. I was touched by a woman who said that she didn't want to lose the singing of the trees' mockingbirds (the state bird). But for the most part, Cuban-Americans have been unwilling to consider that there is anything worthwhile about the Cuban revolution. To me, their successes in the United States pale in comparison to Cuba's achievements: universal literacy, free and excellent schooling, free and exceptional health care, exemplary generosity to poor people around the world (teams of Cuban doctors abroad, free medical school to poor students around the globe, including the United States, aid to countries suffering disasters, and so forth), great advances in organic farming and medical technology, and heroic military aid that helped to end apartheid in South Africa.

Hatred of Castro has also allowed the exiles who have prospered to paper over the considerable inequality and poverty within the Cuban-American community. We read in the *Miami Herald* about brothers Pepe and Alfonso Fanjul. They own one of the world's three largest sugar-growing and refining operations, an enterprise that pollutes Lake Okeechobee and the Everglades, exploits workers, and receives enormous government subsidies. When they complained that the Cuban government had sold some of their paintings that were confiscated when they left the country, the talk was all about Castro's perfidy rather than the activities that had allowed the brothers' family to accumulate the paintings in the first place. The Fanjul family was one of the richest on the island, and its fortune was founded on sugar, which means that it was founded upon slave and near-slave labor. In 1959, here is what they owned:

> ... besides property abroad, an impressive amount in Cuba: four sugar mills, a cattle farm, a rice mill, four apartment buildings (with up to 27 apartments in some), and entire blocks and rows of houses and shops in downtown Havana. They also held stocks and shares and had large quantities of

antiques that included period French furniture, Aubusson tapestries, Chinese export porcelains, and some paintings.

Their art collection included works by Hoppner, Goya, Murillo, Michelangelo, and at least 19 sketches and paintings by Spanish Impressionist artist Joaquín Sorolla y Bastida. . . .

In 1959 the elder Fanjuls and the children owned at least 200 works of art, with a worth presently estimated to be between $20 and $60 million, enough material, when combined with their other art objects, to fully stock two museums in Havana.

When the Fanjuls left, they sold some New York properties and settled in Florida, where they reestablished their sugar business. They receive some $65 million annually in federal government subsidies for their sugar operations.

NUDE BEACH

Karen asked for something special for her birthday in late November. She wanted me to prepare a picnic lunch and then go to the "clothing optional" public beach. This is Haulover Beach, and it is located at Collins Avenue at 108th Street. I prepared a wild rice salad, bought fresh fruit, a French baguette, and a fruit tart—the latter two at the excellent La Provence French Bakery, located in the same building as our apartment (1627 Collins Avenue). We drove to the beach, about twenty minutes north, in mid-morning, paid $5 to park in the public lot, walked through a tunnel under Collins Avenue, made our way through some lush greenery, mainly sea grapes, and came out onto the beach. We set up our blankets and took off our clothes. We thought we would be nervous to do this, but we weren't. Perhaps this was because we had gotten used to seeing topless women on South Beach and around the pool at our building.

The area was uncrowded, but there were naked people all around us. After two short spells of rain, during which we took shelter, the sun came out and we had a fine time. We walked along the ocean, between the signs that demarcate the nude part of the beach, and then we enjoyed our lunch and sunbathed. At one point we had an extended conversation with a fellow nudist. It didn't seem at all peculiar that we were naked. We did wonder if residents in nearby apartment buildings ever used binoculars to spy on the unclothed bodies. They wouldn't have seen much. Many of the beachgoers seemed to be elderly Europeans, no doubt pros at this. I didn't notice any gorgeous bodies, other than Karen's. I concluded that the human body is better left clothed, at least from an aesthetic point of view. Yet there is something liberating about undressing in public. Once you do it, it seems the most natural thing in the world.

THE EVERGLADES

We visited Everglades National Park twice. The Everglades are literally a river of grass, a slow-moving sheet of water fed by rainwater and the overflow of Lake Okeechobee and covering much of south Florida. Today the natural flow of water from the lake is blocked by the Tamiami Highway (which, going east, eventually intersects Little Havana) and must be controlled by human engineering. The results have been wholly deleterious, impacting the ecological health of all of south Florida. Here is how the region was described in 1848 by Buckingham Smith of St. Augustine:

> The appearance of the Everglades is unlike that of any region of which I have ever heard, and certainly it is in some respects the most remarkable on this continent. Imagine a vast lake of fresh water extending in every direction from shore to shore beyond the reach of human vision ordinarily unruffled by a ripple on its surface, studded with thousands of islands of various sizes, from one-fourth of an acre to hundreds of acres in area, and which are generally covered with dense thickets of shrubbery and vines . . . . The surrounding waters, except in places that at first seem like channel ways (but which are

not), are covered with the tall sawgrass, shooting up its straight
and slender stem from the shallow bottom of the lake to the
height of 10 feet above the surface and covering all but a few
rods around from your view. The water is pure and limpid
and almost imperceptibly moves, not in partial currents, but,
as it seems, in a mass, silently and slowly to the southward.

Today's Everglades are wonderful to see but nothing like what
they once were. For at least one hundred years, it was believed that
they had to be drained so that the land could be farmed. This has been
partially done, so they are now much smaller. Pesticides and fertilizers
have leeched into the water and soil causing great damage to wildlife.
Huge colonies of native birds were hunted nearly to extinction for
their plumage, in wanton acts of slaughter reminiscent of the wholesale
killing of bison on the Great Plains. The same fate befell many other
animals, including panthers and wolves, of which only a few survive
today. War was declared on alligators and crocodiles—these two species
can be found in close proximity only here. Lake Okeechobee itself has
been so polluted, drained, and overfished that nothing much is left
of it that is naturally compelling. The islands in the above quote are
called hammocks. They contain many species of trees, the exact type
depending on their elevation. A foot or two can make a tremendous
difference in this flat landscape. Not only were there pine trees, there
were also hardwoods, including mahogany. These were long ago cut
down for their wood, as were most of the pines. The land has been
so altered by human destruction that weather patterns have changed,
making the Everglades drier and the land more disrupted by cycles of
fire and flood. As you drive U.S. Highway 41 (Tamiami Trail and Calle
Ocho in Miami), treeless housing tracts reach far out into what used to
be part of the Everglades. These depressed us, as did the tacky tourist
traps, advertising Indian goods, alligators, snakes, air boat rides, and
worthless trinkets.

Luckily, this special place wasn't completely destroyed. Beginning
in the 1920s and 1930s conservationists began to agitate to protect what
was left of it, and thanks to their valiant efforts, Everglades National Park

was opened in 1947. It is the only national park created especially for
ecological reasons; the land is crucial to the biological health of not just
south Florida but the world. Provided that you go in winter when the
humidity is lower and the mosquitoes won't eat you alive (in a shop
near the one hotel in the park, the Flamingo Lodge, there is a mosquito
meter, with the highest rating being "unbearable"), the Everglades are a
must-see. We first visited the southern part of the park, traveling south
from Miami to the agribusiness and military base town of Homestead
and then west to the entrance. The Everglades are not a hiker's paradise,
but there are some good trails. We took short hikes at the Royal Palms
Visitors' Center, viewing many wading birds—some catching fish—and
seeing our first alligators, most close enough to make us a little fearful.
(Karen had to warn a woman about one that seemed to be attracted to
her sub sandwich. The beast swam in tandem to her movements and
kept coming closer to shore). We saw the nation's largest mahogany tree
in a hammock, and we imagined how many of these there must have been
when the Everglades saw fewer humans. Actually, the best way to see the
park is by boat. We didn't have time to take a water tour that day. From
the Gulf Coast Visitors' Center, you can explore the Ten Thousand
Islands, once the province of Indians, pirates, and misfits, and made
famous by writer Peter Matthiessen in *Killing Mister Watson.*

Near the end of the day, we walked along Florida Bay, near the
Flamingo Lodge. We were curious to see the hotel because it was
operated by our Yellowstone employer, Amfac/Xanterra. Oddly
enough, the human resource manager for the park, who lived nearby,
had been the Lake Hotel manager when we worked there. The lodge
was the shabbiest we have seen in a national park. We guessed that my
old boss must have been demoted.

The Shark Valley Visitors' Center is at the northern end of the park.
Here we rented bicycles and took a fifteen-mile loop ride, which gives you
a good feel for the nature of the Everglades—miles of flat land, covered
in sawgrass and water. We watched an alligator scurrying through
the sawgrass, along a well-worn path made by its fellow reptiles. It is
remarkable and scary how fast these ancient creatures can run. About
halfway along the trail, we walked within three feet of a large alligator

lying on the walkway of a tower overlook. From this high vantage point, we saw scores of alligators and wading birds. We had parked our bikes near the tower, with our packed lunches in the bike baskets. When we got back to them, several large and noisy ravens had pecked into our bags and were feasting on bagels and pretzels. We rode back to the center and told a host what we had seen. Of the alligators, she said, "If you don't bother them they won't bother you." I'm not so sure.

THE ENVIRONMENT: ACT SIX, AN
ECOLOGICAL BASKET CASE

In the late 1700s Florida was a natural paradise, heavily forested, with many rivers winding their way through thick tropical foliage, many lakes, hundreds of clear springs, and, of course, the wondrous blue ocean. An early naturalist, William Bartram, traveled the northern and central parts of the state and recorded what he saw. Historian Mark Derr tells us:

> During [Bartram's] travels, he observed every type of vegetative community in the northern two-thirds of the peninsula—from scrub to longleaf pine, hardwood hammocks to bayheads, swamps to marshes, wet prairie to canebrakes, indigo plantations to feral groves of sour oranges, which the Indians roasted and ate with honey, often after cutting down the tree to permit easy harvesting. He seems to have missed the Everglades only because he didn't venture that far south. In his wanderings he identified 400 species of flowers, shrubs, trees, vines, and mosses—125 of which he had not known.

Little of what Bartram and others observed remains today. Most of the trees have been cut down; nearly all the wild animals are gone; many of the rivers and lakes have disappeared altogether, and the rest are heavily contaminated. Today, according to Derr:

> . . . the fish are edible south of Jacksonville, though over the years water quality has declined because of

the influx of industrial waste from pulp mills—half of
the state's total—power plants, and various factories;
raw sewage from towns and cities; fertilizers, pesticides,
and herbicides from agriculture and suburban lawns.
Around Jacksonville, the lower St. Johns can bear
no more human filth: Fish are deformed and cancer-
riddled, the river bottom saturated with heavy metals,
the river itself a receptacle for industrial waste.

In Miami Beach tropical breezes blow continuously. You would think
that the wind and the absence of heavy industry would cleanse the air
and make it sweet. This is not the case. The constant destruction and
erection of hotels, high-rise apartments, and office complexes puts tons
of dust, smoke, and chemicals into the air. Tens of thousands of cars,
trucks, and buses on the streets make things worse. On some days it was
impossible to breathe freely while we walked on the boardwalk because
of construction. Our apartment balcony had to be thoroughly cleaned at
least twice a day, otherwise it became covered with black soot.

The beach itself was often dirty. Visitors threw their trash on the
sand. During the college spring break season, the beach was so cluttered
with beer bottles and cans, along with cups and fast food wrappers, that
it was difficult to take a step without trampling on something. There
were days when I was ashamed to be among my inconsiderate and
destructive fellow humans. We asked a lifeguard why no one ever tried
to stop the littering. He said that, while he was disgusted with it, he
was afraid to confront anyone for fear of being stabbed or otherwise
physically assaulted. Even had he wanted to, however, the lifeguard
couldn't have done anything about the tar balls of oil that periodically
washed up on the beach and which we stepped on and tracked into our
apartment.

We always got excited when we heard a bird singing in the trees
along the boardwalk. But this was because there were so few of them.
There were gulls and pelicans near the water and on the beach, and
these provided a constant source of amusement. Gulls are like human
beings in capitalist society—they steal food from each other's mouths.

We watched a very large gull guarding food on the beach from a small horde of competitors. Another gull served as its flunky, keeping the others away while the dominant gull ate. There were also flocks of squawking green parrots in the trees along Lincoln Road. But for a tropical paradise there were precious few birds. Too many humans, too much pollution, too much noise, too much light, not enough trees, in a word, too much development, kept them away.

You get the feeling in Florida that you are living through an environmental catastrophe, one that is only going to get worse as people keep coming and industry and real estate developers rule the political roost.

KEY WEST

The drive from Miami Beach to Key West takes about four hours. The traffic can be daunting (signs along the way spell out warnings for frustrated drivers: BE—PATIENT—YOU—WILL—BE—ABLE—TO—PASS—IN—TWO—MILES), but if you leave in early morning and the day is sunny, you will be rewarded with fewer travelers and spectacular views of the ocean on your left and the gulf on you right. The highway, completed in 1938, winds it way through Key Largo, Islamorada, Long Key, and several smaller Keys (a key is a low island or reef). On Big Pine Key, we saw signs warning us to watch out for the rare and endangered key deer. I was nervous on the seven-mile bridge that begins at Marathon; three times we saw cars passing other vehicles, leaving oncoming traffic with nowhere to go. Alongside the bridge are the remnants of a railroad span and tracks destroyed by a hurricane in 1935 and never rebuilt.

The railroad was built by Henry Flagler, partner with John D. Rockefeller in the Standard Oil Company, and Florida's most famous entrepreneur. Already by the end of the nineteenth century, rich Northerners were coming to Florida to vacation and to recuperate from illnesses. Flagler saw dollar signs in these well-to-do travelers, and he began building a real estate empire in the Sunshine State. His great wealth and power, along with his ruthlessness, business brilliance, and belief that he was doing God's work, helped him to bully the state's politicians into giving him millions of acres of public lands for building railroads and draining swamps. He then parlayed this property into a remarkable collection of luxury hotels and tens of millions of dollars in land and home sales. His money literally built the cities of Palm Beach, Fort Lauderdale, and Miami.

As Henry Flagler expanded his Florida empire, he moved steadily south, laying tracks along the way. When he got to the southern end of the state, he decided to make his boldest move, a railroad over the Atlantic Ocean and Gulf of Mexico and through the Florida Keys to the southernmost part of the then United States—Key West. He built it with semi-slave labor; in 1907 his company had to defend itself against indictments for forced labor. Those indicted beat the charges, but working conditions were abominable. As the work progressed, it wreaked devastation throughout the Keys, ripping out hardwoods and starting fires in the peat-like soil with sparks from the train engines. The railroad encouraged settlers (prior to it, the Keys were inhabited only by a few loners), and the farms and plantations they established further weakened the fragile ecosystem. Flagler's great work was completed in 1912, not long before he died. He missed the great hurricane.

90 miles from Cuba in Key West, Florida.

Key West is a great place to visit, though the quirky charm of its Old Town is fast disappearing as those with too much disposable income buy houses from the locals at astronomical prices. We saw houses best described as shacks going for more than one million dollars. Longtime residents find these prices hard to resist no matter how much they might like the easygoing life of the city. Key West is a mecca for gay men and women; the city is famous for its gay scene. But within the gay community, there is now a growing split between rich newcomers, typically more conservative and less flamboyant, and poorer locals who have lived in Key West for a long time. Like everywhere else, the rich are winning, and it won't be long before most of the poorer folks, including those who for years have been living rent-free on small boats, are forced to leave. We rented bikes from a small bike repair shop—bicycles are ubiquitous and the best way to see the island—owned by a young man and his father. The son moved to Key West a few years ago, and his father followed after his retirement from a Pittsburgh steel mill. They were nice people, and they were happy to meet two people from "da burgh." We rented bikes for six dollars apiece for the entire day. I wonder how long they'll be able to live in the new "higher class" Key West.

Tourism is the main industry. The weather is beautiful most of the year. There are many motels and guest houses, bars, good restaurants, gift shops, and beaches, although visitors are surprised to realize that Key West isn't like Miami Beach or any of Florida's renowned beach towns. Most of the shoreline is rock; the only wide sand beach is Smathers Beach, and this is human-made. There is a narrow one at the Fort Zachary Taylor Historic Site, which also has a hiking trail and picnic areas. President Harry Truman's vacation "White House" is in a beautiful set of tree-lined blocks. There is a decent museum. When we visited, there was an interesting exhibit linking the works of Ernest Hemingway—once the island's most famous resident, his house is now a museum—and photographer Walker Evans. Both artists are great role models for writers and photographers, though Hemingway got caught up in the fame machine, as have so many modern male artists: a larger-than-life personality, a macho persona, a feeling that social norms don't apply to them, all whipped up by the media into the iconic individualistic artist whose life is thought to be as interesting as his art.

Every evening, hundreds of people gather at Mallory Square, along the old waterfront, to watch the sunset: "the sun sets and the fun begins." The sunsets are often sensational, and all around the square entertainers put on shows for the crowd. There are jugglers, animal acts, acrobats, magic shows, arts and crafts, and food. Members of the audience are often asked to participate, which adds to the fun. One fellow balances enormous loads of everyday objects on various parts of his body. I had my back to him one night when he was preparing to balance a shopping cart on his forehead. While he was building up to his finale, he was juggling balls and one of them hit me hard in the head. I wanted to throw it in the harbor, but he was a muscular fellow, and well, what the hell, he was just making a living. The one thing that mars the festivities on the square is the presence of gigantic cruise ships, which park in the harbor while their vacationers disembark for a few hours of shopping and dining. They often block good views of the setting sun, and the entertainers sometimes have to operate in their shadows, which is not good for business.

WORK: ACT FIVE, SUNNY WEATHER, GLOOMY LABOR

At Government Cut, it was exciting to watch the huge container and cruise ships enter and leave the harbor. The container boats delivered cargo to the port at Miami and carried goods out to the far corners of the earth. The cruise vessels took tourists to exotic places or out on the ocean a few miles to gamble legally. The travelers waved to the people on the pier, and at night the ships looked like decorated mansions as they made their way out to sea. However, underlying this tranquil scene was a reality of harsh and dangerous labor. The work of loading and unloading the container ships has been radically transformed by technological change. No longer do skilled and strong stevedores pack and unpack the cargo holds, instead, large cranes do the work, placing on board loaded containers that are the size and shape of truck trailers and railroad cars, already loaded. When the containers are unloaded, they can be attached directly onto trains and trucks for delivery. Thousands of longshore workers have been displaced by the new technology, but at least many of them were represented by unions, which were able to negotiate income guarantees for those no longer needed. In the big ports of the United States, there are workers who get a good yearly income whether they work or not. Unfortunately, the unions have also agreed to a tiered system of work classification, so that most port employees are still the exploited casual workers they were in the 1930s before there were unions on the waterfront.

Work on the cruise ships is another matter. These ships usually register in countries such as Liberia and are therefore immune to U.S. labor law. The employees who do the most onerous work are invariably people of color, typically from poor countries. Their pay is low and their hours are long. If they get severely injured on the job and need hospital attention, they are often forced to fly back to their home countries, even if better care is available in the United States. One worker from a Caribbean nation slipped on a kitchen floor while carrying a large pot of oil. The oil severely burned his leg and foot. He was discharged from the hospital in Anchorage, Alaska, and forced to take a flight home, with several stopovers. He was in excruciating pain. At a layover in Miami, he called his mother in desperation, and she told him to contact a lawyer she knew through a friend. The attorney managed to get him care in Miami and then sued the cruise line. The company retaliated by contacting the immigration authorities who promptly deported him.

Labor in Florida has an inglorious history: plantation slave labor in the Panhandle region and prison labor, overwhelmingly black (often put in prison on vagrancy charges, the vagrancy laws being aimed at taking away the freedom of former slaves), leased to private companies in the turpentine camps. Here is how Mark Derr describes labor in the camps early in the twetieth century:

> In the turpentine camps, work was performed at a trot from dawn to dusk. Each man was expected to box—cut a square and affix a collector into which the sap would run—sixty to ninety trees a day. Armed guards watched over the prisoners,

who at night were chained into their beds and by day were manacled. Convicts who collapsed during the week were seldom given any but rudimentary treatment: There were no doctors in the woods. Punishment for anything a guard or captain considered offensive ranged from floggings to consignment to a sweatbox—a lightless, unventilated trap. Camp captains and guards employed a torture method called "watering" in which water was forced through a tube into a prisoner's stomach. Some convicts had permanently distended thumbs from being hung just off the ground by rope tied to their thumbs. Food—pork fat, corn, beans, and often no more than sweet potatoes—provided scant nourishment. Women in the camps were at the mercy of guards, trustees, and every other male around. Every prisoner suffered from malnutrition, filth, vermin, and abuse—whether working in a turpentine camp, on a farm, in a phosphate mine, or on a railroad. The convict-lease system was common throughout the South, but Florida's was particularly inhumane, as witnessed in the title it earned for the peninsula—the American Siberia.

How has the state repaid black workers for these past heinous crimes? With continuous discrimination: locking them in crime-ridden urban ghettoes like Miami's Liberty City, subjecting them to police brutality, discriminating against them in employment, denying them the right to vote after they get out of prison, and trying to prevent them from voting even when they have the legal right to do so. What might have happened to black people if the Radical Reconstruction legitimately imposed on the South after the Civil War had not ended in the inglorious deal of 1877, when to win a contested presidential election the Republican Party agreed to remove federal troops, ending any chance for black political equality? What might be the case today if blacks had been offered the same aid given to the Cubans who came to Florida after 1959? What if the land given away to rich "entrepreneurs" like Flagler had been given to the former slaves?

Work in Miami Beach is like work in almost any "service" economy. The poor serve the rich. Unions are rare. However, there is no reason why Miami Beach cannot be organized like Las Vegas. In the state there have been some hopeful signs. The custodians at the University of Miami organized a successful strike in early 2006. And farm workers at Immokalee, southwest of Lake Okeechobee, won a significant victory with a boycott of Taco Bell, the main buyer of the tomatoes the workers harvest.

Key West wasn't always a tourist town. We were surprised to learn that for much of the nineteenth century it was one of the richest cities in the United States. Early fortunes were made by salvagers, selling goods taken from the many ships that sank in the unforgiving waters off the coast. Key West was also an international center of cigar production, with craftsmen from Cuba making world-renowned smokes. Sponge production was another lucrative industry. In the early twentieth century the city's fortunes turned downward as lighthouses and steamships meant fewer wrecks, as the cigar industry fled labor unrest and moved to the mainland, and as the sponge beds were exhausted. Even Flagler's railroad failed to reverse Key West's economic fortunes. The city went bankrupt during the Great Depression, but things got better as New Deal aid, the opening of the highway from the mainland, and the infusion of federal money during the Second World War paved the way for renewed prosperity. Today, if anything, there is too much prosperity, as the wealthy make Key West another unwelcome destination for the less well-off.

CASINO

When our daughter visited in February, she wanted to go to a casino. We took her to the Seminole Hard Rock Casino near the town of Hollywood, north of Miami. Hollywood is another town cut out of the mangrove swamps of the southern Florida coast. There is a long narrow beach and a paved boardwalk, though both are a good distance from the downtown. Hollywood is a poor man's Miami Beach and the Florida destination of choice for French Canadians, who come in droves. We saw French cafés and diners, with menus in English and French, and middle-aged men with large bellies and skimpy European bathing suits sunbathing, riding bicycles, having picnics with their families, playing handball on outdoor courts, and just enjoying themselves.

The casino is in a large complex of retail stores, restaurants, hotel, concert hall, and parking lots. Everything is connected by an outside promenade. Compared to some Indian casinos we have seen, it is reasonably attractive, with trees, flowers, and an artificial lake. We planned to give the casino a quick look and then spend a couple of hours in the sunshine while our daughter played the slots. We picked a meeting place and told her we'd be there in two hours.

This casino is owned by the Seminole Indians and is supposed to bring money and employment to a tribe now suffering extreme poverty and its attendant evils: poor health, disease, crime, drugs, and early death. Gambling does generate a good deal of revenue; the American appetite for wagering seems to know no bounds. But whether the casinos are the economic and social salvation of Indians is another matter. Tribal government is often corrupt and dominated by a few families well connected with the Bureau of Indian Affairs (BIA). Unless it is made more democratic by grassroots organizing, casino monies are bound to flow mainly to the top and the majority will not benefit much. We do know that where there are casinos, there is crime (organized rackets, robberies, and thefts); there is chronic gambling by those who cannot afford it; and there is bankruptcy. In purely economic terms, it is not obvious that the benefits are greater than the costs, the increase in employment notwithstanding. According to unpublished research done by my friend Jim Craven, Blackfoot Indian and activist:

> From every gross profit casino dollar (keep in mind that non-Indians control the accounting as well as supplies of inputs— vertical integration—at inflated prices thus making paper profits appear smaller than they actually are) subtract 51 cents for "investors" (Bally, Harrah's, etc., all non-Indian), leaving

49 cents. Then subtract 31 cents (consultants, licensing, taxes, lawyers etc., all non-Indian), leaving 18 cents. Then subtract 5 cents (BIA/DIA "holding, transactions and other fees"), leaving 13 cents. Then subtract 5 cents (skimming by BIA/DIA or "Vichy" Indians on the Tribal Councils), leaving around 8 cents of every gross profit dollar for per capita distributions and tribal "programs," often themselves dominated by the traitors and their families.

And it is certainly not clear that whatever economic gains there might be can negate the assault that casinos must inevitably make upon the values and beliefs of so many Indians. It is surely ironic that the political sovereignty enjoyed by Indian tribes has allowed them to embrace the gaming industry. It would be a kind of rough justice if Indian communities could take money from the people who killed their ancestors and stole their land and distribute this money in such a way that Indian communities could thrive. But that is a big *if*.

We had been walking around the casino for five minutes when we saw our daughter motioning us to come over to where she was playing the slots. The light above her machine was whirring and flashing. She had won a large jackpot. We waited until the paperwork was done and the check was cut. Then we left and went back to South Beach.

EXIT NORTH

Although we knew our lease expired at the end of April, we had no destination in mind. We were going to make another long road trip, in a generally western direction, and had bought all the supplies we would need, but we couldn't agree upon an itinerary. For the first time since my retirement, we had no specific place to go. We were both uneasy.

But as often happened in our unstructured lives, a chance event— this time, a phone call—focused our decision. Two days before we left, I got a call from Los Angeles asking me to appear on public television's Tavis Smiley talk show. The caller told me that the program would air in a few days and we could tape an interview in Miami. When I informed her that we were leaving before this would be possible, she said that we could tape it in any city where they had an agreement with a studio. I didn't think we could manage this on such short notice, but I told her we'd consult a map and call back. We looked in our atlas and saw that Gainesville and Tallahassee were possibilities. We settled on the latter (Gainesville was too close) and phoned the contact person. She said Tallahassee would be fine. I wrote down the address, time, and phone number. Once this was settled, we were off and running. Karen had once taken a trip to New Orleans and along the Gulf Coast. Every time she talked about it, I wanted to do the same thing. So we decided to drive north and west through Florida, then ride leisurely along the Gulf coast, stopping in Mobile and New Orleans, on our way to Big Bend National Park in southwest Texas. Back to the West!

SUGGESTED READING

An excellent and readable account of Florida history, from which I have liberally quoted in this chapter, is Mark Derr, *Some Kind of Paradise: A Chronicle of Man and the Land in Florida* (Gainesville, FL: University Press of Florida, 1998). On Cubans in Florida, see Maria Cristina Garcia, *Havana USA: Cuban Exiles and Cuban Americans in South Florida* (Berkeley, CA: University of California Press, 1996). Some good insights into the Cuban-American experience can be found in David Rieff's *Going to Miami: Exiles, Tourists and Refugees in the New America* (Gainesville, FL: University Press of Florida, 1999). Many novels are set in Florida. An exceptional one, set in the Ten Thousand Islands of the southwest coast, is Peter Matthiessen, *Killing Mister Watson* (New York, NY: Vintage, 1991). Check out any novel by longtime Florida resident and *Miami Herald* columnist Carl Hiassen. Also Elmore Leonard, *Get Shorty* (New York, NY: Harper Torch, 2002). A list of terrorist acts against Cuba can be found at *http://www.letcubalive.org/TERRFACT. htm*. The information on cruise ship workers is from "Screwed If by Sea: Cruise Lines Throw Workers Overboard When It Comes to Providing Urgent Medical Care," by Forrest Norman in the *Miami New Times*, available at *http://www.miaminewtimes.com/issues/2004-*

11-11/news/feature.html. On the 1926 real estate bubble see John Kenneth Galbraith, *The Great Crash* (Boston, MA: Houghton Mifflin, 1988).

CHAPTER SEVEN

CHEAP MOTELS AND A HOT PLATE II

TALLAHASSEE, FLORIDA

Population in 2003 153,938
Population in 2000
    White 60.4%
    Black 34.2%
    Asian 2.4%
    Hispanic (all races) 4.2%

Median household income in 2000 .... $30,571
Median rent in 2000 .... $490
Median mortgage, including associated costs $990
People below poverty level of income 20%

A good view of the city can be seen from the observation deck of the New Capitol at Pensacola and Duval Streets, (850) 488-6167. The Old Capitol at 400 South Monroe Street is a museum, worth a visit, (850) 487-1902. We learned that there had been a slave market nearby.

MOBILE, ALABAMA

Population in 2003 193,464
Population in 2000
    White 50.4%

Black 46.3%
Asian 1.5%
Hispanic (all races) 1.4%

Median household income in 2000 .... $31,445
Median rent in 2000 .... $384
Median mortgage, including associated costs $790
People below poverty level of income 21.2%

Get a map at the Visitors' Center, 150 South Royal Street, (251) 208-7658, and walk around. The volunteers there are friendly and helpful. The Dauphin Street Historic District contains some architecturally interesting homes and buildings.

VAN HORN, TEXAS

Population in 2003 2,271
Population in 2000
    White 64.6%
    Black 0.7%
    Some other race (that's what census respondents said) 31.5%
    Hispanic (all races) 78.6%

Median household income in 2000 .... $24,432
Median rent in 2000 .... $226
Median mortgage, including associated costs $574
People below poverty level of income 28.7%

This bleak west Texas outpost was created because it had water, at the Van Horn Wells, twelve miles south of town. It is the setting for the fine but unpublicized film *The Three Burials of Melchiades Estrada* (probably because it shows the INS in a brutal light). We enjoyed the conversation we had with a clerk at the Motel 6: 1805 North Broadway, (432) 283-2992. For some reason, the extraordinarily uncomfortable bed and the chirping birds had us laughing hysterically at three in the morning.

JOPLIN, MISSOURI

Population in 2003 46,373
Population in 2000
    White 91.4%
    Black 2.7%
    American Indian 1.5%
    Hispanic (all races) 2.5%

Median household income in 2000 .... $30,555
Median rent in 2000 .... $359
Median mortgage, including associated costs $649
People below poverty level of income 18.8%

The Joplin Museum Complex is at 7th Street (Old Route 66—Joplin is mentioned in Nat King Cole's "Get Your Kicks on Route 66") and North Schifferdecker Avenue, (417) 623-1180. A must-visit site is the George Washington Carver National Monument, about twenty miles southeast of Joplin. Visit the monument's website at *http://www.nps.gov/gwca*.

THE GULF COAST

We left Miami Beach on May 1, 2005. We thought that the drive on Interstate 95 would be safer on a Sunday, but we were wrong. Soon after we crossed the causeway and entered the freeway, I noticed a moving van in front of us. I said to Karen, "Look, that van's rear door is open." Just as I finished, a large metal dolly flew out onto the highway, passed close to our bumper, and skidded across the lanes to our right. We came to a stop amidst six lanes of cars and trucks. Mercifully we weren't rear-ended, but we had to reenter traffic with cars swerving all around us.

We proceeded north to Fort Pierce and then went northwest on the Florida Turnpike toward Orlando. I have never been to Disney World, but Karen took our children once, while staying with my uncle and aunt, who lived in nearby Leesburg. Karen hated it, and the kids didn't like it either. They do still talk about the cheap yellow Mickey Mouse rain slickers thousands of visitors donned when it showered. Walt Disney bought much of the land in secret to keep prices from rising. His company transformed the landscape, making it even less like it had been before Disney's progenitors, especially Flagler, had put Florida on its path to dream-land. We noticed a change in the terrain around Orlando; there were trees and hills, and the soil was no longer sandy. Large horse farms were visible from the highway, especially near Ocala, a famous horse-breeding area. We were beginning to relax, away from the hectic traffic of I-95, when a tire retread blew off the car in front of us, hitting our front window.

The Florida Panhandle extends so far west that part of it is in the central time zone. We drove through its pine woods on our way to Tallahassee, and my interview with Tavis Smiley. We spent two days in the state capital, an attractive but dull city, unless you are a lobbyist. We were most impressed by the tree cover, so dense that it was impossible to pick out individual houses from the deck atop the new courthouse building. On a road leading into the city from our motel, there were the usual strip malls and big-box stores, but they were hidden from view by the trees growing along the highway. It was a little more difficult to find a store, but the beauty of the oak trees made it worth the extra effort. Thousands of other towns and cities could take a lesson from Tallahassee.

The small media company we did the taping in was hard to locate, and I was almost late. I arrived sweating, but everything went smoothly. Tavis Smiley interviewed me about the relevance of labor unions. He is one of the few liberal talk show hosts on television. I was impressed by his knowledge and sophistication. It was amusing that I disparaged Wal Mart's hostility to unions, only to hear that the company was one of the program's sponsors. Mr. Smiley's show was one that a Bush administration lackey, chairman of the Corporation for Public Broadcasting, Kenneth Tomlinson, had monitored for political bias. I did my best to give the spies something to get upset about.

From Tallahassee we drove south to Wakulla Springs, one of Florida's largest. The waters were too turbid to take a planned boat ride so we pressed on along U.S. 98, which hugs the Gulf of Mexico. We admired the graceful old houses in the former cotton port town of Apalachicola, walked through the nondescript village of Port St. Joe, and were settling in for a long pleasant drive by the water. Unfortunately, from Panama City (one of the state's "spring break" favorites) to Pensacola, more than a hundred miles, we got another look at Florida development run amok. As we sat hot and frustrated in endless traffic jams, we observed countless strip malls, condominiums blocking the view of the water, and houses on stilts, some destroyed by recent hurricanes and the rest cannon fodder for future storms. Everything seemed built pell-mell and on the cheap, lining the pockets of the developers and realtors while fleecing the buyers. Communities and the natural habitat sacked and pillaged so that "second-homers" could have a place to winter.

We searched for an hour for a state park, designated on our map, to have lunch. To get to it, we drove through miles of "planned" communities, towns laid out in pristine Disney fashion, with overlarge houses and "Mayberry" downtowns. The most famous example of the "new urbanism" (a euphemism for a pseudo-sophisticated and make-believe version of small-town America, complete with large front porches and carless streets) is Seaside, located south of U.S. 98, between Panama City and Ft. Walton Beach. Even small one-bedroom condominiums—less than 1,000 square feet of space—sell for nearly a million dollars, not much different than in Manhattan. Few people live year-round in Seaside (and few nonwhites live there ever), and some owners rent their properties to vacationers, at several hundred dollars per night and up. A man in Mobile, Alabama, later told us that a friend had been offered a long weekend in a Seaside apartment free if he paid the cleaning fee. The friend happily agreed, only to be gouged by a four-hundred-dollar charge. Perhaps the best way to convey to readers the bland, totalitarian feel of Seaside is to tell you that it was the setting for the movie *The Truman Show*. Even worse was the nearby community of Watercolor, where the houses were still larger, the traffic worse, the milieu more artificial, and the street names and houses color-themed. Every street was private, so we didn't stop to look around. People obviously wanted to have homes here—housing prices rise significantly every year—but we couldn't imagine why.

After Pensacola, we returned to Interstate 10 and drove to Mobile,

Alabama. We visited before Hurricane Katrina, but the city still had a down-at-the-heels look, the exceptional setting at the top of Mobile Bay notwithstanding. Friendly people and some pretty houses couldn't compensate for a lifeless central city and a declining economic base. At the Visitors' Center, we met two men who gave us good advice on what to see in the surrounding area. On their recommendations, we decided to drive south on each side of the bay. The eastern border of Mobile Bay is both more tree-covered and prosperous than the barren and industrial western perimeter. On the east side we spent a few pleasant hours walking around Fairhope, a picture-postcard village that attracts writers and artists. We backtracked to Mobile and drove on the west side of the bay all the way to Dauphin Island. There was sand everywhere, and then we learned that the western half of this barrier island was off-limits, demolished by the previous year's hurricanes. Construction vehicles hurried along the makeshift road, delivering materials for home and business rebuilding. Millions of dollars were spent, all of it wasted when the island was nearly obliterated months later by Hurricane Katrina. Yet again plans are in the works and money is being spent for reconstruction. Hundreds of millions of dollars will be needed, most of it from taxpayers. Fewer than two thousand people, mostly affluent second-home owners, will benefit. Perhaps Dauphin Island should be left to its own devices, allowed to return to nature, accessible only by boat and unspoiled by houses. As we drove toward the bridge connecting the island to the mainland, we saw a remarkable sight: a group of buildings two stories tall but barely ten feet wide. They were advertised for sale as "condoMINimums." Only in the United States!

We wound our way northwest toward U.S. 90, stopping in the small fishing village of Bayou La Batre. This town was revitalized—if such a word can be used in this backwoods part of Alabama—by an influx of Vietnamese refugees after the Vietnam War. We admired the fishing fleet, many with names in Vietnamese. Refugees allied with the United States and forced to flee their homeland when U.S. forces were defeated by Ho Chi Minh's army and the National Liberation Front found homes along the Gulf Coast, where they could ply their maritime trades. About a third of the town's residents were Vietnamese. Ironically, the newcomers met with racist violence from the white fishermen who had been so patriotic during the war. But by the time we visited, the Vietnamese had proven their mettle and were making a living fishing for oysters and shrimp. Bayou La Batre was another casualty of Katrina, and it is a long way from recovery. There are many fishing boats still caught in trees close to town. A recent *New York Times* (June 7, 2006) article said that "About two dozen shrimp vessels, some of them 80 feet long and weighing more than 100 tons, list in suspended state amid scrub oak and pine, many yards from the bayou where they belong. Removed from the blue and shoved into the green, their white masts and rigging rise like bleached treetops in a forest." Before Katrina, the poverty rate was nearly 30 percent; it must be a good deal higher now. Public money will be slow to come to poor towns like Bayou La Batre. Not enough second homes and tourists. Not enough money to be made.

Once on U.S. 90, we quickly exited Alabama and entered Mississippi. The Mississippi Gulf Coast is less than one hundred miles in length, but there are interesting places to see. After getting some supplies at a store in Pascagoula, we went to Ocean Springs. This friendly bed-and-breakfast town, with its fine beach and large semi-tropical trees, was also battered by Katrina. Karen asked a clerk in a bakery how long it takes to get to Biloxi. She looked at her quizzically and said, "Oh, it's just across the bridge." That bridge was destroyed by the great storm surges. All along the Mississippi Gulf Coast, the destruction was severe—about half the housing stock was destroyed—and recovery efforts have progressed slowly. The poorer the area to begin with, the less the progress. The profit-generating casinos lining the Gulf side of U.S. 90 in Biloxi—the highway was four-laned through the city, and we couldn't figure out how people crossed over to the beaches—were demolished, but they are rapidly being rebuilt. Nearby, poor communities like Pass Christian and Bay Saint Louis have been shortchanged. We thought that Biloxi was a pitiful sight before Katrina: stately homes, many run-down and across the highway from monstrous-looking casinos, befouled and empty beaches overlooking the brown waters of the Gulf and in sight of oil refineries in Gulfport, and a mess of traffic. I have read reports of widespread drunk-driving and accidents following nights of gambling and drinking, but the recovery plan for Biloxi emphasizes more casino building. Not much room for housing it seems. The night before we arrived in New Orleans, we stayed at a Day's Inn in Slidell, Louisiana. Another town no longer intact. That motel is still closed.

NEW ORLEANS

Like Manhattan, New Orleans is a city shrouded in myth. The Big Easy. A racial gumbo. King Oliver and Louis Armstrong and a hundred other jazz giants. Mardi Gras. Ghosts in the French Quarter. Even Bob Dylan got carried away there:

> New Orleans, unlike a lot of those places you go back to and that don't have the magic anymore, still has got it. Night can swallow you up, yet none of it touches you. Around any corner, there's a promise of something daring and ideal and things are just getting going. There's something obscenely joyful behind every door, either that or somebody crying with their head in their hands. A lazy rhythm looms in the dreamy air and the atmosphere pulsates with bygone duels, past-life romance, comrades requesting comrades to aid them in some way. You can't see it, but you know it's here. Somebody is always sinking. Everyone seems to be from some very old Southern families. Either that or a foreigner. I like the way it is. There are a lot of places I like, but I like New Orleans better.

I had never been to New Orleans, so I was excited when we got downtown and checked into our hotel. Karen visited once; one of her sisters lived in Gretna, married to a man who later won the Nobel Prize in medicine. (When Karen was in the eighth grade, he designed a clay heart for her science project.) She told me about crossing Lake Pontchartrain by rail, the water lapping at the narrow track bed. We checked into a room with a view of the Mississippi River and began a whirlwind two-day visit. The weather was mercifully cool and not too humid, unusual for May.

We did all the expected things. We walked the streets of the French Quarter, admiring the architecture, the cool hidden courtyards, and the hanging flower baskets on the iron-railed balconies. We had beignets at Café du Monde and gumbo at a small market stall. We took the streetcar far out St. Charles Street, past Loyola and Tulane universities, and gawked at the mansions lining both sides of the street. We took a free boat ride across the Mississippi. On our second night I stopped in a casino by the river and within ten minutes I won $250 playing a video poker machine. Who said New Orleans isn't a great town? In Jackson Square we saw a tarot card reader, and Karen said, "I recognize that guy." We went over to his table, and he told us that he had just come from Lincoln Road. He spent half the year in New Orleans and half in South Beach. Later, a gregarious panhandler gave us some Mardi Gras beads. We still have these; when we look at them we hope he survived the great hurricane.

New Orleans's streets will never be mistaken for those of Portland. They were dirty and trash-filled. Portland has its share of "adult" stores, but nothing to compare with the open pandering by scantily clad women on Bourbon Street. This street was filled with drunken men and women imbibing openly on the street—allowed by law—at six in the evening.

Pre-Katrina New Orleans.

I doubt any of them were locals, just tourists acting as if they were getting an authentic New Orleans experience. The residents we did speak to decried the rapid conversion of the French Quarter into a Disney-like attraction.

The people on the streets looked poor, and they were. Overwhelmingly they were black. Sociologists Kristin Lavelle and Joe Feagin tell us that:

> Two-thirds of pre-Katrina New Orleans was black, while just 28 percent was white. It was the sixth-poorest large U.S. city, with more than one in four residents living below the official poverty line. Four in ten black families were in poverty, the highest rate for black urbanites nationwide. Graver still was the fact that the majority of the poor scraped by on incomes of less than half of the official poverty level.

Sixty percent of poor blacks were without cars, compared to 17 percent of poor whites. The school system was irreparably harmed by the white flight that occurred after school desegregation; this exodus reduced the tax base and meant the gradual de-funding of the public schools. Before the hurricane, New Orleans's schools were among the worst in the nation. The dropout rate for black ninth graders was over 50 percent. Cheated out of a decent education and condemned to low-wage service sector jobs, many black men ended up in the infamous Angola prison. This is not to say that every poor person was black. There were plenty of poor whites there too. But black labor built New Orleans, and more than once, beginning when the city was the major slave market in the United States.

We were in Flagstaff, Arizona when Hurricane Katrina hit shore, on Monday, August 29. Like everyone else we watched in horror as the city flooded, people perished, and the U.S. government, along with state and local leaders, let a major American city die. As often happens, a catastrophe exposed the fault lines in a society's social structure. In New Orleans it was possible to see the racist, class-biased, corrupt, and ecologically insane core of the United States. Even Fox News reporters were shocked by what they witnessed and were forced to allow a bit of truth to leak into their propaganda machine. New Orleans was a city completely unprepared, with no evacuation plan, despite knowing full well that most poor residents would not be able to evacuate without help. Buses and trains idled when they could have taken people out of danger. Long lines of poor people were herded into the Superdome and other facilities and then left to their own devices. Prisoners, patients in hospitals, and elderly in nursing homes, were all stuck in their cells, beds, and wheelchairs while the waters rose. Desperate people were trapped in attics and on rooftops, abandoned to die. Black refugees trying to escape across the bridge to Gretna were met by police who threatened to shoot them. Police looted and terrorized flood victims. The callousness of President Bush (out west schmoozing with the rich party faithful and vacationing in Texas the day before all hell broke loose); Bush's mother, Barbara (who said that the people stuck in the Superdome were now better off than they had been before the hurricane hit); FEMA and Homeland Security directors Michael Brown and Michael Chertoff (telling more lies than Pinocchio; Chertoff saying, as we were watching it on television, that the horrific scenes at the Superdome were "rumors and anecdotes"); Vice President Cheney (mansion hunting); Condoleeza Rice (shopping for shoes in Manhattan); Mayor Nagin (whose idea of a plan was to say that people needed to get to higher ground and wait to be rescued); and a host of other minor and major characters behaving badly and murderously, were evident for all the world to see.

The aftermath of Katrina has been a litany of horrors. Toxic chemicals were everywhere. Hundreds of thousands of mainly poor and black residents were dispersed around the country and have little hope of return. Fifty-three percent of black residents lost everything in the hurricane. We have learned that the government knew that New Orleans was ripe for a catastrophe, yet it had cut crucial funding that would have made this less likely and appointed political hacks to run critical agencies. We have found out that decades of catering to the rich and big business had made New Orleans an ecological nightmare in the making. We have discovered that the ill-conceived flood prevention projects of the Army Corps of Engineers weren't even executed properly in the first place. We saw the right-wingers barely able to conceal their glee as they handed out misinformation on what happened and began preparing to implement policies that will complete the process of making New Orleans a whiter city built exclusively on tourism. As Mike Davis put it, "The ultimate goal seems to be a tourist theme-park New Orleans, Las Vegas on the Mississippi, with chronic poverty hidden away in bayous, trailer parks and prisons outside the city limits."

Today, more than a year later, thousands of people are living in small and flimsy FEMA trailers and in their cars. All along the Gulf Coast there are trailer ghettoes; some are calling them "Hoovervilles," after the makeshift slums built by the poor during the Great Depression. Tens of thousands are still living far away from their homes. The government (at all levels) doesn't want them back and will not provide the money for them to return. Billions of reconstruction dollars will go to well-connected contractors (former public officials guilty of gross dereliction of duty are being employed as lobbyists for these companies or starting their own consulting firms). Already two billion dollars have been wasted or stolen. New Orleans has always had a well-deserved reputation for public corruption; it will only get worse as the money available increases.

Foreign countries were quick to offer aid to the United States. Apparently, Canadian help arrived before that of the U.S. military. Among the nations offering aid were Venezuela and Cuba. Both were turned down. It is a pity that Cuban aid was refused. Cuba has an exemplary record of dealing with severe hurricanes. As Marjorie Cohn put it:

> Last September, a Category 5 hurricane battered the small island of Cuba with 160-mile-per-hour winds. More than 1.5 million Cubans were evacuated to higher ground ahead of the storm. Although the hurricane destroyed 20,000 houses, no one died.
>
> What is Cuban President Fidel Castro's secret? According to Dr. Nelson Valdes, a sociology professor at the University

of New Mexico, and specialist in Latin America, "the whole
civil defense is embedded in the community to begin with.
People know ahead of time where they are to go." . . .

After Hurricane Ivan, the United Nations International
Secretariat for Disaster Reduction cited Cuba as a model
for hurricane preparation. ISDR director Salvano Briceno
said, "The Cuban way could easily be applied to other
countries with similar economic conditions and even in
countries with greater resources that do not manage to
protect their population as well as Cuba does."

But, alas, Cuba is a "terrorist" nation.

I had always harbored a fear of being in the deep South: the murders
of the civil rights martyrs, the lynchings, and the gross brutality shown
not just to black people but to union organizers and anyone else who
threatened the society's racist underpinnings. Maybe it was too many
viewings of *Easy Rider*. But these are modern times. No more Senators
Bilbo and Eastland—now we have Trent Lott and Haley Barbour, and
pro-business and white-friendly black politicians like New Orleans
Mayor Ray Nagin. No more Jim Crow—now we just superimpose
the "free market" on extraordinarily unequal and racially skewed
distributions of income and wealth and let it work its magic. Or we wait
for a "natural disaster" to do what couldn't easily be done politically—
getting rid of the troublesome poor from a major city—and then put the
market to work. Without social support (call it reparations if you like),
the poor will disproportionately end up uneducated, sick, diseased,
with dead-end jobs, or in prison. Or they will be forced out of a city by
a hurricane and not allowed back. Then white America can blame the
victims. No wonder the blues were invented here.

INTO TEXAS AND BACK TO THE SOUTHWEST

When we left New Orleans we planned to stop somewhere in Cajun
country. A friend had stayed in Breaux Bridge and recommended

that we visit. We did drive into the town, but it was hot and muggy and we decided to move on. However, we'll go back there someday, to experience the food and music my friend has so enthusiastically enjoyed. By the end of the day, dark clouds threatened heavy rains, so we took a room just east of Houston. We continued west the next morning. As we passed Houston, with its dirty, smoggy air, I thought that Dante would have been inspired by its sight to name a new layer of Hell. I'd know that I must have done something terrible in a former life if I had been condemned to live there. As someone later told us, doctors diagnose patients with a special sinus affliction—"Houstonitis." We were amused by the numerous billboards, dispersed along hundreds of miles of the Interstate, advertising Houston as the place to go to get your vasectomy reversed.

We were on our way to Big Bend National Park, and after a night in Fort Stockton, we took the road south to the park. It was only May 10, but we had seen a lot. For reasons explained below, we drove through Big Bend and continued our journey. We turned north at the dusty border town of Presidio and made our way through the stark West Texas landscape. I thought of the harsh life of those who migrated to this region, and I remembered the vivid descriptions of women's labor that Robert Caro gave in his masterful biography of Lyndon Johnson. But in a fine irony, rich Easterners are building second homes in the desolate town of Marfa, which has been written up so often in the *New York Times* that I suspect someone at the newspaper has real estate interests there. I don't think anything short of wanting to evade a police manhunt could persuade me to live near Marfa, the realistic rendition of a Prada store that has been on exhibit there notwithstanding.

THE ENVIRONMENT: ACT SEVEN, POLLUTION IN THE NATIONAL PARKS

Big Bend National Park is in southern Texas, in the middle of nowhere. To get there from the East, we traveled more than six hundred miles on U.S. 10 from the Texas-Louisiana border to the town of Fort Stockton.

From this outpost in the forbidding expanses of the far west of Texas, we drove south for one hundred miles, passing through the one-time mining and railroad town of Marathon. Marathon was named for the Greek town of the same name; to local resident Albion Shepard, the geography of both places was similar—a high desert basin. We bought a dozen biscuits for a dollar from a kind woman who operated a local bakery and admired the stately Gage Hotel.

We wanted to visit Big Bend mainly because of an essay Edward Abbey wrote about a visit there. It is so isolated and remote, with deserts, mountains, and the Rio Grande River, that we thought its beauty would be hard to resist. But once inside the park, we noticed a haze along the horizon. We thought that it must be low-lying clouds or perhaps fog. We stopped at the Persimmon Gap Visitor Center to pick up literature and examine the exhibits. There was a large window looking out over the park to the south, and through it the haze was clearly visible, occluding the view of the mountains. We spotted a park ranger and asked him about it. To our surprise he told us that the fog was pollution. He said that twenty years earlier, you could see mountains in Mexico two hundred miles away. Now you were lucky to see fifty miles in the distance. This day, he estimated we were seeing mountains thirty miles away. It was first thought that the source of the pollution was power plants in Mexico. But this convenient explanation has since been put to rest; most of the dirty air originates in the United States, some of it from as far away as Ohio. The ranger told us that the problem was only getting worse.

From the Visitor Center we continued our drive southward, thinking that we might try to spend a night at the one lodge inside the park. However, the poor visibility had us wondering what would be the point of hiking here. Why seek a lookout high in the Chisos Mountains if there was little to see? The ninety-degree heat only promised to make the haze thicker. The lodge's accommodations were lackluster, as were those just west of the park boundary, in the nearly deserted towns of Terlingua and Study (pronounced "stoody") Butte. We might have picked a place to stay anyway and explored the park, but the pollution turned us away. We decided to leave and drive west along Highway 170, through the stark and lonely cliffs overlooking the Rio Grande, the first national park we ever left disappointed.

Karen at Glacier National Park, Montana.

I have commented in previous chapters on pollution in our national parks. In Joshua Tree, brown air seeps into the park from Los Angeles and bright lights disturb the plant and animal life. In Rocky Mountain, chemicals from industry (gas and oil, cattle ranching, and mining) and automobile emissions have already fouled the air and streams and begun to affect the wildlife. And *Denver Post* reporters Frank Bass and Rita Beamish tell us that:

> Glacier National Park [in northern Montana] is an island, a sanctuary from the outside world.
>
> For how long? To the west, subdivisions, vacation homes and large chain stores march toward its borders. To the north, bulldozers push deeper through the forests to a planned coal mine in the Canadian Flathead River Valley.
>
> To the south, an emotional debate rages over whether to allow oil and gas interests to explore a sacred Blackfoot Indian plot.

From above, gradual warming continues to nibble away at the park's famed glaciers. Once as many as 150, they barely number 35 today.

The authors go on to state that "Pollution has diminished the average daytime visibility from 90 miles to less than 25 miles at Eastern parks and in the West from 140 miles to between 35 and 90 miles . . . . Even the parks' famed views of starry skies are in jeopardy."

To deal with all this, George W. Bush appointed the former president of the Cody, Wyoming, Chamber of Commerce to oversee the national parks, and this notable devised a plan to open them to all-terrain vehicles (ATVs) and a more thorough commercialization. Funding has been cut so severely that park managers have begun to actively solicit private funding, something bound to make them more beholden to corporate interests. If these trends continue, our grandchildren won't be able to see the parks even as we have seen them, much less as our grandparents did.

But if the future of the parks is uncertain and present trends are disheartening, the mountains of Big Bend hiding behind a cloud of gray were especially dispiriting. It was heartbreaking to see pollution in such a place. It shocked us to think that we would leave a national park without taking a hike.

We continued to tack north, toward New Mexico. The mountains in the distance were obscured by pollution here too, but the air cooled and got clearer as we rose into the Guadalupe Mountains. Just before the New Mexico border, about one hundred miles east of El Paso, we visited Guadalupe National Park. Guadalupe Peak, the highest point in Texas at 8,749 feet, is here. The beauty of this park helped make up for our visit to Big Bend. We hiked among wildflowers and natural springs, the greenery and trees refreshing after the desolation of west Texas. Near the springs, there was a farmer's cabin and outbuildings that had been made into a museum, the Frijoles Ranch History Museum. After the hike, we took our lunches to the picnic tables in the front yard of the house. Two rangers were sitting there. We introduced ourselves and said that we wondered what it must have been like to live here. One ranger said, pointing to his partner, "Ask him." This had been the other ranger's childhood home. He told us about his life on this farm—doing chores, playing by the springs, traveling a long distance by wagon to sell produce in town, and going to a one-room school. We felt his mixed emotions— the National Park Service had bought his family's homestead, and now he was working there. At least he got to see the pleasure this place gave us and no doubt many others. Later we took another hike, in McKittrick Canyon, to a house built by geologist Wallace Pratt. Pratt so loved the area that he donated the house and his property to the National Park Service. All the building materials had to be hauled in by horseback, and Pratt designed the house himself. It was a beautiful place, rustic and comfortable, with a stone roof. We sat on the porch amidst the trees and were at peace. We hated to leave.

Smog in Big Bend National Park, Texas.

Carlsbad, New Mexico, is not very far from the Guadalupe Mountains, but it is in another world geographically—flat, hot, nondescript, and smelling of sulphur from oil drilling and refining. In the nearby town of Artesia, the odor is called "the smell of money." In Carlsbad, summer temperatures are often in the low hundreds, yet the heat and the drabness of the land have not stopped retirees from making the town one of New Mexico's fastest growing. There is such a fetish about owning a home in this country that people will live anywhere if a big house and a plot of land can be bought cheaply.

The good thing about Carlsbad is that it is half an hour away from Carlsbad Caverns. This labyrinth of underground caverns is remarkable; a visit is an experience not to be missed. We took a guided tour and an unguided walk. The unguided hike took us through the cave's natural entrance; it is through this that hundreds of thousands of Mexican free-tailed bats make their nightly exodus, from April through October, in search of bugs. Soon after the entrance section began to be exploited for its bat guano fertilizer, one of the guano miners, James Larkin White, began to explore other sections of the cave and make them known to others. When we were on the tour of the Big Room (8.2 acres in area) and the ranger turned out all the lights, the absolute darkness that enveloped us made me think that Mr. White was a very brave man indeed. In describing the caverns, I can't do better than Will Rogers, who called them the "Grand Canyon with a Roof on It." As we try to do in every national park, we spoke to workers at the concession stands. Here they worked seventy-five stories underground in constant fifty-six-degree weather. Yet they weren't allowed to wear jackets.

That evening, around eight o'clock, we sat in the large amphitheater by the natural entrance and watched entranced as the bats made their food run. First we smelled the guano, and then we saw wave after wave of bats, their numbers getting progressively larger, leave the cave. In the dusk they looked like phantoms, and all you could hear was the movement of a million wings. We looked up at the moon and the stars and were happy to be alive.

Next morning, we drove north to Roswell, where extraterrestrials are claimed to have landed, and then west, as the flat hot land gave way to cool hills and mountains. Trees fill the land by the Hondo and Bonito rivers to the south, and we passed beautiful horse farms as we rose toward the resort town of Ruidoso, where the quarter horses race at Ruidoso Downs. We rested and pressed on toward Las Cruces, stopping at a pistachio orchard. New Mexico is a major producer of pistachios and pecans; the largest pecan ranch in the country is near the town of Alamogordo. We sampled the wares at the gift shop until we nearly got sick—plain and spiced nuts, brittle, cookies, and ice cream. Approaching Las Cruces we saw the White Sands National Monument, 275 square miles of gypsum, a spooky dune-filled space surrounded by mountains. The Trinity Site, where the first atomic blast occurred, is close by. The U.S. military machine loves the deserts.

We thought Las Cruces, and especially the adjacent village of Mesilla, with its Mexican feel and history, might be good places to live were it not for the scorching summer heat. The city boasts a large university, New Mexico State; it is ringed by desert mountains; it is forty-two miles from El Paso and Mexico; and housing is not prohibitively expensive. We met friendly people at the local farmers' and artists' market, where Karen bought me a sleek turquoise and silver money clip made by a local artisan (buyers beware: while turquoise has been mined in the Southwest for centuries and is a central feature of much American Indian art, many jewelers use an inferior type of the gem mined in China). Sadly, I lost it seven months later during a winter hike in Rocky Mountain National Park.

New Mexico is called the "Enchanted State" and, although I think Utah is more enthralling, New Mexico is a special place. We have loved every place we visited there. So we decided to go back to an old favorite for an extended stay—Santa Fe. We took Interstate 25 from Las Cruces and made the 275-mile trip north. We slowly drove through our second Border Patrol checkpoint (the first was near Marfa) and shortly after stopped at a rest area on stilts—built so the desert's "walking sands" could blow under rather than pile up against it.

Once in the city, I told the clerk at a Best Western motel that I was a journalist and writer gathering material for a book, and she gave me the "corporate rate," less than fifty dollars per night, a remarkably low price for a city as popular with tourists as Santa Fe. We kept the room from May 15 to May 31. We hiked in the mountains, restocked our organic food supply (mainly at our old favorite, Trader Joe's), promenaded on the square eating tamales, discovered the lilac-draped yards and fine old houses along the road known as La Acequia Madre (the "Mother

Ditch," it originally served as an irrigation canal), admired an ancient cottonwood tree on Canyon Road, and visited art museums (an exhibit trying to show connections between the paintings of Georgia O'Keeffe and Andy Warhol was a good example of the desperation curators must feel to do something different) and galleries. A restaurant owner told us to be sure to go to the Fenn Gallery on Paseo de Peralta. Good advice. The gallery has a fine collection of art-and-craft works, but what makes it special is the garden. Here there is a large fish-filled pond surrounded by enormous sculptures, including a full-scale elephant spouting water from its trunk.

INEQUALITY: ACT SEVEN, THE LONG SHADOW OF RACE

I have always lived in the long shadow of race. Johnstown, Pittsburgh, Portland, Miami Beach, in every city racist remarks and racist actions were commonplace. You didn't have to look for them; they were hard to escape. And on our road trips, no matter where we went or for how few days, it was not at all unusual for a white person to offer a racist comment. It is almost as if there is an understanding among whites that they are all fellow conspirators in the race war.

In Johnstown, daily racism—in bars, at the college where I taught, even in union halls—was a fact of life. A colleague complained in the faculty dining room that he didn't know why his daughter had to pay for work done at the university's dental school clinic when all those "niggers" got it for free. In the college gym, students told me they cheered for the Boston Celtics because they were the "white team." A man in a bowling alley threatened to assault me because I said that Michael Jordan was a great basketball player. In a union class, I got a complaint on the student evaluation forms: too many blacks in the class. There was *one*.

Black people call the Steel City "Pittsburgh South." In our first home there, in an apartment building complex, the college kids got drunk on weekends and hurled racial epithets at passersby from their balconies.

When we moved to another part of town, an old neighborhood woman warned us to keep our curtains closed. She said that black people looked in windows trying to spot something to steal.

I have already commented on the racism of Portland. In Miami Beach, during our six-week stay in 2002, while we were talking to the Cuban-American manager of a realty office, she began to berate the city's Haitian immigrants as dirty criminals. She automatically assumed that I would have no sympathy for these wretched souls who, desperately poor to start with, have been denied asylum, put in detention centers, forced to take the worst jobs, and subjected to vicious racial discrimination.

I got a haircut in a small shop in a mall along Santa Fe's Cerillos Road. I struck up a conversation with the white woman cutting my hair. She was a single mother with a teenage son, and beginning to plan for his college education. Out of the blue she said she was angry that the local schools were biased in favor of Hispanics and Indians. They got all the breaks. This astounded me. We had been reading about—and seen—the dismal conditions faced by the city's people of color. They were poor; they lived in substandard housing; they did the worst jobs; their neighborhoods were ravaged by drugs and alcohol. Many went hungry. The whole history of New Mexico and its capital city was awash in racism and violence against nonwhites. Yet here was a woman who had no hesitance to tell a stranger that the oppressors were really the victims.

In Flagstaff, Arizona, we went to a party organized by a progressive organization called the Friends of Flagstaff. Over its potluck dinner, we met a woman from Boston. She decried the lack of diversity in Flagstaff, saying without irony that she wished it was more like Boston, with its many ethnic restaurants. What was remarkable was her seeming unawareness that Flagstaff is a diverse city, with large Hispanic and Indian populations—Indians comprise nearly 20 percent of all residents. They must have been invisible to her.

Again in Flagstaff, we were enjoying the exhibits in the Museum of Northern Arizona. We ended our visit with a stop at the museum's bookstore. We were admiring the Indian-made works of art for sale when an Indian artist came in and showed the manager some of his jewelry and asked if the museum was interested in buying his pieces. Apparently the craftsmanship was good, but the Indian had been drinking and was known to the manager. The manager and his assistant treated this man as if he were a pathetic drunk unworthy of their time. He kept lowering his price, giving up whatever pride he had to these white people with money. A few minutes later, he was dismissed. After he left, the two museum staffers mocked him. The assistant, not realizing her ignorance, said that perhaps it was time for the Indian to join AAA. We left the museum with heavy hearts. It was as if the history of white oppression of Indians had been reenacted in microcosm before our eyes.

In Estes Park, people smugly said about a group of shabby riverside shacks not far from our cabin, "Oh, that's where the Mexicans live." The local peace group didn't bother to solicit support from local Mexicans because "They probably wouldn't be interested. They have to work too hard and wouldn't have time." We were talking to a jewelry store owner who, after remarking on how much safer (often a code word for "whiter") Estes Park was than his former home in Memphis, Tennessee, said that the Estes Park crime report was pretty small and those arrested always had names you couldn't pronounce. (Those damned Mexicans again.) In the laundromat we met a woman from the Bay Ridge section of Brooklyn, and she said that she had moved here because you couldn't recognize her Brooklyn neighborhood anymore. She told us, without I think realizing how racist she sounded, that there were so many Arabs there now that locals call it "Bay Root." "Get it?," she said, "Bay Root."

There are numerous inconvenient facts that racists are unwilling to confront. The following data compare mainly blacks and white. This is because these are the most readily available and the ones I know best. Comparisons between whites and other minorities such as Hispanics or Indians would show the same trends.

More than one million black men and women are in our jails and prisons, about the same number as whites, though the black share of the population is less than one-sixth that of whites. It is more likely that a black person of college age is in prison than in college. There are no economic indicators showing a black (or Hispanic or American Indian) advantage. Black median income, whether for families or individuals, is less than whites, as is wealth. Black wages are lower. Black poverty rates are higher, by wide margins. Black unemployment rates are typically double white rates. All of these indicators show differences between blacks and whites even after variables that might influence them are held constant. For example, on average, black workers with the same education, the same experience, working in the same industry, and living in the same region of the country as whites still earn less money.

These racial inequalities can be simply explained. A common argument made by whites is that, since more than 150 years have passed since the end of slavery, there has been more than enough time for blacks to catch up with whites economically. However, recent economic research show the flaws in such arguments. Economists have shown that economic advantages carry over from generation to generation and disadvantages do the same. As economist Austin Goolsbee put it, "The recent evidence shows quite clearly that in today's economy starting at the bottom is a recipe for being underpaid for a long time to come." Across generations, we find:

> Although Americans still think of their land as a place of exceptional opportunity—in contrast to class-bound Europe—the evidence suggests otherwise. And scholars have, over the past decade, come to see America as a less mobile society than they once believed. As recently as the later 1980s, economists argued that not much advantage passed from parent to child, perhaps as little as 20 percent. By that measure, a rich man's grandchild would have barely any edge over a poor man's grandchild. . . . But over the last 10 years, better data and more number crunching have led economists and sociologists to a new consensus: The escalators of mobility move much more slowly. A substantial body of research finds that at least 45 percent of parents' advantage in income is passed along to their children, and perhaps as much as 60 percent. With the higher estimate, it's not only how much money your parents have that matters—

even your great-great-grandfather's wealth might give you a
noticeable edge today.

Imagine my own great-great-grandfather and suppose he had been
a black slave in Mississippi. He would have been denied education,
had his family destroyed, been worked nearly to death, suffered severe
privation during the Civil War, and been considered less than human.
Then in 1865 he would have been "freed," to fend for himself and
whatever family he had. No job, no land, no schools, no nothing. For
twelve short years, he might have had some protection provided by the
federal government against the murderous rage of white Southerners. But
in 1877 even that ended, and afterward he would have been confronted
with the full force of Jim Crow and the Ku Klux Klan. What chance
would his children have had? How likely would they have been to catch
up with their white overlords? Isn't zero the most likely probability? His
grandchildren might have migrated north, but again with no wealth and
not much schooling. His great-grandchildren would have lived through
the Great Depression. How much property would they have been likely
to accumulate? Finally, through the heroic struggle of my ancestors and
my own generation, I would have seen the victories of the civil rights
movement, the desegregation of the schools, the end of lynchings, and
the opening up of a few decent jobs. I might have been an auto worker
in Detroit for a dozen years, but then in the 1970s everything would have
come crashing down again.

Too many whites, and a few blacks, cannot confront such facts and
analysis. They'd rather comfort themselves with the notion that what
lies behind these data is social pathology. When a local black minister
wrote that black people in New Orleans were themselves responsible
for the misery inflicted by Hurricane Katrina, Denver's talk show hosts
had a field day. They said that he was heroic for having the courage to
say such a thing, and they hoped for the day when a white politician like
President Bush could say the same.

We took two scenic drives from Santa Fe. First we drove the "high road" to Taos, through verdant farms and past Hispanic cemeteries brightly decorated with plastic flowers. As we climbed into the mountains, we passed the old Spanish settler towns—Cordova, Truchas, Las Trampas, and Penasco—and admired the adobe and wood churches. In Taos we again enjoyed the square and the bridge 650 feet above the deep ravine made by the Rio Grande. It is the second highest suspension bridge in the United States, and I was nervous crossing it on foot. I had thought about visiting the Kit Carson Museum (he lived in Taos) because of the favorable portrait Willa Cather gave him in *Death Comes to the Archbishop*. But I learned that Carson led the slaughter and forcible relocation of the Navajo when the U.S. government waged war against them. I couldn't patronize such a place. We returned to Santa Fe on the more traveled highway, along the Rio Grande, and stopped to watch rafters and kayakers overturning in the raging waters, made so by the early snowmelt.

The second drive took us first to Los Alamos, home of the atomic bomb's Manhattan Project and where William S. Burroughs was sent away to school from his home in St. Louis. The town was attractive and the citizens were solidly middle class, but the place had a spooky, Stepford-wife feel to it. We learned that the town has a population of 12,000, with 10,000 people working at the research center. We backtracked from Los Alamos, first stopping at the Rio Grande overlook at White Rock, which gave a sweeping view of the river's cliffs and the nearby mountains. Then we rode high up into the Jemez Mountains, the land becoming greener as we gained altitude. All of a sudden we were in the Valle Grande, a colossal caldera, one of the largest in the world. Far off in this treeless meadow we saw elk grazing. We descended the mountain through the Jemez River Canyon, gazing up at the sheer cliffs. Past the town of Jemez Springs and into the Jemez Pueblo, we marveled at the red rocks—reminding us of Sedona—and were saddened by how their beauty contrasted with the shacks and mud houses of the Pueblo. The last town we saw before Interstate 25 took us back to Santa Fe was Bernalillo, a suburb of Albuquerque, growing rapidly as thousands of unattractive tan-colored homes are being built as quickly and cheaply as possible. The development we drove by was called "Enchanted Hills."

A few days before we were to leave Santa Fe, I called a real estate agent in Estes Park, Colorado, to see if we could get a summer rental for June. None were available, so I phoned the Discovery Lodge, a motel we had once stayed in, and got a one-month rental at a good discount. We spent the next month in a hiking frenzy. We bought a laminated map of Rocky Mountain National Park at the Alpine Visitors Center, near the highest point on Trail Ridge Road, which traverses the park. Our map showed us most of the hiking trails in the park, and we plotted a new hike nearly every day. I loved the cool dry air, the clarity of the mountains in the clear atmosphere, and the sense of doing something just because I liked it. The contrasts were so pleasing—walking through snow on a hot afternoon; seeing the tiny yet resplendent flowers on the rocky tundra (spotted saxifrage, alp lilies, alpine avens, daisies, sunflowers, and forget-me-nots) growing close to the ground where it was warmer, protected with their own antifreeze; the camaraderie of the hikers amidst the indifference of the stone.

Elk near Estes Park, Colorado.

We took the Peak-to-Peak Highway to the town of Ward to visit a Buddhist poet, friend of Allen Ginsberg and the Beats, and now newly married and blessed with an infant daughter. Ward's citizens are wary of strangers, and a man gave us deliberately false directions to the poet's house, warning us of wild dogs and bears and leading us down a steep, rutted dirt road crowded with abandoned houses, trailers, and bicycles. We backed out, drove to the town where our wordsmith worked, discovered it was his day off, got directions to his house from a coworker, went back, and found the house. The prayer flags and the crying baby told us we were at the right place. We spent an enjoyable two hours visiting, admiring daughter Francesca, and learning about Ward and the Beats. Our new friend told us that the abandoned detritus everywhere helped to keep the second-homers and real estate agents away. He regaled us with a story about Naropa, the famous Beat college in Boulder, Colorado, not far from Ward, where he was urged off the speaker's stage by Allen Ginsberg when, at a fund-raiser among the city's wealthy literati, he read a poem sharply attacking such money-grubbing.

During our hikes, we met many friendly people. Neither Karen nor I had known anyone from Nebraska, but we met several people, including a lovely couple, Bill and Evie, from Clarkson, with whom we built a friendship. After Miami Beach, this was so refreshing (and the trails so beautiful) that we began to entertain the idea of living here for awhile. We needed a place to rest and for me to write this book. Each day, the idea gained traction, and in mid-month we put a "house wanted" ad in the local newspaper and called several rental agencies. The day our ad appeared, we saw another with a house for rent exactly matching what we said we wanted in ours. We called the owners, and after some negotiations, we took a one-year lease, beginning in September, on our cottage along the Big Thompson River. We spent the rest of the month in a happy daze.

MY HOMETOWN

Once we found our new home in Estes Park, we decided to go east on July 1 and visit family. We feel guilty sometimes that we don't have a home our children can visit regularly, one to which they attach special memories. When the guilt gets too great, we make the long drive to western Pennsylvania and Virginia. Sometimes these trips go well and sometimes they don't. But each time we go back, I think about the mining and factory towns that shaped my youth and young adulthood. None of them are anything close to what they used to be. The past thirty years have devastated small-town America. In the nation's industrial heartlands, there have been successive waves of plant closings, as intense international competition has been met by outsourcing, offshoring, and cost-cutting. In the farm belt, overproduction has driven prices down to the point where small farms cannot survive.

When Route 66 was built, it was possible to travel across the United States visiting vibrant small communities. Today this is no longer possible. Towns across the country have become shells of their former selves, filled with abandoned stores and factories and home now to the elderly and those whom "progress" has left behind.

I grew up in the small former factory town of Ford City (population about 3,500) in western Pennsylvania, about forty miles north of Pittsburgh. The town was dominated by a plate glass factory (Pittsburgh Plate Glass Company; everyone called it PPG), at one time the largest in the world, and a sizeable pottery (Elger). From its founding in the late nineteenth century until the end of the 1930s, Ford City was a company town, with everything that this meant in terms of all aspects of daily life. Then the workers formed unions, as part of the great wave of unionization that marked the second half of the Great Depression. They hit the picket lines after the Second World War and won some control not only over what went on in the factory but what happened in the town.

My youth was marked by the town's greatest prosperity, during the 1950s and 1960s. High wages and benefits helped to support a lively downtown, with two banks, two drugstores, two movie theaters, locally owned department stores, shoe stores, furniture stores, grocery stores, bowling alleys, restaurants, and bars. Workers took out government-guaranteed mortgages and built homes on the hills overlooking the town. They bought new appliances, including modern furnaces, refrigerators, stoves, and televisions. They bought cars and took their families on Sunday drives and vacations. They sent their kids to college for the first time. Even the small black community benefited, as black glass and pottery workers got higher wages and benefits too and began to occupy some jobs previously denied them. I remember a town in which there were not grossly obvious disparities in income and wealth. Of course, there were rich and poor, but in my schools, differences were not very marked. There were no elite private schools or exclusive clubs.

There wasn't much working-class culture in the town, if by culture we mean art, literature, music, and the like, as there was in larger union-dominated cities such as New York, but there was a lively culture of sports and clubs.

A big difference that the unions made was in daily work life. Workers were no longer industrial serfs but human beings who demanded to be treated with respect. My parents were afraid of many things, but they did not have the fear of the bosses (or even the police, who are controlled by companies in company towns) that marks life in a nonunion company town. Nobody had to do favors for the foremen to keep their jobs. I worked at the glass factory two summers while I was in college. I did mainly clerical work in the safety department. The plant's fire hall was here, and I spent many days talking about things with the firemen and with the union officers who stopped in every day for coffee. The supervisor was next door, but no one kept quiet about the company. And the men were relatively well-informed about what was going on in the plant, in the union, and in the larger society. A union is an educating organization, not just in the direct sense of informing members of what is happening, sponsoring classes, holding elections, and the like, but also in the indirect sense of giving workers enough time and money to learn on their own.

Things have changed dramatically. The glass factory shut its doors some fifteen years ago, and the pottery is now on its last legs, the union having offered so many concessions over the years that there is now not much difference between a union and a nonunion plant. No industry has come to town to put people back to work; the glass company (PPG Industries) can't sell the land to the town for development because it is laced with deadly chemicals. A walk around town tells you that things are not right there. In fact, most of the downtown is gone, ripped up and replaced by a drive-through bank and the business complex of a prosperous local pharmacist. The housing stock is deteriorating.

Median household income is just 60 percent of the national average. The people don't look good either. Kids coming out of the local high school in the afternoon look poor. The adults in the Wal-Mart a few miles from town look poor too: badly dressed, grossly overweight, looking for bargains. Old people go there every day just to hang out; it is apparently one of the busiest in the country. Young people with any prospects leave town as quickly as they can. Those with none stick around and get by with odd jobs and poverty-level wage work. I have never seen a town where long-term unemployment is such a way of life. If it weren't for the money of the pensioners (who help support their middle-aged children and grandchildren), social security, disability money, and the like, I don't know how far things would fall. Prosperity used to radiate out from the town into rural areas, but no longer. Drive just a few miles from town and you are in the middle of real Appalachian poverty. Drug use and alcohol abuse are rampant.

Matters have come to such a sorry pass that local leaders a few years ago tapped an NFL football player from that town, a young man of no known economics acumen, to be its economic spokesperson. Much hope was placed upon the construction of a new bridge linking the town with the former mining and mill towns to the south. It was actually believed that this bridge would bring in new commerce. The cultural malaise into which the town has fallen was on display this past summer when, during the town's heritage days, an excellent jazz ensemble was brought in from Pittsburgh by a town booster. The booster had bought and renovated the old National Guard armory, fitting it up nicely for dances, concerts, and other events. He sold tickets to the concert for the remarkably low price of $5.00 and offered free beer and soft drinks. My wife, my sister, and I were among the twelve people who showed up to hear a three-hour concert.

In my hometown what has taken the place of the community cohesion and sense of well-being once buttressed by the unions is drugs, alcohol, alienation, and despair. Part-time jobs, dependence on aging parents, and dependence on unemployment compensation and disability payments, these are the new life supports. Another one is religion. In an article published in *Monthly Review*, Jim Straub examined the state of Ohio,

once a union stronghold and pillar of New Deal politics and rock-ribbed
support for the Democratic Party, but now a key to the dominance of the
Republican Party. After detailing the role of Ohio's workers in building
the CIO, in heroic struggles in cities like Akron, Toledo, and Cleveland,
he told the sad story of Ohio's economic unraveling and the collapse
of what had once been models of prosperous blue-collar communities
and lives. He says:

> Ohio's cities, manufacturing industries, and unions have
> been on life support ever since. The old interlocking forms
> of New Deal social democracy—urban machine/social
> safety net/unionized mass-production industry—are on a
> terminal slide to extinction. As all over America, they are
> gradually being replaced by a new comprehensive social
> organization—nonunion Wal-Mart jobs/antisocial exurban
> sprawl/hyper-individualist consumerism—whose value
> system is as oriented towards the Republican right as the
> old New Deal was to FDR Democrats. In this equation, the
> role of ideological prime movers has switched: just as left-
> wing CIO unions used to be the instigators and organizers
> of the discontent that created the rest of the social structure,
> now it is the equally (but oppositely) ideological evangelical
> churches that stoke the fires of blue-collar anger in Ohio. Wal-
> Mart has replaced the steel companies as the state's largest
> employer; the sprawling exurbs of Columbus and Cincinnati
> have replaced Cleveland as its fastest growing areas; and the
> Assemblies of God and Church of the Nazarene are the new
> Steelworkers and Autoworkers.
>
> Ohio has always been a devout place—there are
> more Methodist churches than post offices in the state.
> However, as all over the country, more liberal, old, mainline
> denominations like the Methodists have lost parishioners
> just as the industrial cities have bled jobs. Taking their
> place is a mass movement of largely fundamentalist, right-
> wing Protestant churches—the born again, or evangelical,

movement. And while not every born-again Christian is either a fundamentalist or a conservative, there is no denying that this conservative evangelical movement is leading to both a growth in adherents and a shift to the right for mainstream Christianity. Such churches operate as a more decentralized network than their proprietary forefathers, and their common denominator is not just traditionalist social conservatism. It is a missionary zeal for spreading the word, recruiting in large numbers, and developing members' emotional commitment and ability to further proselytize. This is, by the way, a classic grassroots organizing model, one that is unused not just by the dwindling mainline churches, but also by the dying industrial unions and the left in general. Stepping assertively into a vacuum of grassroots organization in so many communities, evangelical churches have flexed awesome political muscle, and they have become the political foot soldiers of a far-right Republican new world order in the same way unions used to secure the New Deal. In an episode of the television show Frontline about Karl Rove's Republican organization, Dana Milbank of the *Washington Post* said, "Now, where Karl's interest is, is in the mechanics of this. And I think it's fair to say that religious conservatives, evangelical churches, have become sort of the new labor unions."

The small towns of western Pennsylvania and Ohio are paradigmatic of places everywhere in the United States. And if you think Ford City's "bridge to prosperity" story is pathetic, consider the town of Deadwood, South Dakota, where Wild Bill Hickok was gunned down. To encourage tourism—the supposed cure-all for every poor place's economic woes— the town's elected officials wanted to have a "running of the buffalo" on a Deadwood street, hoping to provide an American version of Pamplona's "running of the bulls."

The tiring drive across the nation's heartland, and the visits to my hometown, Pittsburgh, and Virginia, left us desperate to return to the West. It was late July, and we worried that there was no place we could go without facing searing heat. Then we remembered Flagstaff, the coolest town in Arizona. We spent a night in Indianapolis, drove in hundred-degree heat and endless road construction to St. Louis, and then slogged through Missouri on U.S. 44. We noticed the innumerable megachurches along the way, testament to the demise of the area's mines and factories and perhaps the boredom of life in this nondescript and humid region. We bought gas in Rolla, a sad and hapless example of small-town America, and ended up in Joplin, where we visited Karen's sister and brother-in-law, Patty and Jeff. They showed us all the sights, including the garage-top apartment at 3447 ½ Oak Ridge Drive where the outlaw icons, Bonnie Parker and Clyde Barrow, holed up for awhile and had a shoot-out with police. (They escaped.) We visited the Museum Complex's mineral museum, which gave chapter and verse on zinc and lead mining (Joplin was once the center of this), and all the everyday products containing these two minerals, but told us nothing about the miners. In the museum there is a photograph of Mickey Mantle, who grew up in Spavinaw, Oklahoma, about sixty miles southwest of Joplin and whose father, Elvin, was a zinc miner.

After Joplin, we crossed Oklahoma, past Indian casinos, cattle ranches, and the nation's largest McDonald's. We spent a night in the Route 66 town of Tucumcari and made it to Flagstaff by late afternoon. After a two-hour search, we located another cheap motel, this time a Howard Johnson. We stayed four weeks, until the end of August, hiking in the Grand Canyon, Sedona, and near the San Francisco peaks. Flagstaff's weather was mild, cool, and rainy—it was the "monsoon" season—and we often got muddy. In late summer, the mountains here take thousands of lightning strikes, and many afternoons found us hunkering down under rock ledges or deep in ravines, trying to stay dry and safe. There is a ski area near town, sacred ground to Navajo and Zuni, but likely to be desecrated with waste water piped in to make artificial snow. Indians are fighting the water project in court. Bruce Babbitt, scion of one of Arizona's most prominent business and political families, a former member of President Clinton's cabinet and a supposed environmentalist, led the pro-development forces. This is beautiful country; you can look out over the mountains and dry plateaus and feel the spirit of the land and the peoples who once thrived here but now do not. Far off in the distance, the Grand Canyon awaits to surprise and astonish. The trails here are among the best in the country, and the groves of aspen trees whisper to you as you walk among them, and in fall their leaves turn brilliant yellow and red.

Our friend Dwight in Bryce Canyon National Park, Utah.

The last leg of our trip took us again to Mormon country, north from Flagstaff on Highway 89, the roadsides brilliant with sunflowers until the stark canyonlands rose up before us. We marveled at the Vermilion Cliffs and mourned the loss of Glen Canyon, sacrificed to another useless dam, built by the workers who settled the pollution-plagued town of Page in the late 1950s. We drove into Utah and up the Long Valley, staying two nights to visit our Yellowstone friend Dwight in Richfield. We hiked with him there and among the enormous aspen groves of Fish Lake. Then east along Interstate 70, in Utah and Colorado the most beautiful interstate in the United States, into the Rocky Mountains, across the high passes and north to Boulder. We met our landlord, got our keys, and moved to Estes Park.

INEQUALITY: ACT EIGHT, ALAN GREENSPAN'S REVENGE

We met a wealthy man in a midwestern town on our trip from Pittsburgh to Flagstaff. He was a successful professional, and he had used his earnings to buy real estate. During the past few years, his holdings had risen dramatically. Today he is perhaps the largest real estate owner in town, and he is a man of local prominence.

It occurred to me that a key to this man's ability to accumulate property was the very low interest rates generated by the easy money policy of the Federal Reserve System that has marked the first half decade of the twenty-first century. In 2000, the stock market began a precipitous decline, first in the "dot-com" sector and then, in 2001, the rest of the market. In the late 1990s, there was a sharp run-up in stock prices, which, as often happens in capitalist economies, had become a stock market bubble, with investors buying stock simply because everyone else was. The stocks of companies that had consistently lost money and had limited prospects for future profits were trading at remarkably inflated prices. When the big traders started to sell, the floodgates opened and prices plummeted. The events of September 11 compounded the bear market, and share prices fell further. As those whose wealth had diminished and whose debts had risen were forced to cut their consumer spending and investment, what economists call aggregate demand for the economy's output began to fall and threatened a deep recession.

To forestall a downturn, the Board of Governors of the Federal Reserve System, chaired by Alan Greenspan (called "the Maestro" by Bob Woodward in his hagiography of the same name), began to implement monetary policies that pressured interest rates sharply downward. According to standard economic wisdom, falling interest rates will stimulate both consumer and capital spending, increasing both output and employment. Neither of these things happened. Instead low interest rates (lower than at any time in forty years) encouraged borrowing, not to finance the building of productive capital, but to buy real estate. New home construction boomed, with the socially negative consequences noted throughout this book—deforestation, traffic congestion, continuous road construction, air pollution, and erosion of communities by second (and third and fourth) home owners. Sales of existing homes skyrocketed too, as did the refinancing of mortgages, with the latter fueling a burst of home repairing and remodeling.

The businessman we met was able to leverage his existing properties into much larger holdings without incurring high-interest mortgages. As his wealth increased, so too did his political and social influence in the town. And his ability to purchase still more property rose in tandem with the greater wealth the low interest rates made possible. All across the United States there are businessmen like this one; and in cities large and small, they have gained what we can call "class power." They are not the "ruling class," which owns the "commanding heights" of the economy, but they are closely allied with and take direction from it. Alan Greenspan's low-interest-rate-fueled real estate boom has been in essence a form of class warfare, strengthening the power of large property holders.

For working people, low interest rates have meant something different. Some have been able to refinance mortgages and reduce their monthly payments, but for most, the money saved was simply spent on consumer goods. If money was borrowed against houses that had appreciated in value, the result was still more debt. If new homes were bought, there was a good chance, especially for minority borrowers, that the interest rate was not the low one given to richer borrowers. Instead banks gave so-called subprime loans, with higher rates and thousands of dollars of hidden charges. As real estate growth degenerated into a "bubble," financial institutions engaged in an orgy of dishonest advertising, urging everyone to become a home owner. Thousands of poorer, working-class people were sucked into a bevy of mortgage schemes that promise years of debt dependency, bankruptcy, and foreclosure.

Low interest rates used to be a rallying cry of American populists like William Jennings Bryan. Farmers and small business owners needed low rates, they said, to compete with their larger rivals. But in a society marked by large income and wealth inequalities, low interest rates only serve to make such disparities wider. So, in the end, low interest rates have made the rich richer and the poor poorer. It is difficult to believe that at least some of this wasn't intentional.

THE JOURNEY CONTINUES

Five years is a long time to drift around a country. The writer Thomas Wolfe wrote a story titled "Only the Dead Know Brooklyn." Brooklyn is a complicated place, and no one could live long enough to know everything about it. If Brooklyn is complex, many layered, and always changing, then what can we say about the United States? I don't claim to be on intimate terms with the country. I'm not Tocqueville or even Charles Kuralt. But five years of close observation will reveal some things to anyone not altogether obtuse.

It is one thing to know certain facts. That there is growing inequality in the United States is undeniable. But it is another thing to have an experience that makes the facts palpable, that gives them such emotional power that they become, in a way, part of your being. Having dinner at Hurley's in Portland, seeing the clothes hanging over the motel railing in Redding, seeing the gated communities and palatial houses in Santa Fe not far from poor Indian villages, these made inequality real to us in a way data cannot.

The same can be said for work and the environment. I know the data from the Bureau of Labor Statistics well. There are many more bad jobs than good. And the facts of environmental destruction are readily available. But I actually had a bad job. And I have spoken to and lived near many people who have them too. At the Lake Hotel, my aching legs and weary mind told me something about the reality of work for most of my fellow Americans that the data cannot. I have read plenty of facts about what we are doing to the environment. But these were given an unforgettable reality by our visits to Olympic National Park. The contrast between the Hoh rainforest and the clear-cut hillsides nearby made the facts concrete.

I know that I am lucky. I was able to make a radical change in my life and get out of the work rat race, which has a way of taking over our lives and making us incapable of understanding what is going on in the country. Not many people can do what I have done. But some can, and maybe this book will encourage them to do it. More importantly, what we have seen and done might serve as an inspiration for all of us to struggle to create a world in which the freer way we have been able to live is the norm for everyone.

On August 31, 2006, we left Estes Park. My journey continues.

SUGGESTED READINGS

On New Orleans and Hurricane Katrina, see Kristen Lavelle and Joe Feagin, "Race, Class, and Katrina," *Monthly Review*, July-August 2006; Mike Davis, "Catastrophic Economics: The Predators of New Orleans," *Le Monde Diplomatique*, October 2005; and Marjorie Cohn, "The Two Americas," available at *http://www.truthout.org/docs_2005/090305Y. shtml*. The funniest novel I have ever read, set in New Orleans and evocative of the city's oddness, is John Kennedy Toole, *A Confederacy of Dunces* (Baton Rouge, LA: Louisiana State University Press, 2000). Bob Dylan's remarks on New Orleans are from his memoir, *Chronicles: Volume One* (New York, NY: Simon & Schuster, 2005). Pollution in the national parks is the subject of a good article by Frank Bass and Rita Beamish in the *Denver Post* of June 19, 2006: "National Parks' Preservation Threatened." On the collapse of small towns in the industrial heartland, see Jim Straub, "What Was the Matter with Ohio?: Unions and Evangelicals in the Rust Belt," *Monthly Review*, January 2006. On the gap between rich and poor, and blacks and whites, and the difficulties of "catching up" with those who have more money, see John Bellamy Foster, "An Introduction," *Monthly Review*, July-August 2006; Austin Goolsbee, "Hello Young Workers: One Way to Reach the Top Is to Start There," *New York Times*, May 25, 2006; and Lawrence Mishel, Jared Bernstein, and Sylvia Allegretto, *The State of Working America*, 2004/2005 (Ithaca, NY: Cornell University Press, 2005). On mortgage rip-offs for the poor, see "Double Jeopardy," available at *http://www. aecf.org/publications/advocasey/winter2005/double/double3.htm*. Part of the last section is taken from Michael D. Yates, "The Ghosts of Karl Marx and Edward Abbey," *Monthly Review*, March 2005.

INDEX